Anna Freud's Letters to Eva Rosenfeld

Anna Freud's Letters to Eva Rosenfeld

Peter Heller

Translated by
Mary Weigand

with Contributions by
Günther Bittner and Victor Ross

INTERNATIONAL UNIVERSITIES PRESS, INC.
MADISON   CONNECTICUT

Copyright © 1992, Peter Heller

All rights reserved. No part of this book may be reproduced by any means, nor translated into a machine language, without the written permission of the publisher.

Library of Congress Cataloging-in-Publication Data

Freud, Anna, 1895–
    [Correspondence. Selections. English]
    Anna Freud's letters to Eva Rosenfeld / [edited by] Peter Heller ; translated by Mary Weigand; with contributions by Günther Bittner and Victor Ross.
        p. cm.
    Includes bibliographical references and index.
    ISBN 0-8236-0152-8
    1. Freud, Anna, 1895– —Correspondence. 2. Rosenfeld, Eva Marie, 1892–1977—Correspondence. 3. Psychoanalysts—
Correspondence. 4. Child analysis. I. Heller, Peter, 1920– .
II. Bittner, Günther, 1937– . III. Ross, Victor, 1919– .
IV. Title.
RC339.52.F74A4 1992
618.92′89′0092—dc20
[B]   91-31861
                                                                                        CIP

Manufactured in the United States of America

Contents

About the Contributors   vii
Preface   ix
Acknowledgments   xi
Abbreviations   xiii

Part I
Introduction

Anna Freud's Letters to Eva Rosenfeld: A Reader's Response
    GÜNTHER BITTNER   3
Eva Marie Rosenfeld (1892–1977): A Woman of Valor. A Personal Memoir (with illustrations)
    VICTOR ROSS   23

Part II
Anna Freud: Letters to Eva Rosenfeld

Remarks on the Background and Major Topics of the Letters
    PETER HELLER   63
  I.   1925–1928   100
  II.   1929   108
  III.   1930   132
  IV.   1931   150
  V.   1932   170
  VI.   From a Later Period   180

References   189
Index   195

About the Contributors

Günther Bittner, born 1937 in Prague, received his academic training in psychology and pedagogy at the Universities of Tübingen and Vienna, as well as in psychoanalysis at the Stuttgart Academy of which he is a member. He is currently Professor of Pedagogy at the University of Würzburg, Germany, and a practicing psychoanalyst. His numerous publications include *Tarnungen des Ich. Studien zu einer subjektorientierten Abwehrlehre* (Stuttgart: Bonz, 1977); *Das Unbewusste —ein Mensch im Menschen?* (Würzburg: Königshausen and Neumann, 1988); and, bearing specifically on the history of psychoanalysis and psychoanalytical pedagogy: *Das andere Ich. Rekonstruktionen zu Freud* (München: Piper, 1974); G. Bittner and P. Heller (ed.): *Eine Kinderanalyse bei Anna Freud 1929–1932* (Würzburg: Königshausen and Neumann, 1983); *Vater Freuds unordentliche Kinder. Die Chancen post-orthodoxer Psychoanalyse.* (Würzburg: Königshausen and Neumann, 1989).

Peter Heller, born 1920 in Vienna, emigrated in 1938 to England, and subsequently to the United States. He obtained his Ph.D. at Columbia University in 1951, and has taught since the forties first at Columbia University, then at Harvard, the University of Massachusetts at Amherst, and at the State University of New York at Buffalo until his retirement in 1991. His publications outside the field of literature include *A Child Analysis with Anna Freud* (Madison, CT: International Universities Press, 1990).

Victor Ross, the son of Eva Rosenfeld, was born in Vienna, Austria in 1919 and moved to England in 1936 where he completed his education before going into the army. After the war he combined authorship with a career in administration. He has published a number of books and for many years occupied a senior position at *The Reader's Digest*. He lives in England, is married, and has a grown-up family.

Preface

The spirit and style of graceful sobriety which animate these unassuming letters of a young and idealistic woman are scarcely translatable. Yet Anna Freud in her thirties was an accomplished and highly word-conscious writer. Her letters to Eva Rosenfeld in the 1920s and early 1930s, written in the manner of casual and affectionate chats between intimate friends, touch with quiet precision on a variety of joyous and painful, crucial and challenging experiences and insights. The present collection focuses on this period which comes to an end in December 1932. Extant correspondence from later years (notably, 1946–1977; see pp. 180–187) is restricted, on the part of Anna Freud, to brief and/or businesslike communications, while Eva continues on a largely unrequited quest for their former intimacy.

The introductory section of this book provides perspectives on two lives in an age prior to World War II. The psychoanalyst Günther Bittner, historian of child analysis and the era of "psychoanalytical paedagogy," sees Anna Freud primarily in terms of her attempt at self-realization via and despite self-sacrifice and self-surrender. Victor Ross portrays his mother, Eva Rosenfeld, similarly as a woman of valor overcoming suffering and a threatening loss of self through her commitment of self to others. Yet neither reduces their characterization to a formula of self-assertion through self-dedication. Indeed, to do so would be a betrayal of the complexity of psychoanalytical insight, which both sought to embody, though psychoanalysis encompassed the entire universe of Anna Freud while it was but an integral part of the life of

Eva who was married and lost all but one of her four children.

The commentators who contributed explanatory and interpretive materials to this book differ somewhat in regard to large perspectives as well as in terms of biographical details, many of which are still in doubt. Victor Ross and I were raised in varying degrees under the aegis of Anna Freud, Eva Rosenfeld, and their circle. My own bias has been to regard Anna Freud's single-minded devotion to her father and to the cause of psychoanalysis, as a limiting factor, though productive in helping to create and integrate her impressively homogenous and powerful personality. And while all of us as children respected "Muschi," as we called Eva Rosenfeld, and trusted in her authority and affectionate care, the insightful wit, and the sympathy she lavished on all around her, I also recall the sense of what she would later describe as the touch of ice due to her lifelong mourning.

The present volume does not offer finished portraits of personalities. In the absence of Eva's half of the correspondence, the prefatory remarks and the notes to Anna's letters draw extensively on Eva Rosenfeld's unpublished memoirs and other pertinent material. The main purpose of this edition is to enable sympathetic readers to get in touch with two remarkable human beings and to form their own impressions and images of them. If it achieves its purpose, this will be due in large measure to the help of my friend Victor Ross, the owner of these letters. I should also express my gratitude to Mary Weigand for her tireless efforts, and my indebtedness to W. Ernest Freud, another surviving companion of early years, to my daughter, Didi Heller, Professor of English at Bennington College, to Paul Roazen, who alerted me to the later letters of Eva Rosenfeld at the Library of Congress, and to support by the State University of New York at Buffalo and the American Council of Learned Societies.

P. H.

Acknowledgments

The editor thanks the following for granting permission to reproduce material included in this work: Victor Ross and Sigmund Freud Ltd. for the letters of Anna Freud to Eva Rosenfeld; Victor Ross for the letters of Eva Rosenfeld and for material quoted from Eva Rosenfeld's unpublished memoirs and her correspondence with Obermann. The 57 letters of Anna Freud to Eva Rosenfeld which form the basis of this book are in the possession of Victor Ross. Other letters quoted are stored in the Anna Freud Collection of the Manuscript Division at the Library of Congress in Washington, D.C., unless another source is indicated.

Abbreviations

M. J. Burlingham   Burlingham, Michael John (1989), *The Last Tiffany. A Biography of Dorothy Tiffany Burlingham*. New York: Atheneum, 1989.
ER   Eva Rosenfeld, *Recollected in Tranquillity*. Unpublished memoirs. (Numbers following ER refer to the numbered pages in the editor's copy of the manuscript.)
Gay   Gay, Peter (1988), *Freud. A Life for Our Time*. New York: Norton, 1988.
Jones III   Jones, Ernest (1957), *Sigmund Freud. Life and Work*, Volume 3, *The Last Phase* 1919–1939. London: Hogarth Press, 1957.
L + Arabic numeral   Anna Freud's numbered letters to Eva Rosenfeld.
n   note to a letter by Anna Freud to Eva Rosenfeld (i.e., L1n = Letter 1 and notes to Letter 1. L1n2 = Letter 1 and note 2 to L1. (L1)n2 = note 2 to L1 only).
Peters   Peters, Uwe Henrik (1979), *Anna Freud. Ein Leben für das Kind*, rev. ed. Frankfurt/M: Fischer Taschenbuch Verlag. 1984.
Salber   Salber, Wilhelm (in collaboration with W. E. Freud) (1985), *Anna Freud*. Reinbek bei Hamburg: Rororo.
Writings, I to VIII   *The Writings of Anna Freud*, Volumes I–VIII. New York: International Universities Press, 1966–1981.
Young-Bruehl   Young-Bruehl, Elisabeth (1988), *Anna Freud: A Biography*. New York: Summit Books.

Part I

Introduction

Anna Freud's Letters to Eva Rosenfeld: A Reader's Response

Günther Bittner

The major portion of Anna Freud's letters to Eva Rosenfeld were written between 1924 and 1932 in intervals when the two friends, both living in Vienna, where they saw each other almost daily, were separated. One or the other would be on vacation, or would stay at Dr. Ernst Simmel's psychoanalytic sanitarium in Berlin-Tegel (see pp. 19–21). Anna Freud went there for several months in 1928, 1929, and 1930, to accompany her father, Sigmund Freud, to Berlin where Dr. Schroeder worked on the prosthesis required to alleviate Freud's suffering from a cancer of the palate and jaw. Eva Rosenfeld stayed in Tegel in 1931 and 1932, first to manage the household and housekeeping of the sanitarium, then to help with its liquidation, while gaining distance from her marital crisis as well as psychoanalytic experience useful for her future career as an analyst.

During the years of their correspondence, Anna Freud was occupied both with caring for her ailing father and with building up her own professional identity and career. In 1922 she was accepted as member of the Vienna Psychoanalytic Society. In March 1923, her father reported in a letter, March

23 to his and Anna's friend, Lou Andreas-Salomé: "Anna has now joined the group of practicing analysts" (Freud/Salomé, 1980, p. 133). In the following years she was to undertake much professional travel and to attend numerous congresses. These included the Congress at Bad Homburg (1925); the "anti-Anna Freud Symposium" in London (1927), attacking, under the aegis of Melanie Klein, Anna's approach to child analysis; the Innsbruck Congress (1927); Oxford (1929); a trip to Frankfurt to accept the Goethe Prize for her father (1930); the Wiesbaden Congress (1932); and several lecture tours. Due to the personal nature of the correspondence, there is little mention of these activities, or of Anna Freud's writings of the twenties and early thirties, which include her first publication, the account revealing or paraphrasing her own case history and analysis by her father, "Beating Fantasies and Daydreams" (1922), as well as her *Four Lectures on Child Analysis* (1927), *Four Lectures on Psychoanalysis for Teachers and Parents* (1930); and her groping with and turn toward ego psychology later formulated in her classic, *The Ego and the Mechanisms of Defense (1936)* (Writings, I; see also, Bittner and Heller [1983] concerning the themes of A. Freud's work during this period; Salber [pp. 11–21]; Young-Bruehl [pp. 103–139]).

Important as background, in addition to the miniature castle, the park and the lake at Tegel, are the places where the Freuds spent their vacations: Semmering, a fashionable and picturesque resort in the foothills of the Austrian Alps, Easter and Summer, July 8 to September 27, Villa Schüler, 1924, June 3 to September 3, 1925, and August 1928; Tegel, August to October 1928; March 11 to about March 25, 1929; the Alpine Schneewinkel (Berchtesgaden) at the Königsee, beyond the Austrian borders in Germany, June 18 to September 1929; Tegel again, September 15 to October 20, 1929, and May 4 through July, 1930; the mountain lake and village of Grundlsee (Villa Rebenburg) in the Austrian Salzkammergut, July to end of August 1930; and, in the spring and summer of 1931 and 1932, a villa and garden in Pötzleinsdorf, a suburb of Vienna.

Among Anna Freud's writings and the accounts of her available so far, her letters to Eva Rosenfeld stand out in that they offer direct access to her circumstances, feelings, and thoughts during a crucial period of her life. Unlike some major works of her father, such as the autobiographical *The Interpretation of Dreams* (1900), Anna Freud's publications maintain throughout the stance of impersonal scientific writing. However, her letters to Eva Rosenfeld reveal not a public but a private character, and convey the picture of an affectionate, intensely human Anna Freud without a trace of rigidity or psychoanalytic orthodoxy. Here, rather, is a shy young woman of deep feeling, perhaps with an excessive wish to be good, but certainly a human being amply deserving of respect and sympathy.

ANNA FREUD IN PERSON

What is an analyst like in private, in herself, when she is not sitting behind the couch? Accessible and warm-hearted as Anna Freud appears in these letters, she remains nonetheless unmistakably the analyst.

The letters were written mostly at times of relaxation. Usually, there is a sigh of relief after the cessation of the demands of everyday professional life, or else she finds that she is still wound up too tightly, like a toy engine, needing to be fixed again, before she can unwind and enjoy her days or weeks of strictly limited leisure (see L4). At the same time, she is an ascetic, believing that she "doesn't deserve any more sympathy" (L1), as soon as she is reasonably restored. She is enchanted with the "sense of freedom" that "always comes after one has forced onself to go through with something" ("*wenn man sich durch etwas durchgezwungen hat*", L4). Yet this asceticism does not exclude warmth and empathy. To her friend, grieving for her dead child, she writes: "I would like to be a little bit of Mädi for you. I wish I had a little daughter, I would share her with you" (L4).

In that key word, *share*, Anna Freud touches upon a central motif of her life to which she dedicated some of her most striking theoretical observations: The defense mechanism of "altruistic surrender," she found, yielded instinctual pleasure derived from "sharing in the gratification of others," by employing the mechanisms of projection and identification. "The retiring attitude which the prohibition of her impulses caused [a female patient of hers] to adopt when she herself was concerned, vanished when it was a question of fulfilling the same wishes after they had been projected onto someone else" (Writings II, p. 126). Repudiation of her own sexuality does not prevent" the "young school teacher" or "young governess (*junge Erzieherin*, literally: the young educator) in question "from taking an affectionate interest in the love life of her friends and colleagues. She was an enthusiastic matchmaker and many love affairs were confided to her" (Writings II, p. 125).

Many have suspected that this "young teacher" stands for Anna Freud herself. Biographers Peters and Salber are not sure; nor does Young-Bruehl doubt the existence of the patient in question (Young-Bruehl, p. 128–129); but all agree that the problem of "altruistic surrender" is also Anna Freud's own; and this is certainly made equally manifest in her letters to Eva Rosenfeld. In those years Anna Freud led a life of constant and unquestioning service, sacrifice, and dedication to her father's continuously threatened and increasingly failing health, as well as to the ever more demanding psychoanalytic cause and movement. It was, among other things, a life diminished through obligations and renunciations of all sorts. She writes of her sense of liberation and freedom once she has escaped from the family abode in the Berggasse, her sudden perception of herself "as if something was suddenly illuminated and one could see into it." And she adds: "I hope it won't all close up again by the time I get back to Vienna. It often does" (L8). What she cannot feel any more in the Berggasse because of her altruism, is her "narcissism," which she discovers within her with "astonishment" in the very first of these letters, and finds "certainly not unpleasant," though she wonders: "what am I to do with it in daily life? To survive, it would probably need its own bathroom. That is expensive. But altruism isn't as cheap as one might think either" (L1).

The motif and problem of escape and exemption from everyday life is mirrored in a broadly spun out image (also used by her father (Freud/Andreas-Salomé [1980], p. 157): the fantasy of Tegel as an "island of safety" in the midst of traffic, where "all around me people must dodge cars and be afraid; but none can get near me. I love to stand still and be protected" (L15). As her stay in Tegel draws to a close and she gets ready to step down from her island, she will reflect self-critically that the right to withdraw to such a haven should belong only to those who can move more confidently in traffic than she does. She adds: "But I also realize: it looks much easier from up there, because one is at rest while everything else is in motion. That way you can see through it" (L18). Yet the next year, staying again in Tegel, she no longer feels so positively about the "island," complaining "[we are] two prisoners on a rock in a sea called Tegel" (L30). The island now turns into a symbol of confinement with an ever receding prospect of deliverance, as in Chamisso's ballad of "Salas y Gomez" about a sailor who died of old age in solitude, having waited in vain to be rescued from the desolate shore on which he was cast by shipwreck.

The dreams Anna Freud tells about in the letters likewise reflect the theme of self-surrender: Shall I be "I" or has the "I" died, has it been surrendered to an other? Some of the dreams (L11, L22) refer to Eva as a kind of alter ego for Anna: "you are I and I am you" (L11). A drastic dream toward the end of the correspondence is interpreted very convincingly by the writer: "Last night I dreamt that I murdered our cook, Anna. I chopped off her head and cut her into pieces and had no guilt feelings at all, which was very funny. Now I know why; her name is Anna, and that's me" (L47).

Her relationship to Max Eitingon, the Berlin psychoanalyst, remains to be considered. In Tegel, 1930, she complains that something keeps gnawing at her "drowned friendship" with him. (L25). When she does not feel at ease in the Berlin psychoanalytical circles, she suggests this might be connected with her disappointment in him (L24). In her thoughts on this relationship, the motif of altruistic surrender appears in reverse, namely, as her being abandoned:

> What is hurting me so much is not that I lost him, but that he got over losing me so easily, in other words: that he is giving me up so lightly. This goes back to a time when I was very little and I think I know exactly when it began. From then on I always sought out children who abandoned me, and it had the same effect on me as now. As if I were seeing myself through the eyes of the other and were worth just as little to myself as I was to him [L25].

And this is followed later on by a devastating judgment of him and her years with him, which she characterizes by her feeling: "I was in a desert where nothing grows. Wandering around in it, one dries up" (L47).

There has been a good deal of speculation as to why Anna Freud never married (see, for instance, Kardiner, 1979, p. 92), and, generally, about the apparent absence of all erotic or sexual relationships to men (or women) in her life. Peters rejects rumors connecting Anna Freud with Bernfeld, Lampl, Eitingon and Rank, finding "no evidence to nourish such suspicion" (Peters, p. 84; see also Salber, p. 44). Young-Bruehl deals more thoroughly with the subject, and had access to unpublished correspondence between Eitingon and Anna Freud. However, she also concludes: Anna Freud "remained a vestal, to use the apt word Marie Bonaparte later chose to signal both Anna Freud's virginity and her role as the chief keeper of her father's person and his science, psychoanalysis" (Young-Bruehl, p. 137). See also in this connection, Sigmund Freud on Anna Freud's "sexuality and relationships" (Gay, pp. 433–434, 500), Anna Freud, and Ernest Jones (pp. 438, 441, 443, 541, 613). On p. 618 there is a reference by Freud to Anna as "a passionate woman who almost wholly sublimated her sexuality.") On the basis of Anna Freud's remarks in her letters, it would certainly appear that she was deeply attached to Eitingon and felt deeply disappointed by him.

What was he like? It is difficult to gain an impression of Eitingon's personality from the psychoanalytic literature. He was devoted to Sigmund Freud (Freud/Andreas-Salomé, 1980, p. 128), considered himself a member of the family, was an authority on all questions of psychoanalytic training (Deutsch, 1975, p. 148), a great organizer who "put his entire strength and his business acumen at the disposal of the psychoanalytic movement, always without personal gain" (Peters, p. 75; see also pp. 71–76). But what was it that Anna

Freud found attractive in him, if he was indeed akin to "a desert where nothing grows" (L47)? Why did she choose him? Young-Bruehl suggests that she needed an analyst other than her own father or in addition to her own father (Young-Bruehl, pp. 186–187). Anna Freud herself, however, recognized in her choice of Eitingon as an object of her affection the recurrence of a behavior pattern dating back to her childhood which again leads to the central theme and problem of her life, that is, to renunciation and withdrawal.

It may be objected that it is not permissible to attempt to penetrate into Anna Freud's private and intimate sphere and to open to public view her friendships, her inner life, and even her dreams. Yet we have to recognize that psychoanalysis is not, after all, an objective science, but rather, necessarily and legitimately, a highly subjective undertaking. It is the attempt to bring out verbally the peculiar constellation of conflict in an individual's life (Atwood and Stolorow, 1979; Bittner, 1989a); and given the inevitable involvement of the analyst in this enterprise, the analyst himself or herself must needs be considered an object of inquiry as well. If Freud had been a great physicist or biologist, his biography might be a matter of indifference to us. As it is, one simply has to know what he was like personally for the sake of the truth of psychoanalysis. We must know what stuff his thoughts were made of in order to judge their validity, but if this is so, the same considerations apply also to Sigmund Freud's daughter Anna.

PSYCHOANALYSIS AS A THEME OF THE LETTERS

The letters of Anna Freud to Eva Rosenfeld being primarily private, there is relatively little of "scientific" content in them. However, it is interesting how lightly and playfully the theme of "analysis" is handled; for example, the humorous reflection on the relationship between narcissism and a bathroom (L1); the "psychoanalysis" of her father's prosthesis which is said to be "in resistance" (L17, L19), to have regained "all its symptoms" (L19), or "progressing like an analysis: very slowly"

(L24). A similar sense of humor is suggested by Anna's report on a "peasant woman who still spins and weaves loden cloth. But not while doing analysis," (L34), clearly an allusion to Anna Freud's own knitting during her patients' sessions, a habit criticized and "analyzed" by some of her father's associates as a substitute for "masturbation," as well as objected to by some of her patients, including Erik Erikson. In his "Anna Freud—Reflections" (1983), Erikson gently alludes to this, noting that his objection was allayed by Anna Freud's knitting of a sweater for his little son Kai. (Erikson, 1983, p. 71; Salber, 1985; p. 20).

Of substantive interest are her remarks on the nature of transference, including a theoretical observation in L23 and, above all, her directive to Eva as she was about to begin her analysis with Freud:

> You know, there is no contradiction in your undergoing analysis in a place that you would prefer to go to for love's sake alone. I did the same thing, and perhaps because of it, the two things became inextricably bound together for me. In the end you will realize: it is the only way to go into analysis. Right now you are troubled by the feeling that where you love, you would like to be especially good. You will see that being good and being in analysis finally amount to the same thing [L8].

Many a practitioner and patient would find themselves at variance with these views, including, incidentally, the *later* Eva Rosenfeld, who once observed that analysis never did improve anyone's character (taped interview with P. Heller, July 1975). To me Anna Freud's remarks carried immediate conviction. I see in them a confession that an analytic relationship does include more than the transference, namely an element of actual, positive relationship, a point which Schottländer (1959) was to stress later on.

The interweaving of the "real" and the "analytical" relationships was, moreover, the insoluble crux of the original Viennese group. The strict formulation of the rule of neutrality, it seems, was not to be interpreted literally, but had rather apotropaic character in view of the fact that everybody and everything was actually interwoven with everybody and everything else. The children in analysis with Anna Freud, many living either with Eva Rosenfeld or Dorothy Burlingham, went together to the psychoanalytically oriented school run by Sigmund Freud's patients, his daughter Anna and her close friends, Dorothy Burlingham and Eva Rosenfeld. The most important teacher was Erik Homburger Erikson, in turn a patient of Anna Freud. A nice instance of this interweaving is shown in Anna Freud's question concerning the acceptance into Eva Rosenfeld's family pension of a child coming from Germany to continue analysis in Vienna (L26).

I do not find such interweaving of analysis and reality objectionable. It is good to see how the rule of neutrality was born out of struggle. That is not to invalidate it, or to belittle its importance, but to object to its mindless, or soulless, mechanical application.

The advice about reading the works of Sigmund Freud, which Anna Freud gives to her friend to start her on her way, is beautiful and true. Let the ordinary student begin with the *Introductory Lectures*, and whoever is interested in psychopathology stick to the case histories. But the "third way"—which she wanted her friend to attempt—"is to take everything for granted and to use it as if it had always been meant for you" (L4). And indeed, this is probably the only way one can study, assimilate, and appropriate psychoanalysis, which can be learned only in lively confrontation, not as inanimate book learning. To be sure, Anna Freud herself may be somewhat inconsistent or in conflict with her faith in the scientific character of psychoanalysis when she encourages Eva to take all analysis has to offer "for granted and to use it as if it had always been meant for you." (L4) For at the same time, she wonders how her friend happens to know so much: "Papa was really the first to say it all, and nobody before him. You haven't even read it, yet you know it" (L4).

This brings to mind the innumerable unfortunate disputes in those days among psychoanalysts, as to who said what first; all of which reflected a misconception of the nature of the discipline (see, for example, Ferenczi and Groddeck, 1986, p. 27). The question who first detected the AIDS virus under the microscope may be legitimate; but in the realm of the psyche everyone has within himself some sort of prior knowledge of it all. There is no point to quarrels about priority where no one or everyone may claim to own anything or everything as his domain (Bittner, 1974, p. 9).

Perhaps the most concentrated psychoanalytic letter is L11 which contains an impressive portion of self-analysis. Anna has been unable to reach Eva by phone, and thereupon dreams "sad and oppressive things" about her, the dreams being a substitute for real contact.

She then takes up the subject of Obermann, Eva's friend and lover, who, she claims, found his mother again in Eva, "from whom he should get away, but can't." Bob, Dorothy Burlingham's eldest son, and Anna Freud's patient, she finds, also makes such "futile attempts" to find a substitute in his rapid change of girl friends, such as Herta and Trudl. "There seem to be so many, but it is mere illusion" (L11).

And then Anna herself, where will she find a substitute "when I can no longer remain where I am now, when I am left alone and thus lose all that gives meaning to my life?" (L11), that is, when her ailing father is gone. Then she would rather die. And now the "sad and oppressive" quality of the dreams mentioned at the beginning becomes clear: the friend she could not reach by phone the evening before, dies in a dream. "So now we know: you are I and I am you" (L11).

Perhaps this is what kept Anna bound to analysis and to her father: "You are I and I am you" was also valid for that situation, and she rejected any idea of giving up the meaning of her life, which she had found as Sigmund Freud's faithful Antigone, for any substitute.

ANNA FREUD'S ATTEMPT AT A PSYCHOANALYTIC "REFORM OF LIFE"

In the 1920s, as Salber (pp. 41–43) suggested, Anna Freud also sought to create an enlarged, artificial family as a substitute for a "natural" family of her own. Young-Bruehl (chapters 3 and 5) and M. J. Burlingham (chapters 8–11) have since provided further ample material on this development. The children of Anna Freud's enlarged family, living, as Sigmund Freud put it in a "symbiosis" with his own (Letter to Binswanger, January 1925; Peters, p. 191), were, primarily, the children of Anna's ever closer friend and companion, Dorothy Burlingham (and later on even the children of those children), as well as her nephew Ernst Halberstadt-Freud ("Ernsti," later W. Ernest Freud), the older son of her deceased sister Sophie.

Dorothy Tiffany Burlingham, a wealthy American, had left her manic-depressive husband together with her children, to settle in Vienna, first as patient of Theodor Reik, then as the patient of Sigmund Freud. Her children, Bob, Mabbie, Katrina (Tinky), and Michael (Mikey) were in analysis with Anna Freud, as was Anna Freud's nephew Ernst. The enlarged family also included Eva Rosenfeld's daughter Mädi (who was to die tragically in a mountaineering accident in the summer of 1927), and Eva's son Victor. It encompassed at a further remove some of the foster children (such as Lizzie Wellenstein) and some of the helpers in Eva's care, as well as children Anna Freud had in analysis, including Peter Heller, Reinhard Simmel, Judy de Forest, Adelaide Sweetser, and Bob Sweetser. Most of these children and adolescents were at the same time pupils at the small, private "Hietzing School" (or "Burlingham–Rosenfeld") School, founded by Dorothy Burlingham and Eva Rosenfeld under the aegis of Anna Freud; and so the enlarged family also included some of their teachers, most notably Erik Homburger Erikson. At the school only a small minority, including Victor Rosenfeld and two children of a family opposed to analysis, Elisabeth and Mario Jona, were *not* in analysis. Of management and staff, Dorothy Burlingham, Anna Freud, and Eva Rosenfeld were in analysis with Sigmund Freud; Erik Erikson, who taught art, German and humanities, was in training analysis with Anna Freud; as was the English teacher Mary Briehl (subsequently a child analyst) and the occasional teacher Esther Menaker (who also became an analyst). August Aichhorn, an occasional teacher at the school, was himself an analyst. His son Walter, a pupil at the school, was in analysis with Dorothy

Burlingham. Parents with a positive interest in analysis included, in addition to Aichhorn, Dorothy Burlingham, and Eva Rosenfeld, Izette de Forest (subsequently a therapist), Grete Heller (briefly in analysis with Hanns Sachs), Hans Heller (patient of Ludwig Jekels), Valti Rosenfeld, the analyst Dr. Ernst Simmel, the mother of Adelaide and Bob Sweetser, and Mrs. and Mr. Simeon Tropp (the latter subsequently a Reichean analyst).

Salber's account of Anna Freud's enlarged family, produced in collaboration with W. Ernest Freud, seems valid to me. But there is more to be said on this subject. For Anna Freud was concerned not merely with the creation of an enlarged family, but also with something like a reformed and improved life-style, or rather an "alternative way of life" on the basis of psychoanalysis and guided by psychoanalytic ideas, which assume tangible expression in her conception of institutions inspired by psychoanalysis, notably the psychoanalytic Hietzing School for children in Vienna and the psychoanalytic sanitarium in Berlin-Tegel.

Anna Freud's letters show her most vividly as a pedagogue when she is sharing the children's life with her friend in their "analytic family" and writes about them. The letters reveal her continuous interest in the daily lives of the children: whether Herta (a helper at Eva Rosenfeld's) and Anna's patient Lizzie (a foster child living with Eva) had returned, how the boys' room (for Reinhard, Victor, and Ernsti) had turned out, how the young teachers Peter Blos and Erik Erikson were behaving (it sounds as if she were speaking of children) (L17). In a later letter there is "so much to discuss about all the children": "Couldn't you prevent Trudl [a helper at Eva's] from going to Susy [living in at Eva's]? Somehow it doesn't seem right. And I am concerned about Vera [a foster child at Eva's and patient of Anna]. She doesn't make a good impression at all. I hope she will come to me one of these days, then I will know more and can tell you about it. Through Judy [de Forest, living at Dorothy's and Anna Freud's patient] I also know a lot more about Erszi [half-sister of Vera, foster child at Eva's], and would like to talk it over with you" (L24).

She frequently formulates her impression about the children being in "good" or "less good" shape (L12, L24):

> I feel sorry for Lizzie [patient living at Eva's] that I gave her the opportunity to backslide. She was simply not ready for such a long interruption. If I had suspected that, I would have rather had her come to Berlin. Don't worry about Ernsti [AF's nephew and patient, living as foster child at Eva's], I think Dorothy would be glad to take him on now, despite the fact that, unfortunately, he is so much trouble [L33].

Perhaps her most differentiated and revealing pedagogical judgment is passed on Victor, on the basis of the—interesting—postulate that a boy should have an "ideal." She finds him "flourishing physically, strong, healthy, and manly as never before," eagerly participating in the life at his progressive boarding school in Germany (Marienau) and very glad to be there, much like her nephew Ernst at a similar educationally progressive and "free" establishment at Scharfenberg near Berlin. "But it is a different kind of relationship from Ernstl's at Scharfenberg. There is no underlying ideal of what kind of person one should become" (L47).

Such comments suggest Anna Freud's dream of an extended analytical family in which there could be a conscientious family council and consultation on every individual child. And meanwhile the troop of children is pressing for even more of a group existence. For, as Dorothy's eldest daughter Mabbie puts it, the school is to be only "a beginning." "We should have something even more beautiful together, with all the girls and all the children." "The children," Anna Freud adds, "keep talking about a real farm," and she wonders whether this wish of theirs might not come true, revealing her own dream (L5).

The "free" psychoanalytic Hietzing School—named after its setting in an idyllic suburban district of Vienna—was the part of the dream which Anna Freud was able to realize together with Dorothy Burlingham and Eva Rosenfeld. It emerged, after beginnings restricted to the Burlingham children and two of their American friends (Adelaide and Bob Sweetser), in 1927 and continued through 1931. Together with

Dorothy Burlingham, Eva Rosenfeld initiated the school, as she saw it, as a memorial for her dead daughter. In her memoirs, she asks herself:

> Why a school? I never thought about my reasons for choosing that kind of monument for my daughter; many factors, as I see now, contributed to this decision. I wanted to find comfort for my own sad heart in being with the young ones; it was as if I postponed the time of realizing that I would not find *her* among them. There were also very rational reasons: in the Freudian circle of friends I was the one in no way professionally directed or limited—every field of knowledge was welcome in our home. My husband was widely read, artistically interested in music and the arts, and although he kept away from all activities of the school, he was giving directions to my as yet somewhat narrow school-education [ER, p. 207].

Dorothy Burlingham wished to provide her children with an education other than that offered, as she saw it, by the authoritarian and routine-ridden Austrian public school system. She had hired a son of friends of the Rosenfelds, Peter Blos, then a student of biology, as private tutor first for her eldest son, Bob, then for her eldest daughter and her two younger children. Blos brought along his equally young friend, Erik Homburger Erikson, at that time a "bohemian" and budding artist. This became the nucleus for a small private school financed by Dorothy Burlingham, managed by Eva Rosenfeld, and directed by Peter Blos. It was an educational venture which still remains to be described in detail, though Peter Blos left a manuscript on the subject in the archives of the Library of Congress where it has been inaccessible so far, and Erik Erikson and Joan Serson Erikson, who also taught at the school, have written about it, as did some former pupils (W. Ernest Freud, Peter Heller, Victor Ross), Michael John Burlingham, son of Bob Burlingham, and the pedagogue Dr. Rolf Göppel (Erikson, 1930, 1931a, b, 1974; Erikson and Erikson, 1980; W. E. Freud, 1985, 1987; M. J. Burlingham, 1989, pp. 182–189; Heller, 1990, pp. xxviii–xxxii; Göppel, 1991; this volume, pp. 31–33, 78–90).

The Eriksons wrote:

We believe that to begin with, Dorothy Burlingham as well as Eva Rosenfeld and Anna Freud dreamed the whole idea up together. Dorothy's four children were then being tutored by Peter Blos, a remarkably craftsman-like young teacher with clear concepts about how children learn. But tutoring is, of course, individual and isolated learning, and the children lacked the interplay and companionship with other children which a group setting affords.

So a school was formed of children who were spending some time in Vienna—children of different nationalities whose parents were undergoing analysis or who were perhaps in analysis themselves. It was never a very large group, rarely more than twenty children. All the parents, however, were intensely interested in new pedagogic ways and the impact of psychoanalytic understanding on education in the modern world.

Peter Blos, who became the director of this enterprise, had learned about and become impressed by the kind of curriculum then known as the Project Method which had revolutionized various school systems (first, we think, in Winnetka, Illinois) in America. This educational approach was in accord with John Dewey's theory that children learn only when their interest is fully engaged and centered. They are then amazingly capable of drawing all the facets of learning the mandatory "three R's" into the focus of a given project and of mastering otherwise dreary-to-learn skills. So we taught by the Project Method. The whole school would for a time become, for example, the world of the Eskimos. All subjects were then related to Eskimo life—geography, history, science, math, and, of course, reading and writing. This called for an ingenious combination of playful new experience, careful experiment, and free discussions, while it conveyed a sense of contextuality for all the details learned [Erikson, 1983, pp. 3–4].

The exchange of views about the school and its pedagogic principles is reflected in the letters. "Education without coercion" had been advocated repeatedly as an intrinsic characteristic of a psychoanalytic approach; and this was also one of the main points of contact between psychoanalytic pedagogy and the Montessori system [Bittner, 1989b]. But when the practical problems of the school were faced, it apparently became necessary to modify somewhat the principle of "freedom from coercion."

Cautious not to offend, Anna Freud confided to Eva:

> It would be better to talk about the school than to write about it. We really don't disagree; I also believe that school must be compulsion. Our disagreement concerns only one point. I want the children to be made to want to do what they are supposed to do. You want them to be made to do what they don't want to do as well. But the teachers

don't understand any of that. All they know is compulsion or liberation from compulsion. And the latter results in chaos [L8].

"Teachers don't understand any of that" is unfortunately true! What comes to light here, is the old and ever new deficiency of a pedagogy reduced to slogans and generalizations, instead of being developed in terms of more highly differentiated guidelines. Because opposing slogans always contain only half-truths, they soon have to be withdrawn, and thus give rise to quickly changing and alternating fashions. Quite recently, an "anti-authoritarian" education which was also to be an "education without compulsion," was again in fashion. Anna Freud's discriminating point of view is a welcome change from all this. It may well have been she who sowed the seeds of doubt about the very possibility of any psychoanalytically oriented education. She noted in 1968 (the revised German edition of her book *Normality and Pathology in Childhood* originally published in English, 1965):

> A retrospective look at the first half-century of psychoanalytically oriented education leaves no doubt of its unfinished and contradictory character. Confined to the prevention of neuroses as their goal, the paedagogical precepts given to educators kept changing along with changing notions concerning the origins of neuroses, and in keeping with the advance of analysis into ever deeper and more archaic levels of personality. In their chronological sequence, the notions as to what might guarantee psychic health changed directions, emphasis being first on freedom of drive activity, then on strength of the ego and its functions, then again on the intactness of infantile love relationships—a variety of goals, some of which could hardly be reconciled with one another [1968, pp. 2126–2127].

Or—as Anna Freud put it elsewhere: while "some pieces of advice" given to parents and educators over the years "proved beneficial almost beyond expectation," "others were contradictory and mutually exclusive (1965, Writings VI, pp. 6–7).

A specific problem in connection with the school was its official recognition by way of certification, to be discussed with city councillor Aichhorn (L6). "He too thinks one shouldn't start the next year without it." However, according to the Austrian State School Board and State Archives, no such application for official recognition by the educational authorities was ever made; nor was it required. I was told at the Austrian State Archives that Austria was the only European country with a law which did not require school *attendance* but had a requirement in terms of mandatory instruction only; that is, in terms of subject matter to be mastered. Anybody had the right to have his children privately tutored. The Burlingham–Rosenfeld School was, according to law, a communal private school for children. If such was the case, it would be surprising if Aichhorn, as a city official, had not known this. More likely, he did know, but thought formal official recognition desirable in view of the possible need of pupils to gain accreditation in the public school system in the future. And indeed, one of the major difficulties facing the pupils after the termination of the Hietzing School in 1931 to 1932 was the transition to the public school system for which they had been ill-prepared by a "free" education based primarily on freely chosen projects.

Anna Freud's dream of a psychoanalytic sanitarium may seem strange to us today. Perhaps it was suggested by the *genius loci* as she was living at Tegel-Berlin during her father's treatments. Like the Hietzing School, the Sanitarium Schloss Tegel was quite forgotten until the recent reconstruction of its history (Schultz and Hermanns, 1987). Founded on April 11, 1927 by the Berlin physician and psychoanalyst Dr. Ernst Simmel, who had made a name for himself by using elements of psychoanalytic therapy in the treatment of war neuroses, the sanitarium was to provide psychotherapy for gravely ill neurotics and for patients suffering from organic diseases. The interior was designed by Sigmund Freud's son Ernst, an architect by profession. As Sigmund Freud commented favorably on the concept of treatment underlying this establishment, Anna Freud's critical remarks are of special interest. Father and daughter certainly found the aesthetic and historic atmosphere of the old Humboldt castle particularly appealing (Freud's letter to von Heinz cited in Schultz and Hermanns, 1987, p. 64).

Generally speaking, the ambience in which psychoanalysis developed in Berlin was quite different from that of Vienna, and in keeping with the traditional contrast between

Prussian insistence on exacting discipline and the proverbial Austrian or Viennese mentality. The Psychoanalytical Institute of Berlin, founded in 1920, was the first of its kind. It served as model for the International Movement. Characteristic of it was the nexus between the clinical establishment *Poliklinik* and the teaching institute, as well as the development of a systematic curriculum or mandatory program of instruction (Bannach, 1971, pp. 243, 253). It has been said that the atmosphere in Vienna was more relaxed and friendlier. A considerable number of candidates flocking to Vienna and crowding the Vienna Institute did so, allegedly, to "escape the severe discipline of the Berlin Institute" (Leupold-Löwenthal, 1984, p. 105). It is of interest to compare in this context Anna Freud's remarks about Berlin and about her Berlin seminar (L20).

However, as far as Tegel is concerned, she finds it, in contrast to the demanding and strenuous city of Berlin, to be "ideally beautiful"; and she is as hopeful about a plan to assure the future of the sanitarium as she is disappointed when it finally collapses under the weight of financial problems (L6, L15). Nonetheless she is highly critical in regard to some of its aspects and problems which, she surmises, were due to the inexperienced therapists who made use of psychoanalysis where it was not appropriate to do so.

The patients at Tegel being all "beyond the point where they could get well on their own" suggest to her a parallel to child analysis, but with the difference that there is not "the element of hope which is present with children" who are still malleable and in the process of development. And thus, she thinks, the most difficult thing to accept for the therapists must be the disappointment of their hopes to apply psychoanalysis to these cases (L42).

Even so, she does endorse Dr. Simmel's fundamental notion of a purely analytical sanitarium and, more specifically, his insistent demand for a "closed" institution: For there, "analytically oriented care," which would probably get the better immediate results, could be separated clearly from "analytical therapy" which would perhaps remain disappointing until "the right modification of technique" was found (L42).

Beyond these general considerations, Anna Freud is also

increasingly critical of the way in which Simmel conducted his enterprise and the lack of the proper spirit in the relation between the staff and the director, which she contrasts with the model set in the reformatory for delinquents founded by Aichhorn, a man who was to remain one of her closest and most admired friends for the rest of her life (L47).

All in all, it is astonishing how open and impartial Anna Freud remains concerning the thought of a psychoanalytical institution of this kind. She mentions quite pragmatically the points which can become problematic for such a place: the modification of technique, the choice of patients, a clear, methodologically delineated distinction between therapy and a form of nursing care, which, to be sure, should also be informed by a psychoanalytical orientation. At any rate, she has no doctrinal or dogmatic misgivings about a "psychoanalytical sanitarium." Quite the contrary, the sanitarium was, like the school, part and parcel of her dream of a psychoanalytical community.

THE HUMANISTIC IDEAL OF HUMAN ENNOBLEMENT

"Man can always do a great deal for his inner happiness. All depends on the strength of his resolve and on some habituation to self-control and self-overcoming which are the foundation of all virtue and high-mindedness" (Humboldt, 1910, p. 34). These lines too were addressed to a female friend from the little castle at Tegel, though more than a century prior to Anna's letters to Eva, by its original owner, Wilhelm von Humboldt, the foremost proponent of an educational ideal of human culture and individual self-cultivation in the age of German idealism. The pathos of human ennoblement and sublimation of self is also part of the present correspondence. Indeed, Eva explicitly acknowledged the connection between this ideal and the correspondence of Wilhelm and Caroline von Humboldt, "six volumes bound in turquoise bindings," of which she claimed that they had been her "steady companions" and that she knew "the words, the decades, the events" recorded there "almost by heart," even in her old age (ER, chapter 20, "Tegel").

Once more, Anna Freud's problematic judgment of Victor (see above, p. 15) comes to mind, the critique of defensive evasion, notably into impersonally "technical" considerations or the neutrally "matter of fact," in lieu of a direct confrontation of human concerns, and her misgivings about an educational experience which did not, she thought, affect the substance of the pupil's character, or specifically, the lack of an "ideal" regarding what kind of human being one should become (L47). And there is the contrary judgment of Mädi who, Anna Freud thought, was just as one ought to be at her age, in order to become a "real human being" later on (L13).

Anna and Eva cultivated this ideal of a nobler, truer humanity also for themselves. Anna sought the freedom to be attained "by having forced oneself to go through something" (L4), and attempted a "long retreat" into herself (L22). Eva's contemporary letters to Obermann, and indeed her entire, passionately problematic relation to him, and her attitude toward her own family, are couched in terms of a pathos of elevation and of a questioning as to what a true human being should be like. Hence also her saying: "What matters is not what we did but who we were"; that is, her disparagement of mere specialized activity and insistence on a lived essence (this volume, p. 37; taped interview with Heller, July 1975).

The reform of life through psychoanalysis, traceable in the founding of the school and the wish–dream of a psychoanalytical sanitarium, was in truth meant to be a reform of humanity. What was to be created, was the new, the truly truthful and truly human human being. The early analysts were imbued with a humanistic pathos which Anna Freud interpreted specifically in terms of an ethic of sublimation. Theirs was the conviction of the "healing power of self-knowledge." As Erik Homburger Erikson put it at the time in one of his lectures: This had been the theme and concern of Western ethics ever since Socrates, but only in psychoanalysis had this concern and the hope for human enlightenment found its adequate "method" (Erikson, 1930; see Erikson, 1983, p. 29). Such was the ethos of Anna Freud and her early circle prior to the eclipse of their era in the thirties and the Second World War.

Eva Marie Rosenfeld (1892–1977): A Woman of Valor. A Personal Memoir (with illustrations)

Victor Ross

On July 8, 1927, some two years after the date of Anna Freud's first letter in this volume, Eva Rosenfeld lost the third of her four children, her daughter Rosemarie (Mädi), aged fifteen, in a mountaineering accident. "I am thirty-six years old," Eva remembered thinking at the time, "and I shall probably live another thirty-six years without knowing happiness."

Anna Freud came to the funeral in Aussee (a resort in the province of Styria, Austria) and afterwards helped to pack up Mädi's belongings; Sigmund Freud was to inscribe a copy of his latest book, *The Future of an Illusion* (1927a), in November of the same year with the words: "Der tapferen Eva" (to brave Eva).

Mädi's death followed that of her two little brothers from dysentery at the end of the First World War. Eva had lost three of her four children, echoing the pattern of her own mother's tragedy of losing three out of four children in her own lifetime. Loss and mourning formed the backdrop of despair behind which my mother would withdraw intermittently throughout her life. But on stage, her zest, her star quality, her life-enhancing powers, were given full rein. She retained a fine sense of drama to the end of her days.

The theatre was not far from her experience. Many Rosenfelds had a penchant for the theatrical; Eva's father and two of her uncles made it their careers. Like many Jews they chose the role of impresarios, standing at the intersection of art and business, salving their consciences by devoting some of the profits of popular entertainments to the subsidy of worthy money-losers. All my mother knew about the theater as a young girl, however, was that it provided her three elder brothers with unsuitable companions and fatal temptations. As if to compensate for their early delinquency and capacity to cause their uncomprehending parents anguish, she left school at fifteen, half-educated, to devote herself to the care of underprivileged girls.

The Rosenfelds were a large tribe; Eva's father Theodor was one of eleven brothers and sisters riding high on the coat tails of their parents' move from the ghettos of Eastern Europe to Vienna, Berlin, and points west. Freedom and opportunity, not yet a birthright, had at least become attainable rewards for effort. Some of Theodor's brothers and sisters prospered in the arts, others in commerce and the law; the less successful ones were carried along in the wake of what was so clearly a very close-knit family. There was enough money for the Rosenfelds to quarrel about higher things—Schopenhauer, Nietzsche, Wagner. Arguing was good exercise for minds and lungs: every Sunday afternoon there was a shouting match at one or other of the brothers' homes. The police, called by anxious neighbors, soon learned that these were no ordinary domestic disputes: the Rosenfelds were "at it"—shouting their new-found convictions as vigorously as their grandparents had shouted their wares in the market-place. They weren't proper intellectuals yet, certainly not the menfolk who had to earn a living; the women's minds were more finely tuned and, with more time to read and to think, paved the way for the next generation's (that of my parents) aspirations to culture.

This noisy, happy world was struck asunder when Theodor Rosenfeld, first among unequal brothers, died in

1907, at the age of fifty-six. His widow threw herself into a frenzy of mourning, wearing black to the day she died in 1942, in Oxford, England. At the age of fifteen my mother became head of her immediate family, responsible for a grief-demented mother and three elder brothers sheepishly inadequate in their youthful corruption.

A SOCIAL CONSCIENCE

One year after Theodor Rosenfeld died, my mother, now sixteen years old, decided that she needed a profession and a friend. Her profession she found in the Zellerhaus, an institution caring for orphaned girls of the lower classes. Eva liked to relate the series of chance encounters that led her to the Zellerhaus, and contrast these with the fateful inevitability of what she found there: her life's work—helping, teaching, healing. Workhouse or analyst's couch, not forgetting a few stations in between—henceforth her purpose would never waver: she described it as seeking a cure for the sickness that had destroyed her unhappy brothers.

Imagine the situation: a young girl, catapulted—no, self-propelled—from the protective environment of the nouveau riche Jewish middle-class into the lower depths of Berlin's deprived proletariat. She worked among those of her own age as a teacher and guide, and shared the life and hardships of this community. She soon realized that the worst wounds inflicted upon the young came from inadequacies of parental love, and that one had to tend the whole person, not just the wound. She also learned lessons about herself: the lifelong loyalty she would earn from those she shielded from the harsh discipline of the "establishment," her complete indifference to status when it came to serving the needy—to change a bedwetter's sheet was as honorable as opening a shuttered mind to the beauty of a poem; her fierce sense of justice which could turn her natural deference to authority into formidable opposition.

She also needed a friend, a replacement for the brothers who, fatherless, increasingly and secretively went their own ways. Help was at hand, of course from within the Rosenfeld tribe. Her handsome cousin Valentin, living in Vienna, was ready to introduce her to an unfamiliar world of art and literature, and above all music, one he had discovered for himself. From him also, she heard for the first time the name of Sigmund Freud, who was then exploring hitherto uncharted continents of the mind. As early as 1906 or 1907 her cousin had attended Freud's lectures at the University of Vienna, although Valentin's own subject was not medicine but law, which he was soon to practice.

Eva was torn between the exciting world that beckoned in Vienna, and the grim realities of Berlin, which called her no less strongly. Family affection ignited into love between the cousins, and "Valti," as she called my future father, insisted on a formal commitment. My mother hesitated: was she cut out for marriage? What would happen to her charges if she abandoned them? Was the desire for a family of her own stronger than her loyalty to that larger family of which she had become a part? Or could the two somehow be combined?

The engagement was finally announced in 1909 when my mother was just seventeen, but not until Valentin had written to Sigmund Freud asking for his view on marriage between first cousins. The answer, alas, is not preserved, but it was along the lines of "if you don't mind the characteristics common to both parents being reinforced in the children, go ahead." My parents married in 1911, and my mother moved to Vienna, a few weeks after her nineteenth birthday.

It was a heady time in the capital of the multicultural Austro-Hungarian empire, and an eye-opener to my mother to see concert audiences get into fist fights over the merits of an avant-garde work; to have a house furnished by the architect Adolf Loos; to be asked to model for the painter Oskar Kokoschka. And yet my mother found Vienna wanting both in seriousness and in creative tensions. She observed that to those coming from the east Vienna must indeed have seemed like a paradise, but coming from Berlin, she was conscious of a lack of electricity in the air. Perhaps she missed the Zellerhaus.

Ten years later the subject of Berlin versus Vienna—a favorite talking point between Germans and Austrians—must have reappeared in one of Eva's letters to Anna, because we have the latter's reply in L20 where, with instant insight, she suspects German seriousness to be even further removed from reality than Viennese playfulness. She uses the occasion to permit herself a heartfelt outburst against bourgeois acquisitiveness, a point more wittily made in L6 where she hopes that Vera's elaborately designed ball gown will get at least one more outing at her grandmother's funeral.

Eva's chance to replace the Zellerhaus did not come until after World War I, which left my parents living in a truncated and impoverished Austria, with plenty of electricity generated by social and political conflict, physical hardship, and personal tragedy. Their two little sons had died in 1918 as a result of dysentery; even with my father safely back from the war, the family was cut down from five to three in the space of two days. Only their beloved daughter, Mädi, survived. Eva's father-in-law (and uncle), successful lawyer and principal provider, to whose law practice Valti was to return, lay dying. Inflation was rampant. It was a time of moral and economic disintegration.

When the shock of national and personal catastrophe had become dulled to manageable size, and one more child (the present writer) was born into the family, my mother realized that she would have to take a more active part in securing the family's mental and material well-being. Her husband, disorientated by the loss of his father and his two sons, trapped in a profession he disliked, progressively withdrew into causes and hobbies. What was the answer? Another Zellerhaus?

With her unblinking eye for unpalatable truths, Eva recognized that the old order of leisured prosperity underpinned by servants would not return, and that the New Woman would have to learn to perform household chores while still functioning as wife, mother, and adornment of society.

In her own words, she set out to create "a model of household and gardening management ... with young women pupils for whom my house would provide a sort of research station." The idea caught on quickly, and soon my mother had more girls (or perhaps their parents) clamoring for places than there was room for. Most of them attended from midmorning to midafternoon "to keep them out of my poor husband's way," but a few lived in the house. In all the planning and planting that went on indoors and out, my mother saw a metaphor for deeper psychological functions—plants do after all grow in nurseries. Nor is it surprising that some parents used my mother's facilities to offload difficult youngsters, so that dimensions of helping and healing were added to that of teaching. A bit of Zellerhaus, then, without the squalor.

It was Siegfried Bernfeld, friend of my parents and himself an analyst, who drew Anna Freud's attention to my mother's establishment when a foster home was needed for one of her most difficult patients. Anna came to inspect Eva and our home, and soon the patient, Minna, was installed in our household, showing none of the symptoms that made it impossible for her to live at home. My mother's healing presence asserted itself instantly. Anna Freud was astonished to discover this unusual gift in an untrained mind.

Their friendship appears to start on a high note; there is no mention of a gradual ripening in my mother's unpublished reminiscences, from which I have already quoted several times. They meet some time in 1924 and from that moment on Anna Freud is central to my mother's life, and remains so for at least eight years. At Christmas 1924, Anna presents her with a book by Lou Andreas-Salomé, *Ródinka*; in the following year, for Anna's birthday, my mother strings thirty small gifts on a silver cord stretched through three rooms in the Berggasse, one for each birthday missed by not having known Anna before. Henceforth presents with a high content of loving ingenuity are a feature of their relationship: *Handarbeiten* (and in one case, at least, a poem) from Anna, who discovers a bent for making things with her hands; feats of the imagination from my mother who is all thumbs, but whose nose for unexpressed wishes is uncanny.

The exchange of presents went on even after their relationship had cooled. Long after the Freuds and Rosenfelds had emigrated to England, and indeed when my mother was already an old lady, I was the means of transporting her and some carefully wrapped gift to Anna's house in Maresfield Gardens, London.

The year 1924 was also the year in which my mother first met Sigmund Freud, one day while he was passing through Anna's room on his way to his own. Eva was introduced, the first of many honors and favors Anna Freud was to bestow upon her. I never asked my mother to explain the foundation of her friendship with Anna Freud; I grew up taking it for granted. Throughout her long life, Eva never lacked admirers of either sex who were attracted by the unforced originality of her ideas, her intelligence and wit, her joy in selfless service—perhaps above all her uncompromising scale of values which one might be proud to make one's own were it not for the discomfort of having to maintain them.

For Eva it was the Freud family, represented but not exclusively constituted by Anna, that inspired her and won her allegiance. The Berggasse was neither shrine nor laboratory; it was first and foremost a home, with meals at which the family met, with loyal members and comforting rituals. This was the family of which she was to become a part, in which she had her particular role, and which helped to replace losses already suffered and others yet to come.

Another outsider joined the charmed circle, never to leave it. In 1925, Dorothy Burlingham brought her eldest son, Bob, to Vienna to get help with his asthma and associated symptoms. When Anna Freud agreed to accept him as a patient, Dorothy decided on a permanent move from the United States bringing her three other children with her. The decision was eased by her wish to remove the family from the fallout of her husband's manic-depressive illness which required occasional sojourns in an institution.

Very soon the Burlinghams became part of the Freud solar system. Mabbie, the elder of Bob's two sisters, became Anna's patient too, but these shining, newly unwrapped American children, with their freckles and braces on their teeth, who turned heads in the streets of Vienna of 1925 merely by being themselves, excited more than Anna's clinical interest. They were family material: one wanted to have them for oneself, or at least a share in them. Having only just met the Burlinghams, Anna shows that she looks forward to Dorothy's return—with the children of course—in the postscript to L2. Soon the three women, Anna, Dorothy, and Eva are firm friends.

Strange coincidences fed my mother's appetite for omens. One day in the spring of 1926, the three decided to meet for a walk in the Vienna Woods, a favorite excursion spot for nature-loving Viennese. As my mother joined the other two, she heard Dorothy tell the story of how some weeks previously she had walked through the snow in that very same area and on returning home discovered the loss of a beautiful opal brooch that had been a gift of the Professor (Freud). No amount of searching since had proved successful. This story excited my mother's ambition. I can relate it in her own words, fifty years after the event.

> "Please let me look," I cried out. "I have lost so much—this I shall find." I was laughed at and they tried to make me behave sensibly and not search the Wienerwald for a little brooch. I persevered and said goodbye to them. I walked up a slope. There were no footpaths, one walked in meadows and among trees. I tried hard to recall the picture of that brooch, the dancing blue–red–green colours in their heavy gold setting. Since the snow had melted, tiny strawberry leaves had made their first appearance. I bent down idly to caress one of these little leaves, turned it over, and what did I see? The brooch. Unharmed. I arrived at my companions' table and just opened my hand in front of Dorothy's eyes. They could not believe it: laughter, shouts of delight, and congratulations poured over me. Anna and Dorothy decided at once: we had to return to the Berggasse and tell the Professor the news. We did, and his verdict was: "Eva must keep the brooch; I have already ordered another one for Dorothy, which will be ready in a few days."

This story says a lot about the character of Eva and the circle she inhabited: Freud's generosity not just to one, but two of Anna's friends; his soft spot for my mother; my mother's romantic notions anchored in the experience of loss; her joy to be of service, bringing back the lost brooch like a puppy dog that has dug up a bone.

There was a sequel: in the summer of 1930, when the Freuds, the Burlinghams, and the Rosenfelds, attended by a cast of dozens—friends, patients, children, dogs—moved their summer quarters to Grundlsee, the lakeside village near Aussee from which my sister had set out three years earlier on her fateful excursion, my mother had the habit of going for an early morning walk round the lake. One day she decided to venture further afield, halfway up the mountain that casts its shadow into the lake. The sun had risen and, feeling hot, she took off her scarf, secured by the Freud brooch. On returning home for breakfast, she discovered that she had left it lying next to her on the bench where she had taken her rest. Up at five the following morning, she retraced her steps and found the brooch for a second time. My mother liked nothing better than shaking the hand proffered by the long arm of coincidence.

THE SCHOOL

Eva Rosenfeld's fame as an educator, or at least as a willing steward of other people's difficult children, spread, no doubt in part thanks to Anna Freud's friendship and recommendation.

In L6 Anna Freud commends Eva for her success with the children in her care, particularly her own nephew Ernst, and asks: "Aren't you proud of your fine establishment?"

The household research station gave way to something rather more complex, and soon some fairly exotic companions were sharing our home. Among them was Kyra, the daughter of the immortal Nijinsky, herself a dancer who taught me to box and play poker; there was her beautiful friend who refused all food at table but stuffed herself with cream cakes and raw meat as soon as she was alone; there was Reinhard, son of Ernst Simmel, famed Berlin psychoanalyst. Reinhard had such an excess of "Berliner Schnauze" that my mother had to curb his garrulousness with the inspired rule that he was allowed to speak during mealtimes only after his near-autistic neighbor had spoken. It is not surprising that my father increasingly avoided the strange family wished upon him—we were rarely fewer than twelve at table—and found culinary and other consolations outside the home.

The most tangible result of the Freud–Burlingham–Rosenfeld relationship at that time was the school, or perhaps better, the Rosenfeld–Burlingham school. The school tends to be referred to by different names according to the perspective of the viewer. To my mother it was a straightforward matter: the flowering of her educational mission, given substance as a monument to my sister, with Dorothy's four children and a handful of others (including two of the three contributors to this volume) as a nucleus. My mother provided half our garden as building site and playground; Dorothy put up the money for a log cabin with classrooms on two floors. The plans for this were drawn up by two young men of my mother's acquaintance, Peter Blos and Erik Erikson, who were to remain in the business of "teaching and healing" for the rest of their lives. The teaching plan operated on the project method: at any one time the entire school devoted itself to a single subject, each pupil working on some aspect of it, according to ability and need. There were perhaps twenty students in all, between the ages of eight and fifteen, either formed into small syndicates or working by themselves. Anna Freud was no stranger to project teaching: on a temporary assignment as a schoolteacher in Hungary during World War I, she had tried it out herself.

My mother, having provided much of the impetus, took little part in running the school and none in the teaching, except for music. She sang to us, we sang to her, and once she led us in a grand performance of Haydn's Toy Symphony. But behind the scenes she must have attended regular progress meetings, because some school concerns surface in the correspondence, notably in L8, in which Anna Freud, typically, puts her finger on the point about discipline at issue between them—another aspect of the Berlin–Vienna divide.

Apart from her responsibility for the young people who were actually staying in her house, Eva had found another absorbing interest, another Zellerhaus. It was a place where the children of the poor were given food and shelter for part of the day, and which went under the unexpected, English name of "The Settlement." My mother's gift for serving up practical care with a moral dressing, was exemplified by asking each pupil at our school to bring two lunches—one for him or herself, and one for an unknown child at The Settlement.

And Anna Freud's part in all this? With few exceptions, every child at the school was undergoing analysis, many of them with Anna herself. This fact alone must have made it a unique establishment in its time. The school finally closed its doors in 1932. It became my father's home when, after my parents' separation, my mother and I went to live in Germany, and the big house was rented. During the war, the log cabin was hit by a bomb and went up in flames. There is nothing left of it today.

"A GLUTTON FOR THE TRUTH"

My mother liked to think that she, too, like Freud "discovered" psychoanalysis on the rebound from hypnosis, even if the circumstances were not exactly Freudian. One of her more rascally cousins was a doctor and skilled hypnotist, and my mother had the startling experience, while attending a family party in his house, of one of his patients coming out of a deep trance in the consulting-cum-living room where the guests had gathered—having lain forgotten under a rug on a sofa until one of the aunts sat on her.

It was Anna Freud who decided that my mother needed analysis and that her father had to be the analyst. She saw my mother struggling to turn breadwinner under the twin burdens of a grief that would not be assuaged and a marriage beyond repair. My father's legal practice, never flourishing, had received a further blow when he undertook—from bravado rather than conviction—the defence of the radical socialists who had attacked Vienna's Palace of Justice in July 1928. Henceforth he was himself regarded as politically "unreliable" and indeed spent a short time in protective custody during right-wing Chancellor Dollfuss's regime in the early 1930s. Already in 1927 (L4) there are pointers to what is in Anna's mind when she advises her friend on how to read Freud and how happy she is that Eva is "not afraid of us any more."

To the Professor, my mother—no languid Viennese, but that potent mix, a Prussian Jew—must have appeared an attractive challenge on several counts: apart from wanting to please his daughter he knew my mother well enough to see that her devastating directness would cut out a lot of the pussyfooting he had to endure from his society ladies; my mother's command of a sexual vocabulary, learned from her brothers and at the Zellerhaus, would make a pleasant change. He probably recognized in her an early edition of the New Woman—free-thinking, curious, courageous, yet not bent on strenuous intellectual jousting in the manner of Lou Andreas-Salomé.

From my mother's point of view, there was only one question: was she worthy of so much honor, so much love? "I was to find a 'father' again," she wrote later, "22 years after my own father's death." And again: "I doubt whether any thirty-seven-year-old woman in today's world would be as awestruck as I was then." Finally: "The one feeling which predominated over all the others was perhaps a kind of fear that I was so enviable, that this was so undeserved, so out of proportion to my daily grind of looking after others and not bothering about myself, that I really had to rethink my whole life to find out whether I was worthy of what was happening . . ."

In a sense, my mother must have been worried about how she was going to pay for her sessions with the Professor. There was no question of money changing hands: this alone made her analysis well-nigh unique in the roster of the Professor's patients—the cash nexus being important therapeutically and otherwise. Would the price of Eva being in analysis be the end of the easy intimacy with father and daughter, introducing constraint into a treasured friendship? She need not have worried. Everything went on as before: the affectionate relations with Anna, the loving correspondence when they were apart, the admiring friendship for the Professor, the absorption into the family, partly, it has to be said, in a role which my mother performed all too readily: that of fixer–factotum, booker of holidays, tester of beds, measurer of the height of desks.

But for the present, her cup overflowed, life began anew. Analysis would enable her eventually to find the strength to leave her husband and Vienna; she would find her true vocation as an analyst and supervisor of analysts; she would almost, but never quite, find peace amid the daily, gnawing sense of the loss of her three children. And, perhaps, analysis also bore within itself the seeds of the rift, or drift, from Anna Freud.

It was not a conventional analysis by any standards, not even the easy-going ones of the 1920s, with the Professor confidently making his own rules. To begin with, there were seventy-eight sixty-minute sessions in a row, at the rate of six per week, starting, according to Letter 8 on March 25, 1929. These were followed by irregular "hours" (*Stunden* in German, denoting both the passage of time and the lesson learned therein), sometimes only a single hour per week, taken when the families holidayed together. Finally, there was a late burst of greater frequency in 1931, before my mother left Vienna for good.

Unlike most patients, she claimed to have experienced more joy than pain while undergoing analysis, although she once said that since sixty minutes could feel like eternity, perhaps eternity would feel like sixty minutes. The Professor's insights, sometimes humorously, sometimes gruffly revealed, never ceased to delight and enlighten: she was so eager to learn, so anxious not to obstruct the flow with unworthy hesitations! Of course there were barren, wordless periods, too. During one of these, Freud remarked: "If you were as much of a bore as the man who comes before you, I could understand your silence. But you, with *your* life!"

My mother claimed that with all her enthusiasm, she never felt the sort of dependence on her analysis that patients tend to feel "these days." Just as well, given its sporadic nature! Nevertheless, every "hour" brought new insights, some not until much later—like the thought that throughout her analysis, she must have repressed the wish to be analyzed by Anna, "by my dear friend whom I so loved." A propos of this my mother noted down an exchange that took place between her and the Professor during one of the sessions.

> One day I was lying on the couch, looking up at the chandelier in the centre of Freud's consulting room. There were six glass shades, one of

them different from the other five. I said to Freud: "One of these glass shades is different from the other five."
He said: "No."
I said: "Yes it is."
He insisted: "No, it isn't."
I said: "It really is."
So he got up from his chair, switched on the electric light, and had a look for himself. He switched off, went back and sat down.
"You are right," he said. "This fact will not, however, prevent me from saying that you mean to tell me that Anna's position among my six children is different from that of all the others."

The transference, in my mother's own words, was one of passionate intensity. She describes looking foward to her sessions in the language of a lover going to meet the beloved:

I used to say to him: "I wish I could come here by donkey cart, very very slowly, so that I could indulge all my anticipations and memories turning up mixed with new insights and associative thinking." But then, when one actually lies on the couch, it all happens so very differently. Every analytical session is a little miracle in itself; things belong together which one never knew had any bearing on each other; patterns emerge which make sense in a new, unexpected fashion. . . .
I remember very painful days when I seemed wordless, stayed silent, and one rather sarcastic retort of the Professor's when I once told him, "If this goes on for another three days, I shall not be able to stand it." His reply: "Now let's see, what is it today—Tuesday, so it will be Friday when you give up."

But of course my mother would never give up.

The time came when I could readily co-operate, when I brought ideas and reflections made from hour to hour. . . . That was a phase of great liberation, although one remained always liable to great suffering. What one gradually became aware of is what Nietzsche called prophetically "the transvaluation of all values." Your pride and your self-possession consist mainly and rightly of what you have made of yourself, what you have repressed, what victories your conscience has won over your impulses . . . that is where analysis steps in and reshuffles one's dearest achievements like a pack of playing cards. Top goes to bottom and bottom goes on top. . . . But one's personality, one's character remains untouched. . . . I did not become someone other than who I had always been. . . .
Freud's great mind was the gift of those years to my development, between 1924 and 1932. They were eight years that changed my life completely.

The choice between learning the truth about herself and loving the teacher—that "insatiable glutton for the truth"—never had to be made. Anna Freud was quite right when she wrote on March 22, 1929 (L8): "You know, there is no contradiction in your undergoing analysis in a place where you would prefer to come for love's sake alone. I did the same thing, and perhaps because of it, the two things became inextricably bound together for me."

TEGEL

The core of the correspondence between Anna Freud and Eva covers the years 1929 to 1931, with forty-seven of the fifty-seven letters here reproduced falling into those three years. Of the forty-seven, no less than thirty-two were written either from or to Tegel, a suburb of Berlin.

What was so special about Tegel? My mother would claim it as one more instance of the claws of fate making a grab at her. She put it like this: "Schloss Tegel had for centuries been the home of the Humboldt family, and the Humboldts had been the most deeply loved models of my earlier years."

The Humboldts did indeed represent an ideal close to my mother's heart: they believed in the educational process as a means of creating worthy human beings—the rounded mind having, by definition, fewer holes and corners—and worthy human beings representing in turn the best role models for the young. My mother was fond of claiming that "what we did was less important than who we were" ("we" being Anna, herself, and the circle around them). It was also a way of putting psychoanalysis, consciously or unconsciously, in its place.

In the early 1930s, Schloss Tegel had inhabitants who were very different from the Humboldts. It was being run as a psychoanalytic sanitarium by Ernst Simmel, who had done very important work on war neuroses during and after World War I. An ardent follower of Freud, he took the concept of countertransference to its ultimate conclusion by marrying, one after the other, some of his choicer women patients. It was also a place to which Anna and her father repaired to rest between operations and the treatment of the Professor's cancer by the Berlin surgeon Schroeder. Anna's letters from Tegel were written during the long weeks she spent attending to her father in Tegel while Schroeder made painful explorations and adjustments to the prosthesis.

Her work at the Tegel sanitarium was to give my mother an opportunity to make the break with Vienna and with my father, and to start a new career. Admittedly, it was a humble start, as matron of the sanitarium, but it provided a home, a salary, a challenge—it was another Zellerhaus.

The problem in Tegel was lack of organization, of money, of skilled personnel. My mother was called in by Simmel to try and save the place from disintegration. She had been highly recommended by Anna for her energy and managerial skills, and Simmel jumped at the chance, having seen Eva's work as foster mother to his exceptionally fractious son Reinhard, who had been sent to Vienna while his father traded in his then current wife for a new model. Many of Anna Freud's letters of the period reflect her concern about the future of the sanitarium, both in a practical and a clinical sense. Letter 6 refers to some scheme of financial rescue; L42 written in 1931, shows her making an interesting distinction between the patients' need for "active therapy" and "pure analysis" which carries echoes of earlier preoccupations with her child patients and her differences with Melanie Klein over the need for nonanalytic preparation for analysis. It is noteworthy that this letter, which ends on a very affectionate note, contains, by way of a post scriptum, the firm advice that my mother tear up all Anna's letters. The context suggests that the thought came to her because of her remarks about Tegel rather than because of the warmth of the feelings expressed. The latter do, after all, grace the majority of her letters. But one can never be sure of anything except Anna's desire to cover her tracks, of leaving behind no quotable hostages to fortune, which became ever more marked in later life and ultimately contributed to the change in the relationship between the two women.

On the other hand, Anna wants to know everything. Letter 32 goes straight to the point, telling Eva that she has to make "the great change" even if it means her mother moving to Vienna to take over. There appears to be no reluctance on my mother's part to go into the details of her marital problems. Daily telephone calls supplement the letters, charting the state of the negotiations with my father. In L35 the Professor's answer to my mother's question about a last-minute withdrawal, and Dorothy's offer to take me temporarily off my mother's hands, are conveyed. Everybody is in on the act. In L36 Anna reinforces my mother's resolve to cut the knot by going to Berlin, although she is afraid that "you won't come back, once you are there." Nearly every letter in this sequence, with Eva in Grundlsee negotiating with Simmel about a job in Tegel, and with my father in Vienna about separation, contains references to those two momentous steps which are really one. My mother appears to discuss my father's every move with Anna and even passes on his letters so that Anna and the Professor can read them for themselves (L41).

By mid-1931 the decision had been taken and my mother was installed in Tegel with the title of "Matron" and the assignment to supervise and to act as "link between the doctors, the nurses, and the patients." She described what she found:

> Tegel was in a bad state financially and only very energetic organization could rescue it from the threat of closure. I was expected to provide this and also to be once more a housemother to "children" under analysis. My task was two-fold—to deal with the financial crisis brought about by the crash of the Danat Bank on the one hand, and to cope with the emotional crises between the therapists, patients, and nurses on the other. The latter might have been possible, although the work required immense physical resources: there were no lifts, nor any relief from the everlasting foot marches along the stupendous corridors—but the financial strain could not be borne. Parents and relatives of the patients wrote and declared themselves insolvent: the experiment broke down.

My mother was kept on to manage the dissolution. She did this in her inimitable style by first finding new jobs for all the domestics and then persuading nurses and patients to look after themselves. Those who were too ill to do so were found places elsewhere; the others in their temporary guise as cleaners and cooks, made splendid progress. But in the end there was not enough money even to buy food. Yet my mother stayed on to the last so that she would be able to hand over Schloss Tegel to the owner in perfect condition "with not a spoon missing." She felt that she owed this much to the heir of her beloved Wilhelm von Humboldt. Actually, she, or rather Simmel, also owed him the last quarter's rent. Even my mother was not paid her final salary, but received a prophetic gift instead—a beautiful couch, designed by Freud's architect son Ernst—which was to serve as her patients' couch for the next forty years. And perhaps another reward: by meeting the heirs of the Humboldts she had, in Goethe's words, been allowed to breathe the pure air of German idealism.

THE END OF A CHAPTER

With Tegel gone, Vienna foreclosed, and responsibility for a young son and an aging mother, Eva decided to look in an unexpected direction. Might Russia be the country of the future, or at any rate her future? A six weeks' journey of discovery convinced her otherwise, but it was a bold thought and a brave act to have gone to Moscow on her own.

Anna was sufficiently concerned about this adventure to advise warm clothing and drawing hot water from the engine in an emergency (L55). The correspondence breaks off at this point, as suddenly as it began, without intimation of a change in the relationship, much less of a chapter closed.

Yet the bundle of fifty-seven letters must have been regarded as a chapter by my mother, collected as they were in one manilla envelope, boldly labeled (many years later, in English) "Anna's letters." Even allowing for gaps in the collection due to loss, or missing forerunners or stragglers, it is as difficult to prove as it is to disbelieve that this particular parcel had unity and significance. As to Eva's letters of the 1920s and early 1930s, it is unlikely that Anna Freud kept them, given the injunction to destroy her own. They certainly have not turned up among Anna Freud's papers.

There were good practical reasons why the correspondence might have flagged when it did. Eva's move to Berlin marked the end of almost daily affectionate contact to which the letters had been mere adjuncts. They were never bringers of news so much as messengers of love and mutual support. For a correspondence of this nature to carry the information load that two busy lives produced would have required a daily output for which there just was not time. Perhaps the attempt was made, but if so, it could not have been sustained. Anna was increasingly assuming the duties her father was no longer able to perform; my mother had decided to become an analyst, and set herself a punishing schedule of training and study to reach qualified status within three years so as to be able to emigrate from Germany not later than 1936.

To do so she returned to base, to her mother's home in Berlin which became once more the operational headquarters of the Rosenfelds as it had been so many years ago in her father's lifetime. Her mother, the "indispensable Omi" as Freud had called her in the dedication on a photograph in 1929, was restored to the role of provider of love, spiritual and material support, and the centerpiece of a circle of admiring friends.

But there must have been strains below the surface, and perhaps my mother's choice of profession was one of them. Was she—useful, reliable, ever-available Eva—getting a little above herself? Only circumstantial evidence points to this, but on occasions when my mother sought approval for some independent thinking she had done—showing little more ambition than a performer adding a grace note—she had been rebuffed: casually by Freud, quite hurtfully by Anna.

The first of three rebuffs concerned some ideas on the theme of bisexuality where my mother ventured a more elaborate interpretation of Oedipus's answers to the riddle of the sphinx by suggesting that the crawling child represented bisexuality, upright walk suggested having opted for the active, procreative role, "and in the evening everybody becomes an old woman with a stick, that is to say impotent, with a useless member."

Freud did not think much of these ideas; he brushed them aside with the comment that the sphinx's questions must have been distorted over time, and that to construct interpretative answers was pointless. My mother withdrew, abashed but unrepentant, continuing to believe that the legend threw light on how society coped with homosexuality and incest.

Rebuffs by Anna were more complex and more frequent. My mother wrote a number of papers for the British Psychoanalytical Society's proceedings and gave lectures and talks. Rarely did she fail to submit these in advance to Anna Freud, and even rarer was the occasion when her manuscripts did not come back with critical remarks—as often straightforward putdowns as points of substance. The most hurtful incident of this kind concerned a paper about the Brontës, prepared, not for publication, but as a special present for Anna's seventy-fifth birthday. It was the result of deep immersion in the story of that strange family and, for an interpretation of the sisters' childhood memories, Eva drew on Anna Freud's own teaching. It was altogether a Festschrift of bold conception, in line with the tradition of supergifts, beautifully typed and beribboned for the occasion.

Anna's reaction was deeply wounding to my mother, for Anna treated her tribute like an immature student's work, pointing out errors and accidental misspellings, dismissing altogether both the labor and the love. Perhaps the story of three sisters with its hidden parallel was not the best choice of subject Eva could have made.

Yet if this was a reflection of the Freuds' assessment of my mother's capacity as an original thinker and writer, it did not differ all that much from her own. Reflecting on her analysis, she wrote:

> Both my analysts, Freud and Klein, thought well of me and showed special interest in me. To both I became a disappointment to some extent.... As regards Freud, I blame in the first place my lack of education. I learnt little when my brain was at its most receptive. A free-thinker—and that was my family tradition—may easily appear more intelligent than she is. I think this applies to me, at least where the grasp of theory is concerned.

This piece of frank self-assessment reveals her strength as well as her weaknesses. True, she was not great on theory, nor a stylish writer; she had not absorbed the disciplines of abstract thinking in her youth at the time when the mind is most malleable. But her shrewdness, open-mindedness, and quick wit served her patients better than the scholarly nit-picking of many academically superior colleagues.

Her undeniable success as therapist and trainer of therapists lay in her broad humanity, the size of her heart rather than her head. In this respect she represented a welcome contrast to those of her colleagues who poured their personalities into one particular psychoanalytical speciality. Eva operated on the opposite principle: she suffused her knowledge of the world, her understanding of the condition of man, her sense of what was beautiful and what was good, with the glow of analytic understanding. Freud had widened her horizons; so many of his followers had theirs more sharply defined but narrowed.

Her best thoughts and deftest formulations arrived *ex tempore*. She was a compelling speaker, an effective raconteuse. She told me once how anxious Freud had been to "keep medicine out of psychoanalysis." He wanted it to stand on its own feet. "Now psychoanalysis has invaded medicine: touch a body and you hold a soul." This was her neat way of saying that no physician dares to practice medicine today without arranging for a psychological fallback position. This reality came much closer to her own view of psychoanalysis as one tool among many rather than as the answer to the riddle of the universe.

Less speculative as a factor in the gradual growing apart of Anna Freud and Eva Rosenfeld is the Burlingham effect. As Dorothy's star rose, Eva's waned. There is an early warning in the correspondence. In 1927 Anna Freud can still sound quite patronizing about Dorothy. "She wants so much to be one of us," she writes in L4. Two years later she has to reassure Eva: "Why do you act as the 'foil' for Dorothy? Why do you assume that Dorothy is the only person I worry about and the only person I want to be reassured about?" (L17).

For all that, I am sure that even after 1932 my mother still considered herself part of the Freud family and performed, quite automatically, such services as could be rendered at a distance, one of them being the escorting of Anna's nephew Ernst ("Ernsti") across the border between Germany and Austria on the eve of April 30, 1933, the day of the Nazi boycott of all Jewish shops and offices. This was a risky enterprise for someone with a Moscow visa in her passport, and it nearly ended badly. But it would not have occurred to Eva to shirk such a service, nor to Anna not to expect it.

Emigration to England in 1936, according to plan, and two years before the Freuds' flight from Austria, opened the distance on the map and widened such fissures as had appeared in the relationship. One great gash, deliberately—some would say provocatively—inflicted by my mother was her ripening friendship with Melanie Klein.

MELANIE KLEIN

My mother met Melanie Klein not long after her arrival in London. She could hardly have overlooked her: the British Psycho-Analytical Society was riven by quarrels around the teachings and personality of that singular woman. My mother felt immediately drawn to her: "A lonely woman—I had to look out for such a one. I had to comfort her and show her that she did not frighten *me*.... Far from avoiding her as most colleagues did, I was fascinated by her. Had she a message, which I, unlike many others, could understand?"

Eva's first step toward gaining that understanding was to immerse herself in the teachings of Melanie Klein, particularly the role of the destructive impulse—not an unfruitful field for a Freudian in the act of apostasy. She asked Melanie Klein to send her a suitable case and appoint a supervisor, "who would teach me the technique she thought should be applied in severe illnesses—e.g., in depression and its relation to mourning and manic states."

The treatment of the young girl Klein sent, who was in a near-psychotic state, had a profound effect on both patient and analyst. "Without warning the deep afflictions of my past, the loss of my children, language, landscape ... flared up. I felt I needed another piece of psycho-analysis."

My mother's analysis with Freud had never been properly completed; it was allowed to trickle away. Her young patient became the catalyst in bringing her own needs back to the surface. For a moment she recoiled from the inevitable and wrote to Freud in Vienna, asking for a month's intensive treatment. But Freud was old and ill and, having heard of my mother's relationship with the Kleinians, skeptical about the value of such a refresher course. He replied to my mother in a long (unpublished) hand-written letter dated August 15, 1937, saying:

> You put me in the painful position of having to deny you the fulfillment of a wish. Really, you give your own answer when you say that you know that four weeks' analysis with me would achieve nothing. ... You know my attitude to the teachings of Melanie Klein. I too believe that she has discovered something new, but I do not know whether it means as much as she thinks, and I am sure that it grants no right to put theory and technique on a new basis."

Not long afterwards my mother began an analysis with Melanie Klein which continued in fits and starts from 1938 to 1941, when Mrs. Klein moved to Scotland because of wartime conditions in London, and my mother went to live and practice in Oxford.

The tone of Freud's letter does not suggest a sense of betrayal. Anna Freud's views are not on record but my mother claimed that it was due "to Anna's dignified and humane attitude to me that I was never made to feel that I had lost her friendship."

She certainly lost Melanie Klein's friendship. The latter eventually disowned Eva for lack of obedience. My mother wrote: "One never became friends with Melanie Klein. One was either for her or against her. She fought for her ideas and nothing but true discipleship was acceptable to her. She once said to me: 'You have sacrificed your analysis to the friendship with Anna Freud!' " My mother certainly understood that she had sacrificed all hope of professional advancement by taking up a position midway between Freud and Klein, but she summed up her predicament in her usual succinct way: "I made no career, but I gained a reputation."

EPILOGUE

My mother notes Anna Freud's apparent loyalty with approval. But the reality of an intimate, mutual friendship had long disappeared, even if old habits died hard. When the Freuds arrived in London in 1938, my mother was, of course, on hand, organizing with the best of them, but by that time the helpers outnumbered the survivors and some, in their grandeur, outshone them, too.

When my grandmother, the Omi whom Freud always liked so much, was ushered into the old man's presence, he waved his arms at his library, newly installed behind him with every book in its accustomed place. "Alles ist hier," he said. "Aber ich bin nicht hier." (Everything is here, but I am not here.)

It is possible that the very letters Anna had written cast a blight. The knowledge that they existed but no longer held good, that they were lying somewhere, silent witnesses to another time, another place, may have been profoundly disturbing to her. Anna's fear of indiscretions, her desire to veil all personal matters in secrecy, had grown stronger with every passing year and with every attempt from outside to probe family skeletons. My mother, talkative and indiscreet, was a threat. And she had intimate knowledge of family matters quite apart from the letters.

In a broadcast talk Eva gave for the BBC she reminisced harmlessly about the Freuds. Anna's wrath was quite disproportionate to the offense and suggests deeper apprehensions: if anecdotes today, why not letters tomorrow?

I never heard my mother mention the existence of the letters until some time before her death, nor the cache of gifts from Freud, including a book he had owned and written in when he must have been about twelve. She seemed fearful that Anna would in some way repossess herself of all that her father had given her—a potent threat since she believed that Freud had given her back life itself.

But this is speculation. Most of the story told here is not. As her son, I was eye, ear, and heart witness to the years up to the outbreak of the war. On events of later years, I consulted her friends and colleagues.

The most important resource was her own writings. For the last ten years of her life, my mother had been working on what only half-jokingly she referred to as her memoirs. Ostensibly they were for her grandsons and therefore written in English, but her ambitions were for a wider audience and she was disappointed to be told that the material was not publishable. It consists of a mixture of family history, some of it expurgated; stories and thoughts about the Freuds and her own analysis; and autobiographical notes and reflections. I have quoted freely from the manuscript, with minimal editing where I thought this would help the reader. Wherever the context does not indicate otherwise, all quotations are from that source.

Finally, of course, there are Anna's letters themselves, so strong and evocative. Occasionally, in the original German, they pulse with an intensity of feeling which, in translation, survives mainly in the use of endearments. But there are enough expressions of need, of longing, of shared sorrow and love, to prompt the question whether there was more between the two young women than a bond of friendship. The answer has to be a confident no: the tone is exactly that in which close friends of their class might address one another—without inhibition, with a natural innocence, sometimes even with a touch of poetry that belongs to their common heritage of Goethe and Heine. Anna Freud had a magical way with words; some of the high emotion that shines in these letters is due to her ability to lay bare her feelings in the simplest of language. Reading the letters today, they still sound as natural to me as the stories Anna told and the songs my mother sang when I was a child.

In the end the relationship between them was no longer one of equals. My mother was back in awe of Anna, overanxious to prove devotion through service; Anna was sovereign, distant, graciously pleased now and then to accept such service—not primarily to herself, of course.

Letter 57, written when my mother was eighty-three, says it all. There is the little matter of a bathroom fitting to be ordered for poor, sick Mathilde Hollitscher, and who better to do this than Eva who thought of the idea in the first place and might as well share in the cost to give Anna's sister extra pleasure. It's a long road from the way things were in 1929 when Anna Freud wrote to my mother: "You are I and I am you and any part of me that you can use you must always take, because you have a right to it" (L11).

Anna Freud came to my mother's funeral in 1977. Afterwards she wrote to me that she envied Eva the ease of her dying and hoped for the same for herself. It was the first time in many years that she had thought her former friend worthy of emulation.

Anna Freud, Tegel, 1928. (Sigmund Freud Copyrights Ltd., London.)

Dorothy Burlingham and Anna Freud with Alfred de Forest, Berchtesgaden, 1929. (Photo by Max Halberstadt. Courtesy W. Ernest Freud.)

Anna Freud at age 37 (1932). (Sigmund Freud Copyrights Ltd.)

Schloss Tegel (1935).

Grundlsee: view from the Rebenburg.

Eva, Racker, Omi, Mädi, Victor in Vienna, about 1924. (By courtesy of Victor Ross.)

Pupils at the Burlingham–Rosenfeld ("Hietzing") School, about 1930.

Pupils at the Burlingham–Rosenfeld School in the schoolyard.

Valti Rosenfeld, Eva's husband. (By courtesy of Victor Ross.)

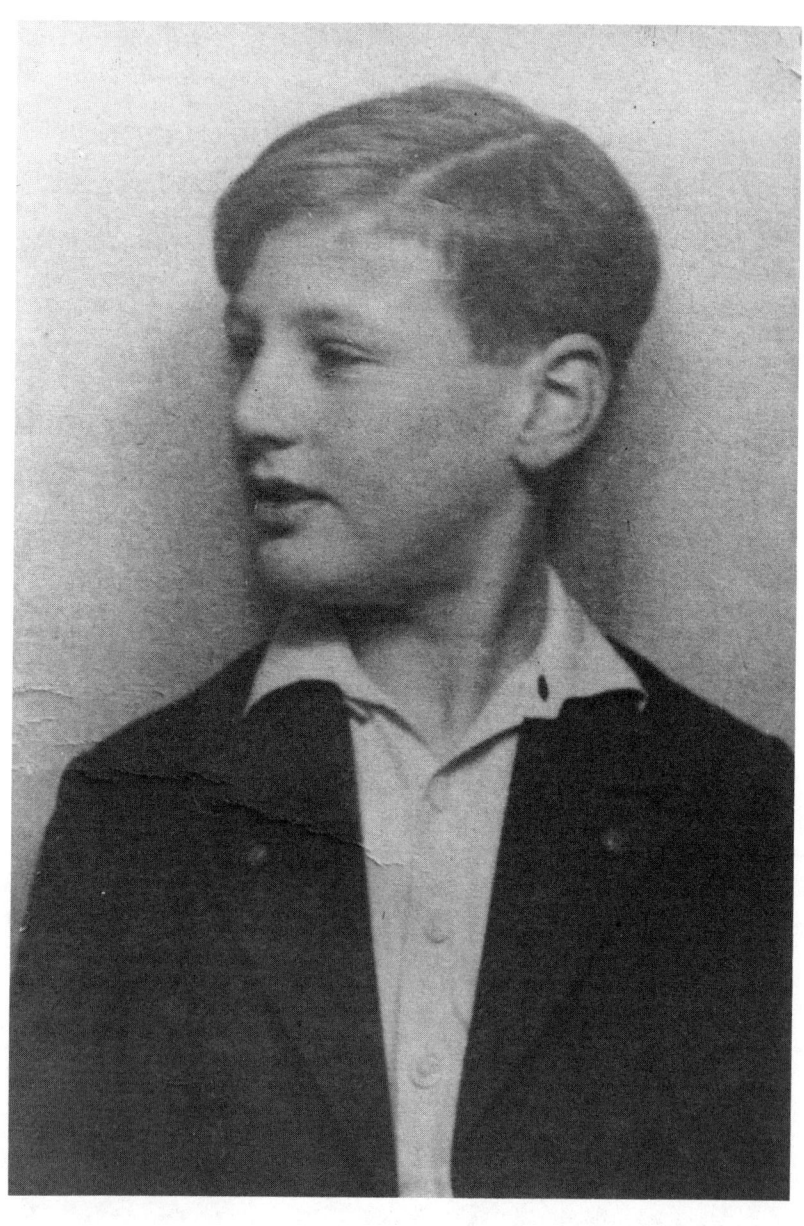

Eva's son, Victor, at about 11 years of age (1930?). (By courtesy of Victor Ross.)

Eva in Grundlsee. (By courtesy of Victor Ross.)

Part II

Anna Freud: Letters to Eva Rosenfeld

Remarks on the Background and Major Topics of the Letters

Peter Heller

In addition to the essays on the major protagonists, the following remarks on recurring themes and characteristic features of the letters may prove helpful to the reader.

According to her memoirs, Eva Rosenfeld met "most of the circle of Freud" between 1924 and 1927, "fairly near the beginning of my friendship with Anna," when the Freud family spent their summers in the Villa Schüler on the Semmering. The circle included the "person who interested" Eva Rosenfeld "more than anybody else," [ER, 200] Lou Andreas-Salomé (Frau Lou) (1861–1937), writer and analyst, formerly Nietzsche's passionately beloved disciple, and the lover of Rilke. "In intellect and heart," Eva recalled some forty years later, "she was a sparkling diamond. None of the men around Freud were her equal in this regard" (to Anna Freud, May 19, 1968). Frau Lou had become an intimate friend of Sigmund Freud, and the elder confidante of his daughter Anna, notwithstanding the difference between Lou who "did only what she felt like doing," and Anna, who led a life of service. The contrast extended also to their views on children. For Lou, as

Anna put it, always wanted to leave children the way they were, while she always wanted "to change them"; and it was apparently Lou's criticism of Anna Freud's "Introduction to the Technique of Child Analysis" (1927) which signaled a cooling down of the relationship, though by no means its extinction (Peters, p. 13).

Eva Rosenfeld recalls:

> [Lou] had arrived [in Vienna] by sleeper from Göttingen and was brought by Anna to my house in the Wattmanngasse one morning at six o'clock for some breakfast. I remember how she brushed her teeth walking up and down the corridor, and then I called her for breakfast in the garden which she enjoyed.... This was shortly after our [private] performance of [Gerhart Hauptmann's play] Hannele, so I guess it must have been in September 1925. I told Lou about the children [who acted the various parts in this drama of a dying child]. She also loved the play and recited to me long passages which she knew by heart [ER, p. 200].

The episode fits the allusion to the breakfast at dawn in L3. However, as Lou visited with the Freuds on the Semmering, where she stayed at the Südbahnhotel from August 15 to the end of the month (Pfeiffer, 1980, p. 175), and we have a letter (see below) about her trip from the Semmering back to Göttingen (via Munich), the breakfast must have occurred on or about August 15 on a stopover on Lou's journey to the Semmering.

A reunion was soon to take place. In a letter to Sigmund Freud (Freud–Andreas-Salomé, 1980, pp. 175–176), dated by the editor "Munich, September 2, 1925.... after Lou's visit with Sigmund and Anna Freud on the Semmering," Lou writes:

> This is only a quick first greeting... I arrived two hours ago in Munich, and in my thoughts I am still in your mountains, with a heart full of gratitude for these long longed-for weeks. When we left the station [on the Semmering]—royally established in our first class compartment—a big and almost full moon looked at us magically. It took Anna's regretful assurance to make me realize that you could not have seen it at the same time on your way home; much as—to my joy—she pointed out to me again and again the Schülervilla or the Südbahn-Hotel, though this seemed like a magic trick, whereby the landscape remained familiar to me, as if it would accompany me to

Germany and even to Göttingen. This way we still had 2 beautiful hours together, arrived—with a delay of 45 minutes—[in Vienna] in an indescribably crowded station, due to children's vacation trains filled with sick people. Nonetheless your son in law [Robert Hollitscher], an immensely cunning scout, tracked us down and brought us to Frau Eva R[osenfeld], where [Siegfried] Bernfeld [psychoanalyst, pedagogue, and friend of Anna Freud; see p. 79] appeared as well, and we had a very pleasant time. Afterwards, at the railroad station, "unfeeling fate" separated Anna and me. Instead of her, a little Parisian lady emerged from my lower berth. She was quite nice, but could not refrain from discussing high politics in the middle of the night, though I assured her vehemently even in my sleep, that I had only partly German blood in my veins, and had only recently indulged my enthusiasm for Napoleon.... Please scratch the hair on the inside of Wolf's ear for me. I was a little unfaithful to him, with the "Racker"—dachshund of the R[osenfeld]s, though he had just robbed and emptied half the dish of meat on the table, without showing the least signs of an ethical indigestion. Nor was he punished. What would Wolf, who is much more capable of civilized refinement, have to say to that?

Eva Rosenfeld relates the same incident,

which happened when, after leaving the Semmering and before Anna accompanied Lou to the Westbahn [railroad station for travel to Munich] in the evening, they were to come to us for supper. While we were chatting before going to supper, the door must have been left open. Our mischievous Dachshund slipped into the room, hopped onto the table, and ate most of the lovely smelling roast. Lou was delighted—I was shocked, but not too upset.... Years later, when Freud's letters to Lou and her replies were published.., I read with pride that my "Racker's" misdemeanours were reported by Lou to Freud, and I remember with satisfaction that she confessed liking "Racker" even better than Anna's "Wolf," the dog who once got lost in the Prater [park in Vienna] and jumped into a taxi, [whereupon the driver looking at his badge, drove him home] [ER, pp. 200–201].

The cheerful and comfortably sentimental tone of these narratives also suggests something about Eva's hospitality. Her means were restricted. Her house was located in Hietzing, a genteel bourgeois suburb of Vienna, in a quiet street reminiscent of the calm, gracefully modest proportions and charm of nineteenth-century Biedermeyer. It was not a large house. Eva's model household was remarkable nonetheless for its scope and spirit. For, as Anna Freud remarked, she did "everything so well," and made "a joy of everything"; and Anna

Freud decided, she herself would like to learn cooking and housekeeping from Eva (to Eitingon, October 21, 1926), which she did, however briefly, for a week in January 1927 (to Eitingon, January 3, 1927).

Apart from guests, Eva's house, with rarely less than twelve persons at mealtimes (see p. 31), was to include at various periods in the 1920s and 1930s as foster children (F) or helpers (H; "Haustöchter," "Pflegetöchter"): Ernst (Ernsti, Ernstl) Halberstadt Freud (F) (W. Ernest Freud), the older son of Anna Freud's deceased older sister Sophie, cared for by and in analysis with Anna Freud; Vera von Freund-Toszeghi (F), patient of Anna Freud, daughter of a wealthy Hungarian industrialist (owner of a chocolate factory), half-sister to Erzsi Toszeghi through their common mother; Herta Huber (H), an illegitimate child of an illegitimate daughter of a Rosenfeld, distantly related to Eva and Valti, without means of her own, temporarily in love with Bob Burlingham; she eventually became a nun; Gusti Körner (H) related to the Rosenfelds, later an analysand of Anna Freud, who became an analyst; Trudi Kraus (H); Minna Mach (H and F), a poor girl with an enlarged aorta, patient of Anna Freud; see p. 28; Ann Nederhoud (F), a girl with eating problems, see p. 31; her mother was the lover of Kyra Nijinski's (F) mother (Kyra being the daughter of the celebrated dancer. Kyra and Ann came together to the Rosenfelds); Reinhard Simmel (F), patient of Anna Freud, son of the analyst Ernst Simmel, who was director of the clinic at Tegel (see p. 31); Erzsi von Toszeghi (F), half-sister of Vera von Freund-Toszeghi); Lizzie Wellenstein (F), a patient of Anna Freud, who had suffered polio (see L1n3).

Yet when the "entire house was asleep," Anna Freud spent "very calm and beautiful evenings" there with Eva, whom Anna described as one of the "ever fewer human beings, who can guess that there is still something else to me than being an analyst" (to Eitingon, February 1, 1926).

MÄDI

Presumably in the fall of 1927, Anna Freud wrote to Eva: "I would like to be a bit of Mädi for you. I wish I had a little daughter, I would share her with you" (L4). As seen in Eva's memoirs (ER, pp. 174–179 passim), Mädi, nearly fifteen in the summer of 1927, was "strong, quick, serious, and purposeful," an outstanding pupil, nicknamed at school "the Amazon." She had, Eva thought:

> a natural religious feeling [expressed in poems and in paintings, including a tryptich showing] Christophorus carrying the baby across the water (a tribute to Grundlsee . . .) [and] the women lamenting beneath Christ's cross. . . . Enthusiastic about the Labour Movement, she wanted to be a labourer herself one day, . . . to master manual skills. . . . [and to lead] a "rough life", . . . of which our urban [existence] had deprived us.

She had started out before dawn on her last day—as the "experienced mountaineer" that she was—to show "her" woods and Alpine realm to a younger city boy. [ER, 174] In the only writing of hers I have, she assumes the voice and dialect of a young farm boy or girl, compelled to work in the fields. She does so in order to celebrate her longing for the life of the lumberjacks ("Holzhacker") in the forests, and on the high plateaus and pastures of the very mountains from which she fell to her death together with her companion. Anna Freud's remark about Mädi having had all it takes to become "a real" or "genuine" "human being" expresses the central, if somewhat undefined, ideal of her circle (Bittner, p. 14).

The death of Mädi, the central tragic event in Eva's life, had occurred on July 8, 1927, on the rocky Trisselwand above the lakes and villages of Alt-Aussee and Grundlsee, two vacation spots in the Austrian Alps. "Together with a young friend," Anna Freud wrote to Eitingon on July 14, "she went on an excursion in the mountains and both fell 150 meters. The search for them lasted for an entire day. Then they found their shattered bodies. This is the third child Eva lost. Harold Sweetser [a patient of Anna Freud] died on the same day and in the same hour."

Called to Grundlsee at the news of Mädi's death by Eva, Anna Freud came from the Semmering "and packed up Mädi's belongings. She knew what had happened to me, but she did not suffer with me. She was a friend in need" (ER, p. 177).

Time and again throughout this correspondence, the letters will refer to the anniversary of the death of Mädi whose "image will no longer change" and "is there every day of the year" for Eva (L5).

In her memoirs she wrote: "Then began my silent mourning. I founded the school in Mädi's honor and worked hard, that is all I know. I thought: 'I shall never have one single sweet moment of gladness again.' That was true."

The year after Mädi's death was one of crisis for Eva. She became pregnant again. Her friend Anna was overjoyed. "I am so happy about this," she wrote to Eitingon on October 12, 1927:

> Evidently, it is ... [Eva's] only way out of mourning and the danger and temptation to live only in the past with her three much beloved dead brothers and her three dead children. She is incredibly brave, maintaining at this moment, in a difficult financial situation, the entire household. She has in addition to 2 young girls, Simmel's boy ... Dorothy's little school is a tenant, and Eva devotes almost her entire morning to work with the schoolchildren in the garden and giving them instruction in home economics. She is even building two additional rooms facing out into the yard. If the child is a girl she will call her Anna Miriam. Anna is me and Miriam was the name of Mädi.

However, on November 4, 1927 Anna Freud reports that Eva is doing very badly and that the pregnancy may have to be terminated. "Then nothing would come of the child to whom I looked forward so very much."

Eva's own account in her memoirs is quite different. It describes her "horror" at finding herself pregnant, "at the idea" that someone "should take the place of Mädi.... I would not let my body be anything but Mädi's resting place." And so she was grateful for Sigmund Freud's advice, that, given her despair, and a colic of the kidneys ("wenn es schon an die Nieren geht") she should have an abortion, which was subsequently performed by Julius Schnitzler (ER, pp. 182–186 *passim*, 371), the brother of the writer Arthur Schnitzler, who, she felt, saved her life.

The mourning for Mädi also led Eva, presumably via Bachofen's *Mother Right* (1861) and the revival of his notion of "Demetrian" matriarchy by Oskar Kokoschka and other German Expressionists (Gordon, 1981, pp. 40–41), into a "mother–daughter cult" patterned on classical mythology. According to Eva's conception of the "mystery of Demeter and Kore," a "mysterious rhythm of life–death," she herself, Eva the mother, had died in place of her dead daughter: "When my daughter died, I did not let her die, I died within myself and let her go on living." All her good times, she wrote, were those when her daughter was living, while her worst were those when Mädi was dead while she, Eva, remained alive: "There are times when *she* dies and *I* am alive, and these are the dark hours of my life, almost unbearable to live through. I crouch in my room and I feel no life within me" (ER, pp. 218–219). Only in her last years, she said, speaking in her eighties, did her lifelong sadness and depression leave her (interview with P. Heller, July 12, 1975). When she was seventy-five, she wrote:

> All this took forty more years for my mind to grasp. . . . I have only recently unravelled the riddle of my existence. . . . I, the mother, did let my daughter be re-born day after day. Now that I am *really* old— "she walks beside me." . . . My analysis from 1929 to 1931 [with Sigmund Freud] revealed none of this mystery [though] it explained to me all other relationships, friendships and maturing processes within my first thirty-seven years of life, and I can never *think* any more without searching for the knowledge of unconscious processes and motivations in my actions and reactions [ER, p. 220].

Even so, it was clearly the unresolved "maternal" half of Eva's life which was to lead her, later on, to the matriarchal analyst, Melanie Klein.

The motifs that went with her continued mourning for Mädi thus constituted a perennial accompaniment or bass to Eva's actively dedicated life and passionately engaged personality. The image of a frozen lake, or inability to "thaw" (see L20), suggest less a mood of Eva Rosenfeld (she was someone who was in command rather than at the mercy of moods) than a basic condition of her existence.

EVA'S ANALYSIS WITH SIGMUND FREUD

According to L8, Eva's first session with Freud was scheduled in March 1929, but her memoirs (ER, pp. 47, 216) have her analysis starting on December 26, 1929. Was there an earlier, preliminary consultation, or is it conceivable that she was meant, originally, to be Anna Freud's patient rather than Sigmund Freud's? The conjecture is unfounded in "reality." It is supported only by a wish of Eva and the fact that it would fit Anna Freud's equation between analysis and love (see L8) more convincingly than an analysis with Anna's father.

Eventually, to quote the memoirs, she did "make a passionate transference" of her feelings for her father onto Freud. He even said "a little sadly: 'and now the same thing has happened to you again. There is a father who singles you out and offers you what nobody else has got.'" Her sense of being preferred above all others, she writes, was "as forbidden and incestuous a feeling as the original feeling had been for my father which was internalised and eternalised when he died unexpectedly, just after I had turned fifteen." Yet in an analysis whose main features were "bitter and dramatic moments," such feelings would be controlled and rectified as the analyst "forced them into the open" (ER, p. 221). She valued the experience of her analysis with Freud immensely (see pp. 34–37), for awakening her creativity, promoting self-realization, enlightening her about everything except the central trauma of her life, the loss of Mädi, and causing a "transvaluation" of all her values, and providing her with a way of thinking which was to affect and change her entire personal and professional life. In keeping with a remark by Eissler, she even credited Freud with having created "a viable universe," and admired his "insatiable" quest for truth. She expressed only mild reservations about his harshness, when, in one of her initial sessions, he responded to her accusation that she had "wanted to tell" him something which he "would not hear," by crying out: "You must be feebleminded!" (an exclamation qualified by his explaining to her why her "reason" had become subject to the service of unreasoning "resistance") (ER, p. 221). At another point he told her: "Had your father lived longer," that is, until she was a grown-up, "you would have hated him." In "today's technique," Eva adds, "we are more cautious, [and] would not say this to a patient unless... his hatred had been transferred blatantly to the analyst" (ER, p. 223). Yet "quite late in life," when she fully understood Freud's assertion, it suddenly did occur to her: "All through my analysis I must have repressed the wish to be analysed by Anna, my dear friend, whom I so loved.... I must have repressed my hatred of father Freud as I had repressed my hatred of my own father. A pity I cannot tell Freud this to-day. He would have been so delighted. He was such a glutton for truth, we would have enjoyed the discovery together" (ER, p. 226).

There is a sting to such qualified sweetness. Blending radical openness with conventional smoothing or semiconcealment of problematic material, Eva's memoirs nowhere contradict her worship of Freud as analyst, thinker, or genius. However, they do suggest something like a disappointment in not having been analyzed by Anna who had first conceived the idea that Eva should undergo analysis: For she had begun "to worry about why I should have accepted my fate with such silent fortitude, and could not believe I could continue my way of life.... And so it happened that I had to learn to attach my attention to my own self" (ER, p. 218). As for Sigmund Freud, Eva writes: "I had not looked for him, but he had come to meet me halfway" (ER, p. 218); and there she was now, at the beginning of her analysis with the "old Professor" in the silence of his room, surrounded by his collection of Egyptian antiques, "awestruck by this seventy-two year old man in whose presence I felt the weight of his deadly illness oppressing me, [while] his undaunted courage filled me with amazement, [and his] interest in me seemed uncanny" (ER, p. 217–218). That was her initial impression. Many years later, she told Paul Roazen (May 30, 1970) as she told me, that she "did not admire his [i.e., Freud's] personality," whereupon Roazen, who quotes her, replied: "A great man is all of a piece, the good with the bad, one cannot have the one without the other" (Roazen, 1971; Heller, interview with Eva Rosenfeld, 1975).

As for L8, the phrase "dass Du gerade dort Analyse machen sollst, wo Du nur lieben möchtest" (literally: "that you should do analysis where you would only like to love") could refer to a person as well as to a place ("wo"), and by extension, to its inhabitants, that is, to a family, such as the Freuds. Even so, Anna Freud's comparison with her own case ("Das habe ich doch auch getan," "I did the same thing"; that is, I went into analysis with the one I loved, meaning her own father) and her conclusion that the relation of patient to analyst should always be one of love, hardly apply to the case of Eva at the time in question. For Eva then loved Anna rather than Anna's still distant father who was ever to remain for her rather formidable (see, however, Bittner, p. 10, and Ross, p. 37).

Thirty-four years later, on November 12, 1963, Anna Freud once more addressed the topic of love and analysis in a letter to Eva Rosenfeld, in which she criticized Eva's German manuscript for a talk on Freud for the BBC. The word "love," she observed, was "of course appropriate with reference to *Übertragungsliebe*, the transference of the patient, but incorrect insofar as it referred to the relation of the analyst to the patient, which should be rather termed "human sympathy, interest, readiness to help or whatever you may want to call it." The earlier and the later statement do not contradict one another, but they do suggest a contrast in mood and attitude.

OBERMANN

In the years following Mädi's death, another crisis occurred in Eva's life. Her marriage, which must have been less than secure for some time, came apart, and, in a sense, released her so that she could enter upon her career as an analyst. The correspondence touches occasionally on Eva's perennial extramarital involvement, her impassioned friendship and turbulently romantic love affair with Julian N. Obermann which was once again to rise to a climax in the summer of 1929 (L9). Poetic and spiritual in emphasis and mode of expression, it coexisted, at times, with Eva's amicable relations with Obermann's fiancée (Lilly Bernfeld), as well as with her own and Obermann's amicable relations with Valti, Eva's cousin and husband. The latter, in turn, had extramarital attachments, including his relationship with Fritzi Löwy (see L44n), a champion swimmer for the Jewish sports club, Hakoah, in which Valti Rosenfeld played a leading part.

Obermann was born in the Warsaw ghetto on June 14, 1888. He died in New Haven, on October 18, 1956, after twenty-five years of service at Yale University, as a distinguished Sterling professor of Semitic Languages. When they met, Eva was twenty-one, he twenty-five. "He thought it my *duty* to leave everything and follow him" (ER, p. 367), she wrote in her memoirs. "What I tried not to see was what Obermann taught me: passion, tearing ... down all laws and conventions ... to obey the highest law: complete fulfillment and complete identity—what was I to do? Sometimes I accepted him and more often I refused and rebuked him. Time and again this happened, and our whole circle of friends burned with the question: how would this end?" (ER, p. 371). But again and again she also felt: "I cannot leave my children and I cannot rob Valti of them" (ER, p. 372). In a characteristic letter marked 1917 (without further date) she writes: "Beloved, dearest friend: From all my suffering emerges, ever new and consoling, my realization that I know you, that I love you, and that I am loved by you with a love that is divine in its greatness." But on the same page, she also writes: "I cannot give any reason for it, not yet, not today, but I feel it and must act accordingly: I am staying with Valti and my children, because I can live and die for them. This is all I can do. But for vying with the gods together with you I am too weak and imperfect." Twelve years later, in the summer of 1929, when Obermann was about to return to the United States, the relationship reached again a dramatic juncture. Settled in New York, Obermann writes on December 13, 1929, in retrospect: "I feel ... as if I had just called out to you my last farewell from the car on the Berchtesgaden Road!" And while he appears to regret that he caused Eva "sorrow and nothing but sorrow" by his mere presence the preceding summer, he also recalls that Eva's letter of mid-October 1929 was "a ray of light in this autumn," the only event which did not leave him "indifferent." "How grateful I was to you for the bit of life, and youth, and Alpine mountains, which you brought to me with this letter! A precious world of bliss—and hopefully not lost to me entirely and forever." For "whatever there was of happiness and beauty in my life, you gave me to hold in my hand, to bear in my mind, and to feel in my heart."

THE BURLINGHAMS AND THE SCHOOL

The Burlinghams

Dorothy Burlingham, née Trimble Tiffany, was born in New York in 1891, and died in London in 1979. She was the youngest daughter of the wealthy artist, interior decorator, and glass designer, Louis Comfort Tiffany and the former Louise Wakeman Knox. Dorothy married Dr. Robert Burlingham in 1914; he was the son of a prominent New York lawyer. They separated after about six years, in part because of his manic-depressive psychosis. Dorothy left for Europe together with her four children, Bob, Mabbie, Tinky, and Mikey, on May 1, 1925. After four months in Geneva, she moved to Vienna, where she met with Anna Freud, and entered analysis with Theodor Reik. The treatment ran into difficulties, and Anna Freud, who found Dorothy's depressions difficult to bear, thought that Reik "mistreated her more than necessary." She discussed the matter with her father (to Eitingon, December 9, 1927) with the result that Dorothy switched to Sigmund Freud. According to Young-Bruehl, the Freuds negotiated this move "by carefully engaging Eitingon as the mediator, so they would not be directly involved." Only then did Dorothy begin to flourish and to develop her "strong productive" capacity for analytical work (Young-Bruehl, p. 190). With Sigmund Freud her personal analysis developed into a training analysis, qualifying her in 1932 as member of the Psychoanalytical Society. In the twenties she soon became an intimate associate of the

Freuds. Freud, according to Gay, was "much taken with this 'quite congenial American woman'," but referred to this mother of four nonetheless as "an unhappy virgin" (Gay, p. 540). As early as fall 1927 Freud thought that Anna was totally absorbed in her friendship with Dorothy (S. Freud to Eitingon, October 11, 1927; Young-Bruehl, p. 188). Their lifelong companionship was to eclipse Anna's relationship to Eva Rosenfeld (see p. 43, pp. 32–33). Dorothy's (husbandless) family came to live increasingly in close proximity with the Freud household, which consisted during the period in question, basically or minimally, of Sigmund Freud; his daughter Anna; his wife Martha Bernays Freud, (born 1861, Wandsbek, died 1951, London); her unmarried sister Minna Bernays (born 1865, Wandsbek, died 1941, London); and their perennial maid Paula Fichtl. Anna Freud became a superior maternal friend to the Burlingham children. She was, at the same time, their analyst, and their major educational authority; the latter also via the private school founded for the benefit of the Burlingham children under Anna Freud's aegis by Dorothy Burlingham and Eva Rosenfeld (see Bittner, pp. 10–11; Ross, p. 32). In the fall of 1929 the Burlinghams moved to an apartment above the Freuds at Berggasse 19; the Freuds and the Burlinghams spent summer vacations together; in 1930 Anna and Dorothy bought a small farmhouse in Hochrotherd near Vienna (which replaced their earlier rented weekend place in Neuhaus near Vienna). In 1938 Dorothy was to share the experience of the Freuds' emigration to London, and eventually to live there with Anna Freud in the Freud house at 20 Maresfield Gardens to the end of their lives, Dorothy preceding Anna Freud in death by four years. Though Anna Freud's life in the late twenties and thirties centered on the care for her father and her pioneering work in child analysis, it was sustained as well by the Freud–Burlingham symbiosis.

In her letters, notably to Eitingon, Anna Freud mentions her analyses of the Burlingham children—in Bob's case the search for a mother substitute (see below L11). Mabbie, she thought, needed help rather than analysis proper for the wish for masculinity, and difficulties with sibling rivalry. She also mentions Tinky's resistance and Mikey's longing for his father. Her relation to these children, she feels, differs from her relation to other patients in which she does not feel the need for personal recognition or gratification. She does not only want to make them well, but also to have at least part of them for herself. This attitude, she adds self-critically, is helpful at this stage for her work with them, but is bound to interfere with it later on. Moreover, Anna feels possessive also about the children's mother, and is ashamed of all this, "especially in front of papa," and therefore does not tell him anything about it (to Eitingon February 5 and 19, 1926), even though she was in 1924 (to Eitingon October 5, 1925), and still continued, on and off, to be her father's patient. With reference to the Burlinghams, she observes, it is all an instance of her dependency on others, her always wanting something for herself, except in her profession, even when she is doing things for others. She had hoped this "stupid way of life" would change once she grew up. But apparently being an adult had little to do with it (to Eitingon, February 19, 1925). These remarks, characteristic of Anna Freud's severity, also suggest the later, problematic aspects of her dominant position in the lives of the Burlingham children and her symbiotic relationship with this family, which was to last to the end of her life.

During the late twenties and early thirties the problems of the Burlingham family seemed to be caused, in Dorothy's and Anna's view, entirely by the father of the children. Dr. Robert Burlingham, a physician, son of the impressive and prominent New York lawyer and kingmaker of the Democratic party, Charles Cult Burlingham, was suffering from a "manic-depressive syndrome" entailing psychotic episodes, and was to be treated in various institutions in America. He committed suicide in May 1938. After his wife had left him and taken the children with her, he repeatedly sought them out in Europe, hoping, pleading, threatening legal action, or putting on other pressure to have them return to him and to the United States (see M. J. Burlingham, pp. 157–267 passim).

In 1926, Anna Freud, aware of the longing of the Burlingham children for their father, mentions a plan to get Robert Burlingham in analysis with Eitingon, in order to try to "save a bit of a father for the children or a bit of a husband for the wife" (to Eitingon, August 29, 1926). At the end of that year the plan is to get Robert together with analyst Sàndor Ferenczi (to Eitingon, November 16, 1926). Robert, though an opponent of analysis, did, in fact, consult Ferenczi somewhat later. Robert and his father continued to hope that the family would be reunited. Concerning the summer of 1928, Anna Freud wrote to Simmel that, as far as the Burlingham children were concerned, this was a time reserved entirely for their father (to Simmel, June 6, 1928). In June and August she reports to Eitingon that the Burlinghams are "lovely to Robert," who was, apparently, a man of great charm when he was well; but she also writes about the undependable and uncanny side of his personality. Robert and his father, who came to Austria several times during 1928 and 1929, attempted, according to Young-Bruehl, "to draw the children away" from their mother, from "psychoanalysis and the Jewish Freuds," creating an upheaval "for Anna Freud's patients" and "their frail mother," who was, in the words of Anna Freud, "worn down by the constant torment" of her husband's behavior. Robert was then cared for by Amsden, an American analyst in Budapest, "and the Freuds pressured both Amsden and Ferenczi to do their best to keep [Robert] Burlingham in Budapest, and to convince him not to sue for the custody of his children after Dorothy Burlingham finally gave up any hope for his cure" (Young-Bruehl, p. 190). Their idyllic summer vacation in Schneewinkel (Berchtesgaden) was disturbed by the visit of the "Burlinghams (father and son)" who finally departed on August 29 "after many unpleasant impressions" (to Eitingon, August 29, 1929). "The real battle for the children," Anna Freud thought, would "probably take place in the course of next year" (to Eitingon, September 7, 1929). Dorothy Burlingham, apparently, gradually developed a firm attitude in this struggle. In L25 Anna observed of her friend that even the need to communicate a final negative decision to Robert could no longer daunt Dorothy. And indeed, she did prevail, despite her precarious health, of which her biographer M. J. Burlingham said that "her life seemed to be at stake in those years" (M. J. Burlingham, p. 221). However, I should add that the image of Dorothy, especially that suggested in Young-Bruehl's biography, is quite at variance with my own extensive recollections of this woman, who, her brittle and haggard appearance notwithstanding, was rather an energetic and aggressive matriarch endowed with uncommon tenacity. Fanatical in her allegiance to Anna and Sigmund Freud, she was as ethical, noble-minded, and generous as she was intolerant, self-righteous, severe, and judgmental in her Puritanical and patrician pride. It is appropriate that M. J. Burlingham should have called her "the last Tiffany," and so is the description of her as a person "with an almost terrifying confidence in her own judgment" (M. J. Burlingham, p. 155), to which should be added stubborn will-power, independent wealth, and the kind of tough endurance which allowed her to live to the ripe old age of eighty-eight. In retrospect it seems a foregone conclusion that she was to win the battle for her children and to proceed to enclose them by keeping them dependent upon her.

The School

It was as characteristic of Dorothy Burlingham as it was in keeping with progressive educational trends in education of the twenties, that she decided to give her children an education of a kind not to be had in the Austrian public school system with its exacting routines and requirements, its coarse texture, and authoritarian discipline.

An affinity to progressive trends was also part of the Freudian environment. Prior to the First World War a powerful Youth Movement manifested itself in critiques of obsolete traditions and the hypocrisy of Wilhelminian society and its conventions. It glorified nature, espoused a new freedom in erotic relationships, and fostered an idealistic spirit favoring radical social change. Subsequently the Movement was politicized. It split into parties of the right and parties of the left, ranging from Socialism and Communism to Zionism, from moderate Christian Nationalism to the precursors of Nazi organizations such as the Hitler Youth. In the context of Anna

Freud's letters, Siegfried Bernfeld, formerly a leader in the Youth Movement, appears as a prominent and original representative of progressive education as conceived on a Marxist basis by a left-wing Freudian. Also, it was he who brought Anna Freud, in search of a home for her patient Minna, to Eva Rosenfeld's house. Bernfeld was a champion of antiauthoritarian experiments in the education of underprivileged children (notably those who were displaced and homeless), in his Kinderheim Baumgarten, and an influential writer on education (including *Sisyphus or the Limits of Education*, 1925). A disciple favored by Sigmund Freud, he was among the close friends of Anna Freud, and she continued to acknowledge his influence on her conceptions of the relation between psychoanalysis and pedagogy, in spite of her own and Freud's marked divergence from Bernfeld's permissive and politically radical (socialist) educational ideology.

With his move to Berlin in 1925, Bernfeld (see L25) entered into an emphatically political phase, a rapprochement to Communists and Communism which this early proponent of a fusion between Marxism and psychoanalysis nonetheless did not cease to criticize. The need for radical transformation of the educational process was predicated in his mind on the need for a radical transformation of society and the abolition of capitalism. Progressive pedagogy was to contribute to the class struggle. However, in the late twenties and early thirties Bernfeld's interest shifted from the relations between psyche, society, and education to "psychophysiology," notably, the possibility of a "libidometer" measuring quantities of libido (in collaboration with physicist Feitelberg). In exile (after 1933) he turned to the investigation of Sigmund Freud and the beginnings of psychoanalysis.

The Burlingham–Rosenfeld or Hietzing School was established by the wealthy, if rebellious descendant of American millionaires and Eva Rosenfeld, who, her "progressive" leanings notwithstanding, was thoroughly imbued, both in lifestyle and cultural ideals, with a sense of traditional values. Neither the founders nor the teachers, nor Anna Freud, shared the radical political or sexual orientation of the left-wing Freudians, though the Hietzing School was not in any sense explicitly procapitalist. It was progressive in favoring verbal sexual enlightenment, though not at all, as the Reichians did, in encouraging sexual activity. As W. Ernest Freud suggested to me, it may well have been the intention of the founders of the school to achieve a middle road between the orientation toward uninhibited drive gratification, characteristic of some early analysts, and the restrictive, disciplinarian, and coercive spirit of the state-approved educational system, which all the major educators at the Hietzing School, with the possible exception of August Aichhorn (who worked within the state system), rejected and treated with principled contempt.

A characteristic passage in L8 addresses this central issue of a balance between the "progressive" emphasis on freedom, the freely chosen "creative" projects, the release from the oppressive routine and compulsory learning required by the official educational establishments, *and* the need to "set limits," to inculcate habits conducive to learning and to disciplined mastery of required skills, information, and behavior. Psychoanalysts, as suggested above, were counted among the protagonists of "progressive" education in those days. When, at the opening of the Frankfurt Psychoanalytic Institute in 1929, Siegfried Bernfeld gave a lecture on the significance of psychoanalysis for pedagogy, a Frankfurt newspaper (*Frankfurter Zeitung, Abendblatt*, February 25, 1929; Peters, pp. 183, 383) reported: Psychoanalysis would provide decisive arguments in favor of endeavors in modern education to promote the independent creative activity of the child and the retrenchment of authority and punishment.

However, from early on, and notwithstanding her abiding appreciation of the efforts of some radically "progressive" educational projects by Bernfeld and others, Anna Freud took the position of a relatively conservative "progressive," favoring an educational process leading to "sublimation." In L8 she stresses, specifically, the enjoyment of required tasks which are initially remote from the demand for immediate gratification, but capable of being enjoyed, given a process of voluntary acceptance of the required work. "Bernfeld," she wrote to Eitingon on April 17, 1928, "draws the wrong conclusions from correct observations. Otherwise one might as well spare oneself the trouble of therapy." The remark suggests the crux of her opposition to the left-wing Freudians who, she implied, advocated in education as well as in analysis and life-style a fallacious short-cut by seeking to suspend or circumvent all inhibition, repression, and coercion, as if the mere absence of restraints and limits, or the pretense to such an absence (letting one and all act on their impulses) could provide a universal panacea.

On the other hand, Anna Freud, in a quest for an intermediate position between coercion and liberation, typically (see L8) invoked as a positive model the approach which her lifelong friend August Aichhorn had developed in his establishment for delinquent youths. August Aichhorn, psychoanalyst and Social Democratic City Councillor (Stadtrat) of Vienna, initiated the application of psychoanalysis to the treatment of juvenile delinquents (see his classic *Wayward Youth* [1935]. Aichhorn's concept was, in a sense, one of pedagogical seduction, compelling his disciples in Anna Freud's phrase "to want to do what they are supposed to do" (L8). He rejected emphatically the notion of his being motivated by "altruism" or "Christian love." "Verwahrlosung" (delinquency), he explained, became personified in his own mind, and made him want to wrest the youth entrusted to him from this personified "delinquency" by winning him for himself; that is, by creating the same dependency on *him* which the youth had experienced before in his relation to "delinquency." To accomplish this, Aichhorn must identify with the delinquent. The delinquent would then identify, in turn, with Aichhorn, and in this way Aichhorn, could "take him away from delinquency." Once this was accomplished, Aichhorn claimed, he lost interest in the youth. The boy's socialization was from Aichhorn's perspective only a "not unpleasant" secondary gain (to Anna Freud May 17, 1948). This remarkable confession concerning the pedagogical eros of a distinguished pedagogue is of interest also in that it offers a close analogy to the conception or practice of therapy by both Sigmund and Anna Freud and by some of their analysands and disciples.

In the context of the twenties, Eva Rosenfeld was likewise of a relatively "progressive" persuasion. When, partly due to her departure for Berlin, the school folded up, she sent her son to Marienau, a coeducational boarding school in the vanguard of the progressive movement. As late as the 1970s, when she was a grandmother, she thought of herself as endowed with a special gift for creating "character" in educating the young "by being exactly as young as they are, only with a richer mind to feed their hungry starved personalities." She would not do so by yielding to the devouring "oral sadism" of the new generation of "regressed adults" of the seventies, but with a creatively maternal touch on the basis of her psychoanalytic insight. (The latter apparently, did not extend to her daughter-in-law who was sternly instructed by her that neither command nor prohibition ["befehlen" or "verbieten"] should ever cross the lips of an educator). Convinced, at age eighty-three, of her successes in educating her grandchildren, she added: "The long and short of this is my regret that we three, Dorothy, you [Anna] and I are now too old to start what we left off in 1932 in Vienna [i.e., the Hietzing School], because I was too ignorant, too immature, too un-analysed and too immersed in my own grief." (To Anna Freud, April 17, 1975) However, in the twenties, as L8 suggests, Eva's insistence on the need to impose tasks without regard to the pupils' enjoyment of their performance, assumed a position further to the "right" than Anna Freud's (see also p. 32), though both she and Anna criticized the teachers Peter Blos and Erik Homburger Erikson, who, Anna Freud claims, recognize only a simplistic alternative between "liberation" and "compulsion." Their bias, she implies, is in favor of mere, hence chaotic "liberation," though, in fact, the Hietzing School, while deficient in scholastic discipline and standards, was far from ever being "chaotic."

Peter Blos was a German who in due course became an analyst and expert on adolescence. He was, I think, by temperament a pedant, and would have been inclined to act the disciplinarian, had it not been for his "progressive" convictions in keeping with the prevalent mood and ideology of the Freudians at the time. Quite unlike him, was his imaginative and versatile friend, Erik. The celebrated psychoanalyst, social psychologist, and psychohistorian of later years was at that time a young artist about to enter into a training analysis with Anna Freud. He delineated his own identity crisis at that juncture in "An Autobiographic Perspective" (Erikson, 1970). He was brought into the circle of Dorothy Burlingham, Anna Freud, and Eva Rosenfeld when Peter Blos, the son of friends of the Rosenfelds, assumed the function of director of the Hietzing School.

Pupils and Child Patients

As pointed out in Bittner's essay, most of the teachers and pupils at the Hietzing School were or had been in analysis. In fact, the enterprise, initiated to provide a congenial educational environment for Bob Burlingham and his siblings, had a secondary aim, namely, to find out what might be done with children undergoing analysis, and taught by an analytically oriented staff; though this, earlier statements and rumors to the contrary, was denied later on.

Some responses of those who attended the school may serve as examples for varied reactions to its educational and social environment, and suggest the dual role the children played as pupils and patients.

The response of Judy de Forest Taves to a questionnaire illustrates a fairly negative reaction to the exclusive style of unadorned, and somewhat austere, though graceful patrician simplicity which was considered de rigueur by the dominant family group (the Burlinghams) in keeping with the quietly judgmental spirit of Anna Freud.

At age fourteen, Judy, an American girl distantly related to the Burlinghams "went to live in Dorothy's Viennese household" where she stayed from January 1929 until June 1930. She found it difficult to get along "in the Burlingham household and with the children at [Hietzing] school." "I was constantly wrestling," she recalled in 1983, "with trying to be liked, esp. *accepted* and *fitting in*." She had been criticized, unfairly, she thought, in private talks with "aunt Dorothy" for being unsocial, not outgoing enough, not sharing with others, and "for not being as I was at the age of 9" when she had gone to school in Geneva where Dorothy had lived at the time. In an atmosphere lacking in "warmth and gaiety" ("Life was serious"), she found Anna Freud, though generally also "quite serious," to be "warm, *lively*, and delightful"; and only "after/during work with her" ("for about 6 mos"), did she feel "finally accepted into the Burlingham family." This, in turn, affected her relationship to her mother, in which there had been for some time "a good deal of love–hate" along with dependency and devotion. For when Izette Taber de Forest (a former patient of Ferenczi who was to become a lay analyst) came to Austria to pick up her daughter, and "A.F. requested that she have some sessions with her," she "wore lipstick and dressed attractively," and so, Mrs. Taves recalls, "I was very critical of my mother because she looked so unlike Dorothy and Anna Freud."

> This [typefied] my difficulty when I went back to the U.S.A. I felt (at last) like an accepted member of the Berggasse family, their standard of thought and behavior, so I was critical of my family and wished they were different. Dorothy and A.F., I felt, did not much like Americans, in general regarding them as superficial, out for quick rewards, and unconcerned with basic human values. Indeed my mother felt she was scolded for bringing me up as she did. [de Forest, personal communication, 1983].

By contrast the retrospective evaluation of the psychoanalyst W. Ernest Freud is entirely positive and enthusiastic. After the early death of his mother, Sophie Freud Halberstadt, Anna Freud took charge of the upbringing of her frail nephew, "the closest thing to a son I ever had" (to Eitingon, December 8, 1934), though Ernstl was eventually to live au pair in Eva's house. "The school," he recalled, was "the most wonderful experience for me." It was a surprise to him that this was not so for all the pupils. He surmised that they had a "full and fully nutrient family life." For a good many others, though, who came from disturbed families, the school did provide additional stimulation which they had lacked. For while all came from professional middle-class or affluent upper middle-class families, these children, like Ernst himself, were somewhat starved, emotionally or intellectually, or semineglected, and thus resembled somewhat disadvantaged children from less privileged strata. He thought the school a model in that it allowed free play to the imagination, setting essay questions on the pattern of "what would you do if—"; for example, "What would you do if you were suddenly alone in the world?", in answer to which twelve children described the death of fifteen parents, three of them murdered, four dying in accidents, and two in prisons. Was the school an "experiment" with child analysis? No, but "at the very least, analysis did introduce a dimension of honesty and insight into things which other people did not have or denied, and this made a difference in the atmosphere and mood of the school community and to the way one learned."

The community of pupils was amicable, aggression at a minimum. He recalled only one instance of aggression in his own experience, and in that case the fight was formalized, even ritualized, a proper boxing match in the yard of the school, according to rules. Learning at that school was, for once, a delight. How did the teachers ever manage to accomplish this? They allowed free rein to curiosity and fantasizing, but not to acting out. The secret of their success was, in part at least, that they provided substitute gratifications:

> close to our instinctual needs, yet much more accessible than others.... If you can harness the natural component instinct of curiosity, you have an easy time, because the child wants to know more about this or that; and maybe that was the gist of the "project method" of teaching. For example: They offered us the study of the Eskimos in all aspects of their lives. This aroused our curiosity: What were Eskimos like? What were they doing?

"The topic," he continues "is relatively uncontaminated," not fraught with previous, possibly traumatic experiences, or prohibitions. And thus, he finds, the best "preconditions for learning" were utilized to the full, and, unlike in the public schools, praise was given for achievement and even for effort at achievement. "The emotional climate in our school was utterly unlike that of the state schools which were really an impediment to learning." It was relaxed, friendly, conducive to giving one's best.

"In the Hietzing school, the teachers had the satisfaction of seeing their pupils grow and unfold, and learn, giving them a lot of feedback in reward for their teaching. And a good many of their pupils, as my recollections and those of others prove, would remember them gratefully for the rest of their lives" (W. Ernest Freud, personal communication).

As I (Peter Heller) was also a pupil at the school, and, in fact appreciative of it and worshipfully enamored of the Burlingham style, and of the freedom and liberating ease of the place, I will insert here my own retrospective critique. W. Ernest Freud's unmitigated praise of this enterprise includes even the excessive and idiosyncratic preoccupation with relatively remote topics, such as the implements, life-styles, igloos, artefacts, hunting, rituals, and myths of the Eskimos. His eulogy culminates in an emphatic notion that learning should be simply or basically "a pleasurable experience," a form of intake comparable to breast-feeding. "Education, it seems to me, is itself a form of feeding and learning an extension of mothering" (W. Ernest Freud; personal communication).

This infantilizing and infantile as well as utopian notion of learning and education was largely shared by some of the teachers at the school. I concede gladly that my own experience of the years at that school was delightful as well, especially when compared to the experience at other educational establishments before or after; though it was not as free from fights or aggression, or even from tragedy as W. Ernest's sunny picture implies. (One older student committed suicide, an event hardly even mentioned, let alone discussed in this liberally "open-minded" educational community.) However, when Erikson, in an essay on the school observed playfully, that "we" (meaning the teachers) had been accused by the students of being "too nice" (Erikson, 1980, p. 13) because the students felt they had no outlet for their aggressions, he seemed to underestimate the gravity of that criticism. In a well-known passage of *Civilization and its Discontents* (1930), Freud observed of our education that in addition to failing to prepare the young for the role of sexuality, "its other sin" was that it did "not prepare them for the aggressiveness of which they are destined to become the objects. In sending the young out into life with such a false psychological orientation, education is behaving as though one were to equip people starting on a Polar expedition with summer clothing and maps of the Italian Lakes" (chapter 8, footnote 1). This applied doubly and threefold to our school, and is applicable even beyond the issue of preparation for aggression. For this school of ours failed utterly to habituate the pupils to the need to tolerate routine, the discipline of strenuous, at times painful effort which are requirements not only imposed by work for any social establishment (i.e., by professions), but equally by autonomously chosen creative efforts. The task of education is less than half done if the pupils have learned only to choose what gratifies, and have not become inured to discipline, to unpleasure, even to the very routine aspects of learning which the public institutions stressed and imposed. The result of the public schools' system was that one could not help but learn, albeit in a somewhat dehumanized manner, far more than was learned at our all too nice school. We were miserably unprepared for later scholastic requirements, let alone for the "Polar expedition" aspect that is part of every extraordinary achievement. Most of us had a difficult time meeting the requirements of public education once our special school was dissolved; and some, I believe, never acquired the discipline necessary for a substantial professional contribution. It was evidently because of the lopsidedness of our ideally pleasant school that Dorothy Burlingham, in a 1940 letter to Bob, was to claim that the Hietzing School (initiated by her largely for the benefit of her eldest son) had been "a mistake" (M. J. Burlingham, p. 230). To be sure, that mistake was due merely to the common illusion and folly of "progressive" education as inverted mirror-image of the folly and illusions of the authoritarian establishments which went about their business by imprisoning and dulling the minds and distorting the character of their pupils.

As for W. Ernest Freud, a new home had to be found for him once Eva was about to leave Vienna for Berlin. On October 10, 1930, Anna Freud told Dr. Simmel of Berlin-Tegel, that the "greatest wish of our Ernst" was to enter the free school community at Scharfenberg. "Now that he has at last become more manly and independent, the thought of a community of big boys and the primitive conditions at Scharfenberg in all external matters are especially attractive to him." As the island of Scharfenberg was close by, she asked Dr. Simmel "to row across the lake" at Tegel and to intervene with the director of the school in order to get Ernst admitted (to Simmel, October 11, 1930); which Simmel did to her great satisfaction. Anna thought entrance into that school would mean for Ernst a "step into reality," provided his delicate health would hold out. Impressed with Scharfenberg's mix of rural and scholastic activities, she added: "I would like to be a boy myself, to study Latin there together with raising chickens" (to Simmel, October 25, 1930). With Ernst's entry there, a period in which Anna Freud was totally in charge of him—financially and physically, as well as spiritually through analysis—must have come to an end, though in much the same way as the Burlingham children, he remained in her orbit for decades to come.

While there were at least two model pupils at the Hietzing School who were not in analysis, and alienated by it, the pupil–patient status was characteristic of the great majority. Reinhard Simmel (born 1920), son of the founder of the psychoanalytic clinic in Berlin-Tegel, is another case in point. Anna Freud's reports to his father illustrate the conscientious spirit in which she conducted the analyses of the children at the school. Their cases (see to Eitingon, December 12, 1928) were evidently also discussed at her seminal seminar in child analysis, the Kinderseminar, so that every member would know and would be able to follow every case; and they provided material for her lectures (such as the lengthy presentation of the case of Peter Heller in Budapest in 1930).

In 1927 Dr. Ernst Simmel sent an urgent request from Berlin to Anna Freud to accept as her patient his thin, pale, nervous, and extraordinarily brash little son, who was "inwardly suffering" (presumably also in connection with the separation of his parents). Anna Freud agreed, recommending the Rosenfeld house as foster home in Vienna and the school housed in her backyard in a suburb near the park of Schönbrunn Castle, established, as she put it, by a private circle of families on friendly terms with one another (to Simmel, June 14 and August 10, 1927). Reinhard's mother was thereupon deceived by her husband regarding the probable length of the treatment (she initially agreed only to an absence of three to four months; Simmel to Anna Freud, [September 23, 1927]). Toward the end of the year, Anna Freud reports to Dr. Simmel that the analysis is complicated by the fact that Reinhard had already had an analysis in Berlin with Melanie Klein. This analysis had uncovered the "deepest" reasons for or layers of his difficulties but had left the surface untouched, and consequently also the application of interpretation and of his self-knowledge to actual behavior and to his relation to the world. Therefore she must go with him the reverse way from deep down up, instead of, as usual, from the top down. Meanwhile the boy is preoccupied, she writes, with his ambivalent relation to God and grown-ups (to Simmel, November 4 and December 27, 1927). The next year (1928) she reports an improvement in his "most important" relation to his mother. She will tell Dr. Simmel orally about the hour in which Reinhard's transformation began (to Simmel, January 11, 1928). Gradually, in constant friendly struggle with him, he is learning that all his "jokes, impertinences and bragging" are but defenses (to Simmel, February 15, 1928). By the summer of 1928 he himself considers the most important change that he can now find "friends and playmates everywhere." A large portion of his "super-imposed, distorted character" has fallen away. "One can speak to him now like to a reasonable human being" (to Simmel, June 6, 1928). She confirms his new "calm, serene and tender ways, without distortion," in November, and adds: "Now I finally know what anxieties he fends off with his pranks and stories, and their position in his Oedipus complex. I was very proud to see suddenly through all this in our last hour and to get a glimpse of the 'real' Reinhard." As for Dr. Simmel's financial straits, she asks him not to send her any money he owes for the treatment, but to use it instead for Reinhard's education, which will be expensive, especially if the boy is not to live with his mother. She adds: "and he is still so small and his analysis as yet offers so little that is tangible" (to Simmel, November 28, 1928). Anxiously, she warns against taking him away from the house and school in Vienna, where, in contrast to earlier times, all are so satisfied with him and he is in the process of truly fitting in and understanding his difficulties (to Simmel, December 12, 1928). The next year, when he is back in Berlin, she warns his father how easily Reinhard tends to fall back on his neurotic mechanisms in the face of a "real" obstacle; how it needs only one word to dissolve this danger, but that one word needs to be spoken. And so she recommends that he, the father, should continue to offer him "analytical help" which will be all the easier if Reinhard does not live with him (to Simmel, March 5, 1929). Dr. Simmel himself appears to confirm the success of this procedure. Meanwhile, Anna Freud dreams that Reinhard has misbehaved badly and that Dr. S. merely did not tell her, in order to spare her (to Simmel, May 10, 1929). She continues to take an active interest in Reinhard's well-being, writing in 1931 that he should become "inwardly somewhat more robust and learn a little to defend himself against the various injuries" of life (to Simmel, January 1, 1931). Finally, in 1934, she writes that she is happy to hear that Reinhard, by then in California, has turned into a "tall, radiant, Germanic blond youth" though she cannot quite believe it (to Simmel, December 13, 1934).

A comparable sense of involvement, including the humanistic, moralistic, and pedagogical fervor in the quest for the "real," the true, or genuine personality, presumed to have been obscured by neurotic distortions and ignoble defenses, is also a characteristic of her concern with her other child patients, even outside the charmed circle of the Burlinghams with their special claim on her preference and affection.

TEGEL

In his suffering, since 1923, Anna Freud was the only nurse her father accepted. She was to care for him, willingly and soberly, for the remaining sixteen years of his life (Jones III, p. 120; Peters, p. 101). In addition to constant treatments and frequent operations, a prosthesis was required. When the fourth and fifth of these, provided by a Viennese oral surgeon, proved inadequate, Freud was persuaded to seek relief from his "prosthesis misery" in Berlin from the eminent Professor Schroeder (Gay, p. 538); hence the repeated visits to Berlin-Tegel, in close vicinity to the city, where father and daughter stayed in a small chateau or palatial "villa" on beautiful park-like grounds, as guests of a Psychoanalytical Clinic for about twenty to thirty patients, the first of its kind, founded in April 1927, and directed by the socialist, physician, and psychoanalyst Ernst Simmel until its demise in 1931. After their first visit to Tegel, Anna Freud wrote to Simmel (on November 15, 1929) that she and her father had rarely had such a wonderful time, which included her learning to ride a bike. She would "never forget this." Her thoughts still went back to Tegel right after her father's death—"how beautiful you made everything there for my father" (to Simmel, November 25, 1939).

EITINGON

Closely connected with Berlin was Anna Freud's strange and close friendship with Max Eitingon, who founded the Berlin Psychoanalytical Polyclinic in 1919, as he was later on to found the Psychoanalytical Association of Palestine. After the end of World War I he had supported the Freuds with a large monetary gift, and in 1920 he received from Freud the symbolic "ring" as a token of acceptance into the psychoanalytic movement's inner circle, formerly the "Committee," whose first members were Ferenczi, Abraham, Jones, Sachs, and Rank. (Anna Freud received the ring in 1928; later on both Eva Rosenfeld and Dorothy Burlingham [Peters, p. 192] were similarly honored, though this token had, perhaps, ceased to have some of its earlier significance.)

Whatever its degree of mental or physical intimacy, Anna Freud's relationship to Eitingon touched her closely enough, to make his "loss" the cause of a depression and of a regression to her preanalytical phase, the Anna of the daydreams, whose problems she described in her account of her own analysis in her earliest publication, dealing successively with masturbatory, beatified, and "sublimated" beating phantasies, daydreams, and their literary transformation (A. Freud, 1922,; L33n).

Her letters to Eitingon suggest that he wanted a sexual relationship and that she refused until he "gave her up" (see L25), which hurt her deeply. From early on (to Eitingon, November 16, 1923) she insists that she has the same answer to his often repeated question, which he, to her surprise, refuses to accept, even though he knows so well the people concerned in the matter (referring, one surmises, to herself, her father, to Eitingon himself, and to his wife). There are some faintly flirtatious twists and turns. She confesses she has a hard time whenever he leaves ("I am not so easily controlled and cool, as I am thought to be. What is awakened in me on one day, wants to live on the next, and then is at a loss where it should turn.") Yet, while he seems to find her not accommodating enough, she cannot help being always afraid of being too much so (to Eitingon, July 15, 1926). She appears to tease him occasionally about his rationalistic faith in "the supremacy of reason" and "anxiety-free cognition," telling him that reason, by going too far, turns into its opposite; and that, although he does not believe this, he should be glad that she does (December 12, 1927). But perhaps her own rational, ascetic, and filial ideal precludes all passionate proximity: Papa, she writes to him (on November 10, 1925), would like her to be "more reasonable and clearer than the women he gets to know in analysis, with all their moods, discontent, and passionate peculiarities." And she would like to be that way for his sake, and because it is one's only chance to be at all useful rather than a worry and burden to others. In 1928 they apparently had a decisive conversation in Berlin. Afterwards she observes somewhat wistfully that she always thought he was there to help her (September 15, 1928). In 1929 it is he who complains that she waited for a business matter to come up before writing to him; whereupon she replies, she thought this was exactly what he wanted her to do (September 7, 1929).

No interpretation of the relationship seems satisfactory. Conceivably, some have thought, she also underwent a kind of supplemental analysis with him (a letter of September 19, 1925 may suggest this). But this seems hardly in keeping with the keen sense of loss she suffers with regard to a man whom she compares to a barren desert (L47), nor with her resentment of the fact that he gave her up so easily (see L25). By 1931 she expresses, albeit in the context of communications from which "all the important things" were to be eliminated (see to Eitingon, November 15, 1928), the wish that the ill-feeling and irritations which clouded their relationship in the past year, should clear up (to Eitingon, June 24, 1931). Thereafter her letters betray no emotions other than those of a cordial, collegial friendship, while he keeps sending her roses on her birthdays. The relationship, mediated as it is through Anna Freud's and Eitingon's relationship to her father, remains puzzling. Perhaps it is even more so than in the case of Aichhorn, another self-styled "son" of Sigmund Freud, who confessed in the letters of his last years a passionate, lifelong attachment to Anna Freud. This love affair had ever been predicated on renunciation of its fulfillment in "reality" and conducted by him—not without some qualified, tacit approval on her part—exclusively *par distance*, in the sphere of phantasy and daydreams. Perhaps this was a condition unacceptable to Eitingon, who urged Anna Freud toward independence (see to Eitingon, February 19, 1926) and, possibly, to a distance from her father which was unacceptable to her.

The view of Eitingon as an ultimately unsatisfactory father substitute is suggested by Young-Bruehl (pp. 186–187), and is in keeping with the thesis of Anna Freud's perennial virginity. To be sure, the virginity of a person who describes the major problem area in her (first) analysis, and occasionally, later on as well, in terms of her difficulty in coping with masturbatory phantasies (A. Freud, 1922; Young-Bruehl, chapter 3) is itself problamatic, unless virginity could be defined as the absence of sexual relations with bodies other than one's own. Also, there were possibilities, like Hans Lampl (recalling after decades: "It did not disturb me that your father went on alone while I was with you" [Young-Bruehl, p. 96]), or Jones who warned Freud of Anna's "sexual repression" (Gay, p. 435), and Bernfeld, and Aichhorn, and the rest. However, none of these encounters led to anything like Anna's later, permanent relation to Dorothy Burlingham, or even to anything comparable in intensity to her relations to some other women friends. The violence of her experience of the break with Eitingon, and some of her remarks about it, would suggest a physical relationship if it were not for one's sense of Anna Freud's status as virginal priestess guarding the paternal temple, a view supported by the absence of any recorded or observable affairs in her life, and the asexual ambience which was part of her presence. Her father, Sigmund Freud himself, worried about her father fixation ("Sometimes I urgently wish her a good man, sometimes I shrink from the loss"; Gay, p. 438); asked himself, "How will she bear the lonely life," once he was gone; wondered whether he could "drive her libido from the hiding place into which it has crawled" (Gay, p. 441), and feared that Anna might turn lesbian. Yet even as he did so, he fostered a sublimated incest with his daughter, negatively by fending off potential lovers (such as Lampl or Jones [Gay, pp. 433–435]); positively, by virtue of his quadruple role as beloved father, analyst, ultimate professional authority, and idolized head of the psychoanalytic movement, and as ailing patient demanding that no one but his "Antigone" should be his nurse.

Anna Freud herself connects her self-devaluation with the Eitingon affair, and analyzes it in terms of her masochistic choice of rejecting partners in childhood (see L25). This tendency, Gay (p. 432) speaks of "bursts of self-denigration," is connected also with her feeling rejected by her sister Sophie, with the masochistic fictions related in "Beating Fantasies and Day Dreams," as well as with a defense mechanism exceeding "altruistic surrender," which she was to describe as identification with the enemy and loss of self.

ANNA FREUD'S SENSE OF A LACK OF "SELF"; HER STYLE; AND HER CHARACTER

A major area of tensions and problems in Anna Freud's personality, especially during the period of the following correspondence, can be characterized in terms of her own sense of a lack of self. Terms which come to mind are defense versus loss of self, integration and assertion of self versus virtues of selflessness. Repeatedly, Anna Freud described problematic aspects of "altruistic surrender" of one's own identity, and the tendency to live vicariously through another (such as Eva; see L9). Yet she is committed equally to rejection of egocentricity and deeply appreciative of an ethic of altruistic sacrifice.

Her use of metaphors is instructive in this regard. She says of Tegel that she feels there "wie auf einer Rettungsinsel im Stadtverkehr." The metaphor of the "island" (literally: "of rescue," i.e., safety, suggesting at the same time "Verkehrsinsel," traffic island; "Verkehr" meaning both "traffic" and "intercourse") is spun out in the letters from Tegel (see L16, L18). It extends from a "literal" range (safety from intrusion of the city) to more recondite levels of intimate and threatening relationships, from which Anna desired to be protected, though not without accusing herself for such abstention from self-involvement or sparing of herself for the sake, ostensibly, of a calm perspective and peace of mind (see Bittner, pp. 5–7).

In L18 the image of the island protecting Anna from the commotion of both city and human relationships, including the one to Eitingon, is developed in a manner which goes to the core of Anna Freud's choice of life-style away from and above the turmoils of some basic kinds of human intercourse. The question arises whether such isolation and its advantage of perspective are all too easy. For they allow the one who evades the movement or dance of life that intertwines with the movements of all the rest, to stand still and merely survey the commotion, and thus to spare herself. This is the same motif as in Anna's deliberations on her empathetic though vicarious experience of Eva's turbulent relationship to Obermann (L9). In L18, the conclusion of the text, concerning Anna Freud's lectures, continues the thread of associations. For the public discussions in her seminar are, in fact, her "movement" and do involve her on one plane with the movements of others, thus introducing an element of the confusion that goes with involvement. What appears negatively as a doubt in the right to spare herself the common commotion and to stay on the island, is related, on the positive side, to the issue of a life of self-dedication versus self-seeking or living according to the pleasure principle. It is the theme of altruistic surrender versus "narcissism" sounded at the outset of the correspondence in L1 (see also pp. 5–6). In its further development into a metaphor of involuntary confinement, the island will form a cluster with the prosthesis of Anna's father, which is first personified (L17, L19), then turns into an analogon of psychoanalysis (L24; Bittner, p. 7), and is finally "reified" so as to become, upon its completion, the "ship" that will rescue daughter and father from being isolated, like castaways, on a rock out in the sea (L30–L33).

Metaphoric treatment can veil objects of discourse, a procedure in keeping with Anna Freud's avoidance of explicit indulgence in self-exposure. The metaphors appear typically when she is dealing with topics of intimate and central concern to her. In L22, for example, she develops a metaphor by taking it literally. Anna Freud there treats her attempted "withdrawal" (Rückzug) into self, or recovery of self, in analogy to children's games (see also the preceding dream of children), where one is "sent back" to the initial point of departure (for instance, a tree), and must start all over again. A similar metaphoric passage occurs at the opening of L23. In both places, as in L24, L25, L26, and L33, the topic is Anna Freud's major depression and, as she suspects, a psychosomatic sickness connected with the breakup of her relationship to Eitingon.

However, Anna Freud's metaphorical style does not express or serve simple self-concealment, but corresponds rather to a compromise between self-revelation and self-effacement, though the latter retains the upper hand. This struggle, in turn, is related to the perennial tension in Anna Freud regarding the issue of service versus self-fulfillment, self-dedication versus narcissism, self-gratification versus sublimation, in which service, dedication, and sublimation keep reasserting their dominance.

The sense of a lack of identity is a major theme in Anna Freud's correspondence with Eitingon. She explains to him (May 20, 1926), that she has made it a rule never to be the first to write to someone or to make presents, not out of reticence, but out of a fear of being at the other's mercy ("aus Ausgeliefertsein"). It goes with her as with the artist Schmutzer's drawing of her father. He won't fix it, because it would get too rigid, and therefore one has to put it quickly under glass and frame it. "Somebody evidently forgot to fix me too. And if the frame selected isn't right—it shouldn't be too heavy, but stiff and protective enough—then the white on the picture flies off into the surroundings and nothing remains." This condition is related to lack self-confidence: She dreams: Tinky and Adelaide are driving. She thinks in the dream, if one lets the children drive, things are bound to go wrong. The two little girls, she interprets, are she. If she is put into the driver's seat, things must go wrong (to Eitingon, October 21, 1927). But there are also positive sides to selflessness. In the same letter, she says it is so much nicer to be shown something, than to have to show others how to do things. She complains (to Eitingon, March 4, 1927): She is tired, overworked, "everyone wants something" of her. "In what remains, noone is really interested. But oddly enough: this remnant is oneself." And this sense of her own fragility and evanescence seems to stay with her and to be related to her ultimate reticence and need for privacy, underlying, I think, also her admonition to Simmel (October 25, 1930): "Will you please see to it a little that no one should get my picture to whom I did not give it in person? It's quite another matter with my father's."

Another related theme is the contrast between Anna Freud's faith in "inwardness" and her credo of "realism." "All that is real takes place within" ("alles Wirkliche geschieht doch immer innen" (L30) is a central tenet of Anna Freud in keeping with a Romantic aspect and the heritage of psychoanalysis as a kind of pan-psychism, and in contrast to its "scientistic" aspect with its stress upon reliance on "external reality." The two coexist, as may be seen in the scientist's credo in Freud's *New Introductory Lectures*, and, in contrast, his note on the eve of death, reducing the "outside world" to an unconscious projection of the psyche ("Psyche ist ausgedehnt, weiss nichts davon") (*Gesammelte Werke*, vol. 17, 1941, p. 152). In the case of Anna Freud one is struck with the proximity to the gospel of her favorite poet, Rilke, who proclaimed it the task of humanity to transform all external reality into internal reality.

Her credo and sense of inwardness, while germane to psychology as such, seems to be associated, not perhaps by logic, but emotionally, with her love or longing for the naive, unconscious, idyllic, and somewhat infantile, as a sort of precerebral condition, including homespun weaving and gardening. All this is glorified by Anna Freud repeatedly as an idealized "other" state of being, germane to the little farmhouse she wishes for, or to the flowerbeds she tends, in short, to an existence away from city, Berggasse, and analysis. Her enjoyment of excursions into the mountains and her pride in how capable and secure she was in mountain climbing (to Eitingon, July 19, 1926) also belong with this glorification and love of unreflexive nature (see L24, L34).

Interestingly, in this connection, one of her metaphoric confessions (see L53) is derived from her recently acquired passion for gardening; but only to lead back to her basic problem: altruistic surrender and loss of self versus narcissism and self assertion, which is alluded to in the very first letter (L1; also, p. 6) and, intermittently, throughout the subsequent correspondence. At the period in question, there are still remnants of the conflict between two aspects or selves of Anna Freud. The earlier Anna of poetic and self-indulgent day-dreams is both more self-centered and selfless, that is, without defined personality and given to "inwardness," than the later analyst, therapist, and capable organizer. Yet the mature Anna Freud, however dedicated with a firm, pedagogical zeal to the credo of her father's later years, "Where id was, there ego shall be," still conceals and contains within herself, as her old friend Eva knew only too well, the earlier, delicate, withdrawn, and fragile Anna of the daydreams.

I: 1925–1928

Letter 1

(Spring 1925?)[1]
Thursday evening
Kurhaus Semmering

Eva dear, why couldn't you come? The train you'd have come on is just whistling down below, and in ten minutes you'd have been here. Shall I tell you what I prepared for you? An apple, a plate of black plums, some yoghurt, and a bunch of Christmas roses (bought, not picked by me). And besides all that, me. I was so sure you were going to come that I counted on my own company only until 9:30. And now I have to get accustomed to myself again. I don't even know who has kept you away from me: Aichhorn after all? Or the Deutsch patient? Or the children? Or Miss Albertini's dark moods? Or Valti? It is too late for the Settlement, but barring that there are so many possibilities one doesn't know who to blame.[2]

I am very well and really don't deserve any more sympathy. I am not doing a thing and live like a lady of leisure between bed, sofa, veranda, and bath. Life is certainly easier when there are no demands except for looking after oneself, but I don't think I'd like it in the long run.

To my astonishment, I discover that I too have a touch of narcissism. It is certainly not unpleasant, but what am I to do with it in daily life? Apparently, it has been developing quietly, because I was not aware of it before. To survive, it would probably need its own bathroom. That is expensive. But altruism isn't as cheap as one might think either. So it's all the same in the end.

Don't be alarmed at my foolishness. That is part of getting well. Just now I had the thought that you did come on the train and left a message that you were not coming in order to surprise me. But then you'd be here by now.

And so good night, and heartfelt greetings. Hasn't Lizzie come yet?³ If I hadn't started with my new patient, the interruption would not be so difficult. But now I am worrying again.

A car is just driving up. Is it you after all? When will you come?

    Your
    Anna

Notes to Letter 1

1. Date and setting: The Freuds, frequent visitors to the Semmering region, then about two-and-a-half hours by train from Vienna, had also stayed at the Kurhaus the preceding year (Jones III, p. 106–107); but L1 presupposes the connection with Eva's household established in the fall of 1924. As Eva wrote some forty-eight years later: "The most important thing in my life was, of course, your first visit to my house in November 1924, and all that followed from it" (to Anna Freud, September 10, 1968).
2. August Aichhorn, see p. 81. The Deutsch patient: patient of analyst Helene Deutsch. The children: Eva's own (Mädi, Victor) and foster children living with Eva, like Lizzie Wellenstein. Valti Rosenfeld: Eva's husband. The Settlement: day care center for neglected and underprivileged children (see pp. 32–33; ER, pp. 206–207).
3. Lizzie Wellenstein: Anna Freud's patient, a Dutch girl who, as a result of polio, could walk only with splints, and needed a special banister to get up and down the stairs in the Rosenfeld house.

Letter 2

    (Summer 1925?)¹
    Friday evening

Eva dear,

Our letters crossed twice. I am so glad you are up and about again, and that you are coming on Monday. When will you arrive? Could I still see you in the evening?

I have decided that you must come to the Congress.² I'll pay all your travel expenses. Write at once to Dr. Landauer³ (Frankfurt, Kettenhofweg 17) and reserve a room. Don't say no. It is a mistake to deprive oneself of things one likes to do, there are so many disagreeable things one has to do.

We can talk over everything else when you are here, but write to Landauer immediately!

Love and kisses,

    Your
      Anna

Good news from Dorothy[4] from on board ship—tomorrow we may have news of her arrival.

Notes to Letter 2

1. Date and setting: The references to a psychoanalytical congress near Frankfurt (see below) suggest summer 1925.
2. Congress: At the 9th Psychoanalytical Congress in Bad Homburg near Frankfurt (September 3–15), Anna Freud was to become secretary of the Viennese Educational Commission of the Psychoanalytical Association, chaired by Max Eitingon (Peters, p. 119).
3. Dr. Karl Landauer, psychoanalyst, in charge of the South-West German Psychoanalytical Society, the nucleus for the later Frankfurt Psychoanalytical Institute (Peters, p. 182).
4. Dorothy Burlingham: see pp. 74–78.

Letter 3

    (Late August, 1925?)[1]
    Semmering, Sunday

Dear Eva!

What are you doing? How many guests have passed through your house by now, and how many people have wanted something from you? I recommend you everywhere as a breakfast stop, open at dawn, with the most exquisite china and the most beautiful napkins. If I ever have a house and if I ever have a daughter—which is even less likely—I will send her to you to be trained.

I just spoke to [Siegfried] Bernfeld[2] on the telephone. He is making sleeping-car reservations for us for September 1. But I would much rather not go at all.

I fell asleep in the car; it took a thunderstorm to wake me. Frau Lou[3] likes it here very much. We have gone for walks and we have so many things to talk about. All goes very well.

But it is cold, 45 degrees, and rainy; so we can't lie under the birches. But when you come, we'll be able to again. You don't need to decide in advance. Any time will do, and there is always a room for you. Just give us a call.

Many greetings
   Your
     Anna

Again many thanks for the good half-day with you! The memory will stay with me—perhaps we will meet again!
   Lou Andreas

Notes to Letter 3

1. Setting and date: see pp. 63–66.
2. Bernfeld: see pp. 78–79.
3. Lou: see pp. 63–65.

Letter 4

(September 1927?)[1]
Friday

Eva dear, you can't imagine what I've been going through for the last few days. I was like the engine on Victor's train[2] when it is wound up too tight: first it runs like mad on its tracks, then it lies on its back for a while with its wheels still spinning in the air, and finally it won't run at all and has to be fixed. That's sort of how it was, and I couldn't bear the sight of a pen or a letter or a typewriter. But now I am all fixed again. I was about to thank you for our lovely Sunday morning when your letter came, in which you say it was you who received a gift. It must have been completely mutual. And then your second letter came, the most beautiful and dearest I have ever received from you, and by way of an answer I would have liked to get on a train and come to you because so many pathways opened out from it, and I wanted to try them all right away. That is difficult to do in writing. You ask what you should read now, and that is not easy to say. Actually there are three ways into the reading of Papa's books. One is the methodical approach of a student, for example, who wants to learn something. He must start with the "[Introductory] Lectures." The other is that of someone motivated by his concern for sick people. He should begin with the "Case Histories." They are difficult but reveal a lot. They are, I think, in volume 8. The third way would be to take everything for granted and to use it as if it had always been meant for you. In that case you could start with the writings on applied psychoanalysis in volume 10, such as "Totem and Taboo," and "Thoughts for the Times on War and Death," and whatever else you may find there. You should also read "Mourning and Melancholia," I don't know in which volume. But I am sure you would enjoy "Totem and Taboo." I would like so much for you to read Group Psychology, because in rereading it, I worked through a huge portion of my own analysis. (When I reread it, it helped me over a giant step in my own analysis.) Suddenly everything was in it, my old daydreams and everything I desired. I am so glad that you are no longer afraid of us.[3]

And, after all, you know all of it, and would only need to describe Vera [von Freund-Toszeghi] or Maria or Erzsi [Toszeghi][4] to them, and every one of our teaching institutes—even under the strict chairmanship of Dr. Eitingon—would have to graduate you at once; unlike poor aunt Kata[5] with her assiduously acquired pseudo-knowledge of analysis. I keep wanting to know how you happen to know all this. Papa was really the first to say it all, and nobody before him. You haven't even read it, yet you know it.

Aren't you expecting too much generosity from Vera? You know we decided that not even I had quite learned to have that kind of generosity. It is probably the most difficult kind to acquire.

But I did learn a great deal at this Congress,[6] a new sense of freedom that always comes after one has forced oneself to go through with something. Now I may almost have a little house for my weekends.[7] And what came afterwards was only weariness, not the loss of anything gained there. Is it possible that Dr. Eitingon was right after all? We were both so sure that he was wrong. But this time we got along with each other very well. Can you come soon? It isn't unpeaceful here now, almost all the visitors are gone, and we see little of those who remain. I would love to have you here.

Tinky was sick again with a high fever, but it lasted only a day. Dorothy is very well. She wants so much to be one of us and is making a tremendous effort to work on herself.[8]

I would like to be a little bit of Mädi[9] for you. I wish I had a little daughter, I would share her with you.

A greeting and a kiss wrapped in nothing but love,

>   Your
>   Anna

Erik[10] is making a drawing of me, but oddly enough I look like Marinka[11] in it.

Notes to Letter 4

1. The date of this typed letter is presumably early September 1927, shortly after the 10th International Psychoanalytical Congress in Innsbruck (September 1–3). An earlier date is precluded by the allusion to Mädi's death in the summer of 1927 (see p. 67) and mention of Erik Erikson (see pp. 82–83) who, according to Robert Coles (1970, p. 21), was not living in Vienna before 1927.
2. A Christmas present received the previous year.
3. Volume numbers refer to Freud's *Gesammelte Schriften* (1924*ff*). Among the "applied" writings recommended by Anna Freud is also "The Moses of Michelangelo" (1914) which later served as the starting point for Eva Rosenfeld's essay "The Pan-Headed Moses—A Parallel" (presented at the British Psycho-Analytical Society in October 1950). This was Eva's attempt to bring together Freud, Klein, and herself by synthesizing the male monotheistic Judaic ethic and the Freudian intellect with a Dionysian, "preOedipal" polytheism and the feminine Mother Goddess. Finally, bearing on Anna Freud's own analysis and inner life, the letter points to "Group

Psychology and the Analysis of the Ego" (1921), a work centered on self-surrender and identification with a dominant collective father figure and the community of his followers.

4. "Housedaughters" at Eva's (see p. 66).

5. According to Young-Bruehl, pp. 79, 114–115, 195, Katá Levy, née Toszeghi, a Hungarian, was an analysand of Sigmund Frued in 1918 (see also Roazen [1976, p. 215]). She was a social worker and the sister of Freud's friend and patron Anton von Freund, a wealthy businessman, who died in 1920. She was married to Dr. Lajos Levy, who himself became an analyst. Katá Levy, who was also to become an analyst, had been a "quasi-maternal companion" of Anna Freud in 1917, at a time when Anna Freud acted as informal tutor for Vera von Freund-Toszeghi, the little daughter of the von Freunds. Later on, Katá was outstripped by Anna Freud from whom, as she wrote in 1952, she was eventually to learn a great deal about psychoanalysis.

The relationship to the von Freund family continued throughout the lives of Anna Freud and Eva. In response to a request for financial support for Anton von Freund's son Tony, then a refugee doctor who needed to prepare for his board examinations to be admitted to medical practice in Britain, Anna Freud wrote on December 12, 1957 to Eva: "I feel that the obligation towards him is greater than towards anybody else in view of the large sums of money which his father has given for psycho-analysis. You know, of course, we could never have had a publishing company nor the Collected Writings (*Gesammelte Schriften*) without Anton von Freund. This is the right time to pay back some of it."

6. At the 10th International Psychoanalytical Congress in Innsbruck (September 1–3, 1925), Anna Freud presented a paper by her father on humor, and, for the first time at a congress, a lecture of her own, "On the Theory of Analysis of Children," later revised as "The Theory of Child Analysis" (1932, *Writings* I, p. 162). Concerning her lecturing on the "Introduction to Child Analysis" in the preceding year, she wrote (to Eitingon, November 8, 1926) that she felt at first as if she was flying about somewhere up in the air but then took great pleasure in speaking, which she did, like her father, without reading from a prepared text, and found very easy. At the congress she was also elected General Secretary of the International Psycho-Analytical Association, her first important position in the organization.

8. Tinky (Katrina Ely Burlingham, born 1919): Dorothy Burlingham's younger daughter. The phrase "[sie] . . . macht so ungeheure Anstrengungen mit sich selber," presumably also referring to Dorothy's analysis with Sigmund Freud, might be translated alternately as "She is trying so very hard in coping with herself."

9. See p. 67.

10. See note 1 above.

11. Marinka Gurewitsch (née Revész), born 1902 in Bratislava, Hungary (now Czechoslovakia), died 1989, New York City.

Letter 5

(July 6, 1928, Semmering?)[1]
Friday evening

Eva dear, I was so happy with your letter, it was just like you. But you know, I have always known what is going on inside you, even when you don't show it. I know it from others, and I would also know it if nobody told me. I would like to be with you always when you are like that, even if I can't help you. But at least I would be with you.

Tomorrow I leave for Vienna. It was like this last year too and when I got back there was the message that I should come to you. I feel as if something immense and alive has turned one year old, our image of Mädi which will no longer change.[2] But it is there every day of the year and I would like to come to you every day, not only today.

Since I have known you, Eva, I have felt certain that I will never be entirely miserable: I will always be able to come to you and feel at home with you, like Marinka [Gurewitsch] and Gusti [Körner]. You have never promised this, yet I feel sure of it.

Every day Mabbie says: Next year we must have three houses next door to each other, one of them for Aunt Eva. The school should just be a beginning, we should have something even more beautiful together, with all the girls and all the children.[3] The children keep talking about a real farm. Do you think that this could come about? That would be your school farm.

The birches have been waiting for you all this time and the children are looking foward to Victor. I wish the Monday child weren't coming and you were having an easier time. But I know that this doesn't make much difference to you right now.

I will call you tomorrow, but on Wednesday, when I come in for my patients, I must see you for a little while.

I am with you every day.

    Your
    Anna

I was told afterwards that there *was* some Adalin[4] in the house. I was so sorry about that. For next time. Love to Omi.[5]

Notes to Letter 5

1. Date: Meant to reach Eva on the first anniversary of Mädi's death, the letter was apparently written the "Friday evening" preceding July 8, 1928.
2. See p. 67.
3. Eva Rosenfeld wrote in her Memoirs: "I founded the school in October 1927, together with Dorothy Burlingham, in . . . memory of my daughter" (ER, p. 187). Dorothy Burlingham said similarly of Eva's part: "I thought it was to replace Mädi" (interview with P. Heller, June 13, 1975).
4. A brand of sleeping pills.
5. Eva's mother, Rose Schiller Rosenfeld.

II. 1929

Letter 6

(March 1929?)[1]
Tegel, Wednesday

My dear Eva,

What are you doing? Are you writing the long letter you promised? How is the house and everybody in it?

Yesterday I spent a long time with Omi and Vera and it was very nice there. I was immediately called on to be Solomon: Should Vera leave immediately because of Regine's last letter?[2] She must, but the letter is so outrageous, that it should be promptly published and circulated. I hope she will save it for you. She spends one page on her terminally ill grandmother and three on a ball in Budapest to which Vera is invited and for which she simply has to have a gown that is longer in the back than in front. Then a lot of directives on how and where the dress is to be made. One doesn't know—is Vera going for grandmother or for the ball? And could she then at least wear the gown that is longer in back to the funeral as well?

Tegel is ideally beautiful but the grounds are not quite usable. If I had wings I could take the loveliest excursions. We are living in the villa again and have been smothered with flowers and fruit. But Berlin is strenuous and keeps calling on the phone, and we ride around a great deal. Frau Lou is coming tomorrow. I look forward to that very much.

Write to me, Eva. Is the Offer plan already dead? We all think it is great, Omi too, and Papa as well.

The visits to Schroeder are not so bad this time, and Papa is very well.

Love and kisses,

>   Your
>   Anna

(Continuation)

My dear Eva,

I wrote this letter to you before breakfast and the minute I was finished, yours came. It made me so happy. I am very sorry I won't be there when the house is taken apart. Where will you put up the boys in the meantime? I can offer you both of my rooms if you need a shelter for the homeless.

Today we are having a quiet morning and will not drive in to see Schroeder until noon, which is very nice. I would like to go out into the wide world with no plans at all. But that isn't so easy.

Omi has an idea how to help the sanitarium.[3] If it succeeds, it would be splendid. I promised her that if it did, she would receive a great psychoanalytical medal of distinction. You write so hopefully about the Offer plan. Will it really come off? It would be nice, but I can't imagine that the difficulties Valti is putting in its way can really be overcome. As for the question of certification for the school, we should also talk to Aichhorn once more. He too thinks one shouldn't start the next year without it.[4]

I am so glad that Ernsti[5] is a good boy. Papa also finds him truly changed for the first time. Aren't you proud of your fine establishment?

It seems to me I have a lot more to say, but I suppose you will have to read it all between the lines.

Another kiss,
　　Your
　　Anna

Notes to Letter 6

1. Date and setting: For Freud seeking relief for his "prosthesis-misery" and his and his daughter's stays in Berlin-Tegel see pp. 20–21. Their second visit there, March 11, 1929, was to last for "only two weeks, during which Lou Salomé came twice from Göttingen to visit Freud and his daughter. At these visits, he wrote later on, he had to leave conversation largely to Anna, not only because he had such a hard time speaking, but also because he could not hear well any more" (Peters, p. 183). Both the remark "we live again in the villa" and the reference to Lou's visit suggest March 1929.
2. Regine Toszeghi: mother of Vera von Freund-Toszeghi. Eva's mother, Omi, lived in Berlin at the time.
3. Lacking public support, Simmel's sanitarium was in constant financial straits.
4. Certification: Presumably, it was recommended that the private Hietzing School (see pp. 79–80 and Bittner, pp. 18–19) should obtain official certification for its curriculum, a matter in which City Councillor Aichhorn could be of assistance.
5. Ernsti, Anna Freud's nephew (see p. 66) had been living au pair at Eva's since 1928.

Letter 7

(March 18, 1929) Sunday
[afternoon][1] contd. evening

My dear Eva!

Max Halberstadt[2] just left. The three of us spent a few very nice and peaceful hours together in the afternoon. Your phone call was a beautiful idea. We were all delighted: I with you, and Max with Ernsti, and Ernsti with Max, and you (I hope) with me, and the people listening at the next table, with our merriment. It was just lovely. Max is so dear and good, you would like him right away if you saw him. I do so want things to go well with him, but he has so many worries, and he is not well at all. He is happy that Ernst is thriving and is terribly grateful to you. He isn't surprised that Ernst doesn't want to come back anymore. I think he would like to come to you too, just like Dr. Simmel.

I have just—it is evening now—had a long talk with Papa, the sort of talk that makes a person wiser. I think the effect has yet to show itself and won't be noticeable in this letter, unfortunately.

I think a great deal about you and your roofless house,[3] and hope it has grown together above your head. I am in love with our villa all over again, and can't imagine that we won't always live like this.

Frau Lou is here and I am very happy about it, because this time I can't seem to get accustomed to all the others. Visiting with Omi was the only thing that felt like a homecoming.

Write me another long letter instead of a Gilly evening. That is my charge for the week, at the very least. I am on the go all the time and will hardly be able to get to all the work which I wanted to finish here.

I send you many greetings and kisses. Papa is well, Schroeder works very slowly.

> Your
> soon-to-return
> Anna

Notes to Letter 7

1. Date: postmarked envelope; [afternoon]: crossed out; setting and persons: see L6.
2. Max Halberstadt, the widowed father of Ernst (W. Ernest Halberstadt Freud). Dr. Simmel's son Reinhard also lived au pair at Eva's.
3. Presumably, the roof of Eva's house was being repaired.

Letter 8

> (March 22, 1929)[1]
> Tegel, early Friday

My dear Eva!

This is a last greeting from Berlin before our return. We arrive early Sunday, and Monday at six you are expected for your first hour.² You know, there is no contradiction in your undergoing analysis in a place that you would prefer to come to for love's sake alone. I did the same thing, and perhaps because of it, the two things became inextricably bound together for me. In the end you will realize: it is the only way to go into analysis. Right now you are troubled by the feeling that where you love you would like to be especially good. You will see that being good and being in analysis finally amount to the same thing.

I am very glad I was in Berlin. It took quite a while, but suddenly—between my last letter and this one—I had again the sense of freedom that I usually get when I am away from the Berggasse. And I learned something about things you have long known about. It was very strange. As if something was suddenly illuminated and one could see into it. It was about what actually happens between those many other people and oneself, and about happiness being not as important as I have always thought it to be, and that quite different things are what really matter. It is much easier to feel this than to put it in words. I hope it won't all close up again by the time I get back to Vienna. It often does.

It would be better to talk about the school than to write about it. We really don't disagree; I also believe that school must be compulsion. Our disagreement concerns only one point. I want the children to be made to want to do what they are supposed to do. You want them to be made to do what they don't want to do as well. But the teachers don't understand any of that. All they know is compulsion or liberation from compulsion. And the latter results in chaos. My example—which you grant—is Aichhorn. But you are right: something has to be accomplished in the school now. Otherwise we simply don't amount to anything.³

I was at Marinka's and met Omi there. I will tell you all about it. It was lovely being with her.

I noticed that Vera wants to get back to Berlin. But I'll leave all that for Sunday or Monday evening when you will be free. I think there is a lot to be said about it.

I got a very nice cheerful letter from Ernsti. Today I will see Mrs. Simmel. I think I already know everything I'm going to feel afterwards. Poor Reinhard [Simmel]![4]

Today you don't need to read between the lines. I've written a lot and everything else I'm saving for you in Vienna.

With a kiss, see you soon,

      Your
      Anna

Frau Lou sends you greetings.

Notes to Letter 8

1. Date: postmarked envelope.
2. This refers, presumably, to Eva Rosenfeld's first analytic session with Sigmund Freud (see p. 70).
3. For a discussion of these remarks on an issue central to this progressive educational venture, see Ross, p. 32, Bittner, pp. 17–18, and Heller, pp. 80–82.
4. This refers to the Simmels' difficulties affecting their son Reinhard (see pp. 41, 88–90).

Letter 9

(after June 18, 1929?)[1]
Schneewinkel, Friday

Eva dear! I just unpacked my fountain pen and am putting it to paper for the first time. So far I have only received news from you and have only replied in thought. And after all there is nothing to be said about this, I just want to know what is going on.

It seems very strange to me that I have known you for such a long time without knowing the one thing your life really revolves around. Now I can't imagine how that could have been possible.[2]

I believe I understand very well how things are with you, and I have an odd, slightly dizzy feeling as if I were experiencing all this or as if you were experiencing it for me and I was sparing myself too much. I would like to relieve you of some of this burden, but I know that isn't possible.

I was in Hofreit yesterday. It is high up and open and has much more of a view than I expected or remembered. But one would have to reserve a room soon because it gets very full here in July.

I would like to help you far more than I am able to. I was at Rosenbichlers yesterday. Perhaps you will like it here, if only things are going better by then.

It is so beautiful here; we never had as nice a place before. But I haven't been able to settle down yet, something still keeps pushing me from within. I'll be all right though. Ernstl[3] is especially sweet and loving and a credit to you.

Now that I have learned to use my pen again, you will hear from me regularly.

Just a kiss,

    Your
    Anna

Notes to Letter 9

1. According to Peters (p. 184), the Freud family moved on June 18, 1929 to their summer resort in Berchtesgaden (of which House Schneewinkel [lehen] and Hofreit are part). Freud was visited there successively by psychoanalysts Ernest Jones, Sándor Ferenczi, A. A. Brill, and later by René Laforgue and Joan Riviere. The opening of the letter suggests that it was written shortly after arrival.
2. All this refers to Eva's perennial friendship and love affair with Julian N. Obermann (see pp. 72–74).
3. Ernstl, otherwise living at Eva's, was on vacation in Berchtesgaden together with the Freud family, Dorothy Burlingham, her children, and others, including Herta Huber, one of Eva's helpers (see p. 117) in a supervisory role, and Peter Heller.

Letter 10

(June 21 or 22, 1929?)[1]
Schneewinkel, Sunday morning

My dear Eva, there is no mail on Sunday and our telephone is out of order. Dorothy will call you from Hofreit where she is visiting Judy and her mother.² I hope all is well and in good order, at least externally.

At last I am beginning to feel as though I am on vacation. I have a bicycle, and the fact that I have leisure for something so utterly superfluous, and can enjoy it, proves most clearly to me that these are vacations. My poor Wolf [her German shepherd] hurt his paw and is much too good about it. Today, with great trouble, the help of a neighboring farmer, and his brother, a village priest, we bought seven laying hens for Mabbie. We have almost digested our first visitors: Jones and wife should be leaving tomorrow morning. Right now fires have been lit on all the mountains in spite of clouds and rain. All these days seem precious to me, and I am afraid they will vanish too quickly.

Tomorrow the letters you promised are supposed to come. You have a breathing spell now before everything starts up again. Maybe it will be easier for you when it does. I am looking forward tremendously to your coming, even if it will be only for a short time initially.

All the best and let's write again soon,

> Your
> Anna

Notes to Letter 10

1. Date: Schneewinkel (Berchtesgaden) indicates summer 1929, *after* the preceding letter when Anna Freud had just unpacked her fountain pen, as does the sense of vacation "finally" setting in. The festive lighting of fires on mountain tops suggests the summer solstice (June 21 or 22).
2. Judy de Forest: see pp. 83–84.

Letter 11

> (June 26, 1929)
> (Schneewinkel [Berchtesgaden](?))[1]
> Wednesday morning

Eva dear, we called you twice with no success. Your phone rattles but there is no answer. Afterwards I dreamed about you and Victor all night long and the dreams were full of sad and oppressive things.

I received all your own letters and the others you sent along as well. I believe I now understand Obermann much better, and I thank you for that. I think you made him relive what every man experiences with the mother from whom he should get away, but can't, endlessly repeating his futile attempts to do so. Basically, it is the same as with Bob and Herta and Trudl.[2] They too represent an attempt to find a substitute that is doomed from the start. There seem to be so many, but it is mere illusion.[3] For the first time I see your whole life now, and our meeting, all in your letter. But there is one thing I must ask you. What am I going to do when I can no longer remain where I am now, when I am left alone and thus lose all that gives meaning to my life? I have always wished that I would then be allowed to die. And now it occurs to me that I dreamed that *you* died last night. I did not want to mention it before, it seemed so senseless.

So now we know: you are I and I am you and any part of me that you can use, you must always take, because you have a right to it. I am sending the letters back to you, there were four, not three, but the first two say the same thing.

Now Obermann is there, and maybe everything is much better. Now we will go look for a room for you.

Here everything is beautiful, in spite of the rain. Ernsti is very well behaved.

With a big kiss

    Your
    Anna

Notes to Letter 11

1. Date and setting: postmarked envelope (Berchtesgaden). Closer acquaintance with Eva's relation to Obermann through his letters, sent by Eva to Anna (see L10), points to L9. The search for a room for Eva in Berchtesgaden

suggesting that the letter was sent from Schneewinkel, is concluded in L12. See p. 12, for a discussion of L11.

2. Herta Huber, a distant relative of the Rosenfelds, remained even in her later life as a nun, a devoted "daughter" to her "dearest Muschi" as evidenced in an affectionate letter she sent on the occasion of Eva's seventieth birthday on January 2, 1968. Trude Pfandl, née Kraus, another "Haustochter" of Eva Rosenfeld, later married a native of Grundlsee where she lived until her death.

3. M. J. Burlingham (p. 212) adds three more (Judy de Forest, Ann Nederhoud, Kira Nijinski) as "his [Bob's] girls." In the context of Obermann's stay with Eva in the summer of 1929 and their impending parting (see p. 73), Anna Freud's analysis of his relation to Eva in analogy to Bob Burlingham's adolescent flirtations with the young women in Eva Rosenfeld's establishment implies a critique and a judgment (see also Bittner, p. 12). The subsequent passage refers, of course, to the death of Anna Freud's father as the event which would take away "meinen ganzen Lebenssinn" (literally: "the entire sense and meaning of my life").

Letter 12

(Early July, 1929,
Schneewinkel [?])[1]
Sunday evening

Eva dear, at last we have found the right room for you and I am very happy about it. It is so near to us that you can see straight across from your balcony to ours. On foot, the way is a little more roundabout, but not much. The room is very large and has many windows; no toilet, as the farmer's wife said, just an outhouse, but a brand new one. The farmhouse is very old, and the stone steps are narrow and slippery from their use by many generations. Right next door is a sawmill that belongs to the same farmers. Suddenly it occurs to me that I didn't hear it because it's Sunday. Will it be noisy on weekdays? But surely not at night, and this was the only chance of getting anything at all close to us. Actually there are even two adjoining rooms, one large and one small.

Our life is rather lively. Yesterday Dorothy and I had supper in the Grand Hotel with the Amsdens[2] who were passing through; early this morning we picked up Dr. Ferenczi and wife from Salzburg. They spent the day with us, on their way to Switzerland. Yesterday we had the first radiantly sunny day in a long time and all of us helped with the haying all day. The neighbor's eight children stay with us continually. For the children it is really paradise. Bob doesn't look bad at all, you delivered him in good shape. Of course, he is again two heads taller than all the others.[3]

I am so glad that you are having a calmer time now. I hope it stays that way until the fourth. We must still arrange precisely how we are to meet and all the rest of it!

Now June is gone, and I regret the passage of each day.[4]
I send you a kiss and many good wishes.

    Your
    Anna

Notes to Letter 12

1. Date: During his stay at Berchtesgaden Freud was visited by analysts, including Ferenczi (Peters, p. 184).
2. Amsden, an American analyst in Budapest, temporarily treated Dr. Robert Burlingham, the mentally ill husband of Dorothy, ever in pursuit of wife and children (see pp. 76–77; M. J. Burlingham, pp. 157–267 passim).
3. Bob Burlingham, as the oldest also the tallest, had been staying at Eva's at the time. Though Dorothy Burlingham claimed she felt never close to Eva, she entrusted her children to her on many occasions.
4. She wrote similarly to Ernst Simmel (July 11, 1929): "We are staying in an indescribably beautiful house in a remarkable location and I lead a marvellous life, bringing in the hay, weeding the vegetable garden, painting windows and doors of a small summer-house. If it weren't for the congress, I would be perfectly happy and think of nothing else . . . I will soon see you in Oxford" and so on.

Letter 13

Schneewinkel, July 7, 1929

My dear Eva, I come to you now in the form of a letter, after all, and I hope I get to you on time, in spite of Sunday. Dorothy and I wanted to surprise you tomorrow in Grundlsee,[1] but failed, partly because Mama[2] sprained her foot and is immobilized, and partly because of the general resistance against our undertakings, which always proves too strong. I am sad about this, but I know you will accept me even as a letter. And anyway, I always have the same thing to say, in whatever form I come.

Since you left, I have read Mädi's notes and she came to life so vividly for me that I was entirely filled with her. She was exactly how one should be at that age, with just the qualities one needs as a basis for becoming a real human being later on.[3] You must feel that you did very well by her in order for her to develop like that. She believes so firmly that the dear Lord had something planned for her. Perhaps she was right and he lifted her out of it all. You know I don't usually speak of the dear Lord because I don't believe in him. But in Mädi's dear Lord even I can believe.

Her mental maturity almost frightened me. But I knew a lot about that before from Minna.[4]

I am happy, Eva, that you found your way back to Grundlsee and can now go to Mädi's grave which you could not do last time. I will be there with you tomorrow, even if not in reality.

I thought of you here during the Salzburg night, but believed that things would turn out as your letter now says they have. There is such a thing as justice after all. First we don't reach out for life, and then it doesn't reach out for us. And at the very end, it may turn out that it was good that way.

Tell Obermann that the thunderstorm he didn't want to take seriously cost a man in a rowboat his life, out on the lake, and a hundred others in a big boat were barely saved. The Königsee[5] is not to be trifled with at such moments.

And also tell him that the farmer's wife from the Doffer house came over here the next day all excited. She suddenly realized that she had made a mistake, and that his room had been reserved for all of July a long time ago. To make up for it, she has found similar lodgings for him in the house next door: two rooms with a large balcony for the same price, with no other guests in the house. We rented it and will still look it over. Do you suppose he didn't make a good impression? I warned him when we went up there. With your farmer's wife everything is all right.

We look forward immensely to seeing you.

And now a kiss that includes all that still remains unsaid.

> Your
> Anna

Notes to Letter 13

1. To join Eva on the second anniversary of Mädi's death in the place from which Mädi had started out on July 8, 1927.
2. Anna Freud's mother, Martha, rarely mentioned by Anna Freud, ran the household impeccably on the plane of daily routines.
3. See p. 67.
4. Minna Mach, Anna's young patient who lived at Eva's.
5. Alpine like at Berchtesgaden. Obermann was apparently staying with Eva at Grundlsee, possibly also in Salzburg, and came together with her to Berchtesgaden, first (see above) on a brief visit, later for a longer period, prior to leaving for the United States (see pp. 73–74). The memory of Schneewinkel stayed with Eva: thirty-six years later, on September 20, 1965, she wrote to Anna: "Being young and fair weather really belong together. Now, for instance, I am thinking of the fragrance of wood and the geraniums your mother used to water in the evenings in Schneewinkel; and how I came racing along on my bike to be with both of you still for one moment. Within me, I guess, all was black as night at that time, except when I thought of the 'family' to which you were my entrance gate."

Letter 14

Schneewinkel, August 2, 1929

Eva dear,

You know our ways. We take little Lün as seriously in death as we did in life, even giving her the right to be mourned, although she may not be entitled to it. What hurts me so is that I could not bring her back to Papa in spite of all the searching for her.[1] And then she suddenly turned into many others for me—into Sophie as my sister and Papa's little daughter,[2] and into Heinerle[3] because he also gave him such joy, and I could not nurse him back to health. But perhaps we can replace her for Papa after a while. You mustn't feel too bad, Eva, your intentions were good, all you wanted to do was to put yourself out for us. It could have happened to any of us.

Somehow my heart aches for her, but I try hard to make it pass.

Why were you sick? And what was wrong?

Martin[4] is here; we want to make at least one excursion into the mountains. Ernsti's father is coming tomorrow after all, to stay for ten days.

I am so pleased about Tegel.[5]

Just decided that Dorothy, Martin, and I will leave for the Glockner region[6] today and spend two days there. I think it will be very beautiful.

Lots of kisses.

    Your
    Anna

Notes to Letter 14

1. Lün: Sigmund Freud's chow, a present from Dorothy Burlingham, was to be taken by Eva from Berchtesgaden to Vienna when she broke loose in the Salzburg station. "We searched for her almost incessantly for three days," Anna wrote to Eitingon (August 29, 1929). "She was finally found run over on the railroad tracks."
2. Heinerle: Heinz Rudolf Halberstadt, Ernstl's little brother, second child of Sigmund Freud's daughter Sophie, stayed in Vienna after her death. He was greatly beloved by his grandfather, as the most enchanting and intelligent child he had ever encountered. Heinerle died of miliary tuberculosis, aged four-and-a-half, on June 19, 1923 (Jones III, p. 96). Gay (p. 436), calls Ernstl (past 6 in 1920) and Heinerle Anna Freud's "first 'patients' " (in quotes) which makes more sense with regard to Ernstl than to Heinerle.
3. Sophie Freud Halberstadt (born 1893 in Vienna), mother of Heinerle and W. Ernest (Ernstl) Halberstadt Freud, died in her early twenties. As an older sister and beauty, Sophie was in Anna Freud's childhood and youth the object of her admiration, jealousy, and rivalry (Young-Bruehl, pp. 43–47; Gay, p. 432).
4. Martin Freud, eldest son of Sigmund Freud.
5. Tegel: The good news presumably referred to hopeful developments in the management of the financially troubled clinic (see also L15).
6. (Gross) Glockner: highest mountain (3798 m) in the Austrian Alps.

Letter 15

Tegel, September 18, 1929

Eva dear,

Tegel is an idyll bordering on the world whose shadows fall upon it. You will probably hear from Omi and Marinka about Edith's visit here; and perhaps also from Mathilde, with whom she is staying at the moment.[1] I would rather tell you more about it in person.

Both of your dear letters have arrived and they are as insightful, clear and brave as you are yourself. I also read to Papa parts which concern him, Ruths[2] and the analysis. But the fact that your strength is failing is not good. That has never been the case before, at least not since I have known you. If only you could be here and lie in the sun out in front of the sanitarium facing the lake. That would be the right kind of Berchtesgaden, the way we meant it to be.[3]

Again I am the one who is having an easy time. I feel as if I were on an island of safety in the midst of city traffic.[4] All around me people must dodge cars and be afraid; but none can get near me. I love to stand still and be protected.

I saw Marinka and talked to Omi several times. Today is our first appointment with Schroeder.

Tegel is ideal and more beautiful than ever, and Dr. Simmel is in high spirits and full of hope. He reports that Reinhard [Simmel][5] is doing very well. Apparently, even his mother is pleased.

I kiss you, you must write again right away.

Your
Anna

Notes to Letter 15

1. Mathilde Freud Hollitscher, Freud's eldest daughter.
2. Ruths: Swedish industrialist, self-made millionaire, inventor of "Ruths Speicher" (for storing steam).
3. "das richtige Berchtesgaden": a reference to the stay there in the preceding summer which did not turn out to be as restful and relaxing (especially for Eva) as intended.
4. For the discussion of this metaphor and Anna Freud's style, see pp. 95–96 and Bittner, p. 7.

5. Reinhard Simmel: See pp. 88–90.

Letter 16

Tegel, September 27, 1929

My dear Eva,

You must not worry about me. The traffic island is intact, the only threat is its connection to the other world by phone. Consequently we had some chaotic days because of Edith, with constant calling back and forth. But every now and then we do hang up the receiver and it is quiet again, within and outside. I also know from Dorothy that she has gotten over her condition and I believe that from now on everything else will go well. But it upsets her very much that Gusti [Körner] saw her in such bad shape. Perhaps you can manage to erase that impression a little.

I just got your call from Berggasse. It really doesn't seem right that I can't be with you now. When everybody has finally moved in, the impression of a "beginning" is no longer the same. But we must keep in mind that spatial distance makes no difference. In reality I am right there with you.[1] I am so glad that you see Mathilde [Hollitscher] and talk to her. I always think that she would have a much better life if we could manage to draw her to us and out of her circle which is quite empty and which does not suit her at all.[2]

I had a very pleasant and peaceful afternoon with Omi, right after the Edith commotion; we got along very well. I will surely see her again soon. Nobody knows how long we will stay. Some time in the first half of October we will suddenly be in Vienna.

Could you ask Peter Heller's father[3] whether he got a letter from me? I wrote to him, but did not know the number in the Karolinengasse and the letter was mailed by mistake. If he didn't get it, I will have to write to him again.

Will you give something really nice to Victor on my behalf? You will have some money of mine. Something that goes with his idea of me.

I am now giving a—weekly—seminar on child analysis here as well,[4] for the rest of my stay. That and reading proofs for my little book[5] are the threads by which, I hope, I shall find my way back to work again. For the time being, doing nothing still pleases me wonderfully. Yesterday I even fell asleep in my boat on the lake.

Of course you must keep Relly.[6] Dorothy can find someone else. How about school activities and lunch? Will Susy and her baby move in on Sunday as well?[7] Isn't that too soon? I am very curious about the shape Lizzie will return in. And what is Ernstl doing? How did the boys' room turn out?[8]

I haven't heard anything about Yvette Guilbert.[9] It would be grand if she came. Are you feeling stronger? If you aren't, how will you stand it all?

It is a good thing, after all, that the island has a telephone.

I greet you and kiss you with all my heart,

    Your
    Anna

Notes to Letter 16

1. The Burlinghams moved into the top floor at Berggasse 19 in the fall of 1929. Eva Rosenfeld helped with the move, and both Dorothy and Eva called Anna. The situation raises again the question of the relationship between Eva and Dorothy. It was perceived by Eva's son, Victor Ross, as a close and lifelong friendship, while Dorothy, in her later years, remarked that Eva was Anna's friend, not hers (interview 1975 with P. Heller).
2. Mathilde, Freud's eldest daughter, was married to the writer Robert Hollitscher.
3. The letter to Hans Heller, father of Anna Freud's patient, Peter Heller, concerned the delay in the treatment caused by her absence.
4. Her seminar on child analysis in Vienna.
5. My little book: presumably *Einführung in die Psychoanalyse für Pädagogen, Vier Vorträge* (1930). See "Four Lectures on Psychoanalysis for Teachers and Parents" (1932, Writings I, pp. 72–133).
6. Relly: a cook.
7. Susy and new baby: lover and daughter of Ruths (see L15n2).
8. The boys' room: shared by Victor, Reinhard Simmel, and Ernstl, though Victor recalls that most of the time there were two rooms, one shared by him and Reinhard, the other occupied by Ernstl.
9. Yvette Guilbert, Eva Rosenfeld's aunt by marriage, was a celebrated French chansonnière, greatly admired by Sigmund and Anna Freud.

Letter 17

Tegel, September 30, 1929

My dear Eva,

I am sorry that I always miss Victor's birthday [October 1]. I hope it was nice, nice for him. For us his birthday will always be connected with that first of October when Mädi, so lovely and strange in her costume, was the center of attraction. Even if he has forgotten, you, probably, see nothing else.

Both times that I heard you on the phone (but did not speak to you), it wasn't you at all. Why do you act as the "foil" for Dorothy? Why do you assume that Dorothy is the only person I worry about and the only person I want to be reassured about?[1] Now I don't know a thing about what is going on with you: Whether Hertha and Lizzie are back; when Susy and her baby will move in; how Peter and Erik are behaving; whether the whole issue of the school is a great burden to you[1]; how the boys' room is standing up. And, above all, what you are doing and how everything is working out these days. It seems as though you haven't written to me in detail for a long time.

At the moment, there is no real progress here. As in analysis, the prosthesis appears to be in a phase of resistance. We live very peacefully in Tegel. As in Vienna, the only interruptions are meetings of the Psychoanalytic Association, or my seminar, or some consultation, and a great deal of paperwork. I have had three hours of analysis[2] and am a bit wiser and feel quite peaceful. You will have to tell me whether or not the wiser is noticeable, when I get back. While patients[3] are here, I go rowing. It is lovely to be alone with the lake.

We are trying to found Tegel Incorporated, but are lacking a few rich people who could buy shares. I hope we bring it off.

Write soon, and at length!
A kiss from

>   Your
>   Anna

Will you remember the money for Gretl Ustobal?[4] Please do!

Notes to Letter 17

1. See p. 43, on the incipient shift in Anna Freud's relationship to Eva Rosenfeld and Dorothy Burlingham, a triumvirate held together by the positive relationship of both Dorothy and Eva to Anna. The passage following in L17 refers to members of Eva's household (Herta Huber, Lizzie Wellenstein, Susy and baby, the boys: Victor, Reinhard Simmel, Ernstl) and to teachers at the Hietzing School (Erik, Peter); four of them (Lizzie, Reinhard, Ernstl, Erik) were Anna Freud's patients.
2. On Anna Freud's analysis with her father, who was certain he had "succeeded well" with his own daughter, see Young-Bruehl and Gay (p. 439). In view of sessions reported here, the biographers' assumption that the analysis was restricted to two periods, 1918 to about 1921 or 1922, and 1924 to 1925, seems neater than reality.
3. Patients of Sigmund Freud, some following him to Berlin from Vienna.
4. Gretl Ustobal (married name Erthal): a young friend or acquaintance, it appears, who Anna Freud had met at an orphanage in Vienna.(?)

Letter 18

> Tegel, October 5, 1929

My dear Eva,

Your letter of yesterday sounds so sad; it made me quite sad too. It isn't enough that we are well, you must be well too. There is no use in my being well, if nothing is left over for you. Maybe it will all be better when we get back, and we really will be back soon. Schroeder thinks he'll be able to finish sometime next week.

I am glad I gave Vicki a nice soccer ball. How is he? Is he getting accustomed to the [Hietzing] school?

Did you ask Peter Heller's father whether he got my letter? It explained the reason for my being delayed, and it would be quite embarrassing for me if he had not received it.

Many thanks for all the things you are taking care of for me. I must have owed you money for a long time; also for Ernsti. I'll get it to you via Dorothy who still owes me money. I am glad all is well with her, and that I get such nice sensible letters from Ernsti.

Now I am looking in all directions, preparing to step down from the island of safety. And as I do so, I think to myself that if I can't walk more skillfully and securely between the cars now, I have no right to step back up again later on. But I also realize: it looks much easier from up there, because one is at rest while everything else is in motion. That way you can see through it. It's only when your own movement is added to it, that you get confused.[1] Sometimes I think, I could do it better if I didn't have to give lectures.

And how will everything turn out for you, Eva? How is it with Valti? Soon I will be sitting with you in your living room again or you will be sitting at my place in the rocking chair.

A kiss

Your
Anna

Notes to Letter 18

1. For the discussion of this metaphor see pp. 95–96.

Letter 19

Tegel, October 10, 1929

My dear Eva,

We were too confident, and perhaps too impatient: we wanted so much to be in Vienna by this Sunday. But now, suddenly, the prosthesis is "in resistance," all its symptoms have come back, and no one knows when it will give them up again. Papa, understandably disappointed, is now, after the first disappointment, quite patient again. The prosthesis is stronger than we are, and we both know it and act accordingly.

Of course I am worried about all my work in Vienna which has been postponed, Erik and Peter Heller and Judy and all the many things connected with the [Psychoanalytic] Association. But I will catch up with things later.

I am glad you did not force yourself to take on an impossible au pair girl. I'll still find something better for you in the course of my work, you'll see. I have a number of consultations here and always make "propaganda" for you. Monday I was at a party with Omi and she sent Papa something for the Jewish holidays. She looks pale and worries about you. I will see her again soon and would like to see Marinka [Gurewitsch] too. I have 200 Mark here for Minna. What did Dr.Schur think about her?[1]

Though I have to worry sometimes that my own work might get away from me if the waiting period gets too long, it is a good thing that I don't have to worry about people in Vienna forgetting us if we stay away too long. It must be dreadful to come back and have nothing waiting for oneself. I feel terrible about your being in such agony. When I get back, you must let everything thaw again and give me half of it to carry.

See you soon, Eva,

Your
Anna

Notes to Letter 19

1. Erik, Judy, Peter, Minna: patients of Anna. Dr. Max Schur was from 1929 on Sigmund Freud's personal physician. He was apparently consulted with regard to the patient Minna Mach.

Letter 20

Tegel, October 14, 1929

My dear Eva,

I really went to see Omi the other day and it was exceptionally nice. After Omi called, Marinka immediately abandoned her husband and was there too, and Lilli [Sachs; Eva's cousin] came a little later, and suddenly I understood, as never before, what sustained you before you came to Vienna, and how you must miss it. Actually, nothing special happened and I really can't say what it was about. But we all belonged together and liked each other, and talked a little and it didn't matter what lay outside the room, whether it was Berlin or Vienna or Paris or any other place. It was quite a unique atmosphere and perhaps worth all the neuroses hidden inside it somewhere. For other people have their neuroses too, and live in a poor atmosphere to boot.

This time I liked your voice on the phone again; you mustn't freeze over anymore until we come back. Then I will chop away a bit of ice every day, as they do in winter for the fish, so they won't freeze to death, and it remains unfrozen.[1]

My seminar here is over now, or at least I decided it should be. But I can't tell you how much I prefer the one in Vienna.[2] You ask if I don't find the people here deeper and more solid than in Vienna. I can't say I do, they are just a bit different. In Vienna, you know, they are more inclined to turn to whatever is easy and pleasurable. Here maybe they cling more to the usable and useful, even if it is not pleasant. But both here and there they neglect what really matters, and the useful may be furthest away from that, just because it is so terribly palpable and commonplace. But what seems most terrible to me are their ideals, what people imagine to be most desirable, that is, their houses and antique furniture and styles and conveniences and everything else that money can buy. I am glad I don't have to live in all this.

I don't mention Eitingon for a very good reason—he has not been here at all. He has been in Switzerland since the Congress[3] and won't be back until the first of November. As we get along so much better at a distance, this is probably a great advantage.

Now I am really coming, though I don't know exactly when. Don't manage too well without me!

With a kiss

Your
Anna

Notes to Letter 20

1. A convincing metaphor for Eva's condition of mourning and depression, though fishermen who cut holes in ice do so not to keep the fish from freezing, but to catch fish.
2. Her Berlin seminar, Anna Freud wrote to Eitingon, would probably last no more than three evenings. It consisted of six to seven people, "all nice and interested," though there were still traces of "Melanie Klein's Berlin period." The participants were collected by car and brought out to her to Tegel. She mentions by name the Bornstein sisters (Steff and Bertl), Melitta Schmideberg, Harnik, Müller-Braunschweig, and Mrs. Wulff; as one-time visitors: Radó, the Princess Bonaparte, and Dr. Simmel (to Eitingon, September 24 and October 15, 1929). For the invidious comparison between the dominant moods of Berlin and Vienna which, unlike the devaluation of both, is in keeping with a tradition of mutual critique and fault-finding on the part of Viennese and Berliners, see also p. 27. Anna Freud herself suggests in L24 a connection with her disappointment in her relations with Eitingon.
3. The 11th International Psychoanalytical Congress took place from July 27th to 31st, in Oxford, under the chairmanship of Eitingon, with Anna Freud again as General Secretary. She wrote to Eitingon afterwards that she thought he behaved badly toward her at the congress, though, she added somewhat sarcastically, she made the mistake of taking herself more seriously than the "International Psycho-Analytical Association," which ought not to happen to a "General Secretary" (to Eitingon, October 3, 1929), a position, which, as she saw it, Eitingon, then President of the Association, had induced her to accept (to Eitingon, December 12, 1928).

Letter21

Tegel, October 20, 1929

My dear Eva,

I was just going to write you about a nice and peaceful afternoon I spent out here with Omi, when the tragic incident occurred that Dorothy may already have told you about. I don't think you know the people concerned, my cousin Tom and her husband Jankew Seidmann.[1] He hung himself last night, committing what I think was the first evil deed or certainly the first unkind deed of his life. He was a young Eastern Jew, very sweet and brotherly and very Russian in his ways. She is the most difficult person you can imagine, melancholy, always thinking of suicide. And in between: a seven-year-old girl who looks like a little elf. Now he is dead, and she in a sanitarium so that she can be monitored, and the child is with the Lampls for the time being.[2] Their business will collapse, and it remains to be seen what can be salvaged from the ruins.

I would have liked best to bring the little girl to Omi the same night, but she knows the Lampls and we don't want to subject her to any more shocks than necessary.

I don't understand why there has to be so much misery. I am going back to her again now.

I am very glad about the plan with Minna. I want her to have something good in her life, not only trouble, and together we will see her through. She needs so little. It was good that you found that out this way. If she can stand Elsa[3] for any length of time, living with her, I believe, would be simpler and freer of conflicts for Minna. Living with you is so strongly tied up with her illness and treatment. Anyway, one would have to try it, and not mind too much, if it doesn't work. For neither of them is really suited to the other.

I am looking forward to talking. So little can be said in writing.

With love

Your
Anna

Notes to Letter 21

1. For Jankew, Anna Freud wrote to Eitingon, "suicide was probably the easiest way out of his difficulties"; his wife, "incapable of living, even in better days," escaped into a daze. She had "decayed" ever since she had her breasts operated on, or rather, removed; she lacked a will to health and hated other human beings (to Eitingon, January 4, 1927, October 22, 1929). Martha Seidmann, who called herself Tom and dressed as a man (Young-Bruehl, p. 97), illustrator, inventor, and author of unique and charming children's books, committed suicide in 1930, one year after her husband.

2. Psychoanalysts Jeanne Lampl-de Groot, a close friend of Anna, and Hans Lampl, a former "suitor" of Anna (see also Young-Bruehl, p. 96–97).
3. Elsa Houtermans, friend of Eva Rosenfeld into whose care Minna [Mach] was to be placed.

III: 1930

Letter 22

Thursday, May 15, 1930
(Tegel)

Eva dear,

I dreamt about you all night, partly about a lot of complicated events in your house, as if on stage, about Vicki, who was very sweet, and about many children. All the while I was writing to you about all this.

I am trying to make a long retreat into myself, and once I almost arrived. But then something sent me back to the beginning and now I must set out again.[1] I don't know whether it's really my body; perhaps it is just joining in, and it certainly has every right to do so. But I will repair everything; it just takes some time. And some peace and quiet, which is not easy to come by, not even in Tegel. Maybe I am asking for too much of it, and therefore it is not available anywhere.

Tonight I will have a talk with Angela's guardian. Her family here has a somewhat problematic attitude toward him. But what isn't problematic with them!

Papa is really recovering visibly here. The care he gets in Tegel is doing him a lot of good, and I believe it will even make him gain some weight. All we want in addition is for the sun to come out. We need it badly.

Could you really come at Pentecost if we were still here? That would be very very very nice. You will have to split yourself in two, so that one half can stay in Tegel and the other half can stay at Omi's, otherwise I won't get enough of you.

I will write soon again. For today just another kiss.

Your
Anna

Notes to Letter 22

1. For a discussion of this passage see p. 96.

Letter 23

(May 24, 1930)[1]
Tegel, Saturday morning

My dear Eva!

The only dog we have here is the dog I turned into early this week. Then I suddenly realized that it's all for the birds; and now I am working my way up to higher animal species, and have become almost human again. If only I can stay this way, I'll be all right. But I still can't stand very much and get tired too quickly.[2] Papa is feeling very well, except that he had to give up again on his attempt to resume his daily ration of two cigars. His heart, which he usually doesn't feel at all, acted up again. But he looks very good, loves Tegel, and has definitely put on some weight. He just misses the dogs a lot, and the old prosthesis is no good any more and painful. Schroeder is so deeply involved with the new one, and so enthusiastic about it, that he can't be bothered with the old one. Dorothy is healthy and blooming as never before and Judy [de Forest] is very good.[3]

So much for the news bulletin. Oddly enough, my thoughts about this summer suddenly revolve completely around Gmunden,[4] and I fantasize about the park, the lake, a boat, riding a bicycle and spending every weekend with you. It would not be far from Grundlsee at all; one could almost get over there on bike. I hope Mama will find something suitable, but actually I don't see why poor Gmunden should all of a sudden offer what all the other places didn't have. But maybe it will! Wouldn't you be pleased?

I am glad you are reading the articles on psychoanalytic technique[5] and feel how wonderful they are. They are perfectly simple, yet one needs to be fairly advanced to understand them properly. Papa himself can no longer remember where he first introduced the [notion of a] "transference neurosis";[6] I made a point of asking him. But the concept is very simple. At first the patient appears to be getting well (like Hertha in her new job), drops his former objects and phantasies, and with them symptoms and conflicts. They are no longer invested with libido. And then he forms everything anew, this time with the analyst as central object. Comparable to an experiment in a laboratory, this new formation of the neurosis under the eyes of the analyst, makes it possible to truly penetrate it. To the outsider it looks as though the patient has only really gotten sick in analysis, which in a way is true. But you know all that.

The day before yesterday I had my little seminar here, and last night Dr. Radó was here and reported on the gigantic American congress.[7] What a good thing that I wasn't there!

We may go to Hiddensee[8] for a couple of days while Schroeder is away.

Hold me very tight and I will be decent again.

      Ever your
      Anna

Notes to Letter 23

1. Date: postmarked envelope.
2. The passage describes Anna's efforts to overcome a near physical breakdown and acute depression. It does so in the manner of ironical understatement and a traditional language of Viennese punning (Kalauer). A concatenation of idioms "auf den Hund kommen" ("going to the dogs") and "für die Katz" (in vain, "for the birds") is taken literally, suggesting a transformation from a human into a "low" animal state of depression and weakness, from which the writer is trying to work her way up and back into a "decent human" state (see end of letter: "Hold me very tight and I will be 'decent' [anständig] again").
3. Dorothy Burlingham, Sigmund Freud's patient left Vienna with the Freuds on May 4. Judy de Forest and Mabbie Burlingham, Anna's patients

also followed them to Tegel (letter from Judy de Forest to Peter Heller, January 22, 1983; M. J. Burlingham, p. 211).

4. Gmunden: vacation town near Grundlsee. The mention of "Mama" trying, probably in vain, to find something suitable there, is another of Anna's few references to her mother. See also L26 where she appears again in a somewhat unflattering context, while her function in L13 is merely that of an innocent impediment.

5. The articles on psychoanalytic technique (mostly in vol. 6 of Sigmund Freud's *Gesammelte Schriften* [1924–1932]) included also the recent deliberations on "The Question of Lay Analysis" (1926; in *Standard Edition* 20: 179–258), which were central to the conflict with the American analysts who insisted on the inadmissibility of lay analysts. In 1929 Freud chastized the English and Dutch representatives, Jones and Ophuijsen, for their "dangerous game" of mediation between the American analysts and the defenders of lay analysis: "Unless you intend to destroy the IPV [International Psycho-Analytical Association] you'd better be careful," he wrote to Ophuijsen. "The first to leave the IPV if it were to yield to the Americans on this issue of lay treatment, am I, the author of 'The Question of Lay Analysis' " (to Ophuijsen, May 26, 1929). Anna Freud, a lay analyst, took an active part in this struggle, which was also a matter of concern for the future lay analyst Eva Rosenfeld.

6. According to Laplanche and Pontalis (1973, p. 463), the notion of transference neurosis as a phenomenon in the process of psychoanalytic therapy, was introduced in Freud's "Remembering, Repeating and Working-Through" (1914).

7. Sàndor Radó, psychoanalyst, a native of Hungary, later active in the United States (Roazen, 1976, pp. 506–509).

8. Island and vacation spot in the Baltic sea where Anna Freud's brother Ernst had a small house (see L24).

Letter 24

Tegel, June 3, 1930

My dear Eva,

I am horrified to see how quickly June is passing and our departure still not in sight. However, I am sure that I'll still get to Vienna before we go to the country (but where?). What if you are in Grundlsee by that time? What is to become of all the matters we haven't talked about these last weeks and that are so difficult to put in writing? Didn't you say once you might come here at Pentecost? But now you have Mabbie again. Couldn't you escape from all of them for a little while?

I am sure you could send Mabbie to Mathilde [Freud Hollitscher] any time.

Now I know exactly what I have been missing all this time: an island. Two days on an island have been enough to make me all well again, and now I am so completely at peace with myself that I don't need to know anything about myself anymore. That is the best way to be. Hiddensee is truly a paradise, uniting all that is beautiful in one small spot with air and wind and freedom.

Now I am not work-weary at all any more. On the contrary. I am sometimes afraid that my whole professional life will peter out, because I have stayed away for too long. I wish summer were not coming now, but rather a working period so that I could first get everything into good order again. This really worries me. So do Lizzie and Erik and little Peter, and especially my seminar. But I don't see what I can do about it.

Also, there is so much to discuss with regard to all the children. I had a letter from Hilde Abraham. She wants you to let her know if anything fails to run smoothly. Possibly with Minna? I also worry about a lot of other things. Couldn't you prevent Trudl [Kraus] from going to Susy [Ruths' girl friend]? Somehow it doesn't seem right. And I am concerned about Vera [Freund-Toszeghi]. She doesn't make a good impression at all. I hope she will come to me one of these days, and then I will know more and can tell you about it. Through Judy [de Forest] I also know a lot more about Erzsi [Toszeghi], and would like to talk this over with you. I think she has reached the point where one won't be able to make any headway without analysis.

The Psychoanalytic Society here gives me no pleasure at all. I feel like a stranger, as if I didn't belong and had nothing to do with it. Perhaps this is, basically, connected with Dr. Eitingon, from whom I feel totally estranged. I don't really know.

Dorothy is really well. I think you will find her greatly changed, much calmer and steadier. They also like her very much here in the sanitarium. Dr. Simmel is in a lot of financial trouble, I don't see how this is to go on.

You see, this is a sort of menu of what is going on here. But eating and digesting it all will take a lot more time.

I am sorry for Ernst, but he should be smarter by now. It is my fault that I did not make him smarter.

Only then will it be your turn, and then mine. Isn't that alone worth a trip to Berlin?[1]

The prosthesis is progressing like an analysis: very slowly.

With a big kiss,

    Your
      Anna

Notes to Letter 24

1. Meaning: The letter contains a "menu" of topics to be discussed; first all the others, then, finally you (Eva) and me. To discuss all these, including us, would be worth a trip to Berlin on your (Eva's) part.

Letter 25

(June 1930 ?)[1]
Tegel, Saturday morning

My dear Eva!
I am very sad that you were sad and that I was not near you. And I am also sad that the little piece of me that I put into your house, our Ernstl, is only a taker and can't give what I would like to give you. It would not have to be that way—but then we probably would not have him, and he would be giving whatever he is capable of giving somewhere else.

The continuation of your letter that you announced, has not arrived yet; perhaps it will still get here today, before Sunday. Our news is that Papa is wearing his new prosthesis for the first time. Of course, it is still unfinished, but what there is of it does not exert any pressure, and we hope it will continue to grow in the same manner. I am now convinced that we will be in Vienna before your departure. Then I'll certainly stay there for a while, if only for Lizzie etc., and the seminar [Kinderseminar]. Besides, we have no prospects for the summer that would lure us away. That is a pity, we used to look forward to our summer place all year long. Now all this traveling back and forth has spoiled our appetite in advance.

Vera is coming to see me tomorrow. Reinhard is behaving impeccably, looks well and is praised by all. Tinky and Mikey are very cheerful. Dorothy is faced with writing a final letter of refusal to Robert [see pp. 76–77], but even that doesn't daunt her. I only talked to Omi on the phone, because I am only half alive due to a maddening hayfever.

My seminar is becoming more human; the last evening was rather pleasant. I have captivated all of them a bit. I am also attending [Siegfried] Bernfeld's pedagogical seminar [see p. 79]. And almost every afternoon I am out on the lake. If I weren't so stupid and if something in me didn't keep gnawing at my drowned friendship with Dr. Eitingon, I would have only good things. But that is more than one can ask for and maybe it is better for the "world-order" this way. I believe I know something now I must confide to you, but nobody else knows about it. I believe what is hurting me so much is not that I lost him but that he got over losing me so easily, in other words: that he is giving me up so lightly. This goes back to a time when I was very little and I think I know exactly when it began. From then on I always sought out children who abandoned me, and it had the same effect on me as now. As if I were seeing myself through the eyes of the other and were worth just as little to myself as I was to him. Now I am almost all right again because I know what it is. Only this time it was not my doing. And it remains a reality which has the right to hurt me [see pp. 91–94].

But it is over, and at least I learned something from it.

Too bad that the time on the island passed so quickly. I would like to go back there or somewhere near the sea. But it doesn't matter, I can go to Reichenau [vacation spot on Lake Constance] just as well.

It worries me that I haven't earned any money, or earned so little, for such a long time. I always need so much, and what will be left over for my farm? It has become smaller, but it does loom large on my horizon.²

I would so much like to turn into someone who would need almost nothing for herself, just as Mädi intended to be. But I am such a big heavy clod of ingrained habits. I wish I could get rid of them and become entirely different.

I send you a kiss by special delivery and am ever

>   Your
>   Anna

Notes to Letter 25

1. Date: Regret that "time on the island passed so quickly" suggests a date after Anna's stay on Hiddensee (see L24).
2. With the help of Dorothy Burlingham the purchase of a six-acre farm in Hochrotherd in the Vienna Woods (then a 45-minute ride from Berggasse) did become a reality in the fall of 1930 (M. J. Burlingham, p. 216).

Letter 26

>   Tegel, June 12, 1930

My dear Eva!

I am worried by your letter of yesterday, and especially by your reference to financial worries. That must mean that something happened which you did not write about. Was it something with Valti? Did his plan to get some money for the house come to nothing?¹ Or did something happen at [Valti Rosenfeld's legal] office? You must write me about it.

Speaking of financial worries, I have a question I was going to write you about anyway. One of the child analysts here would like to come to Vienna for a year, but she would have to take along a little patient of hers, whom she can't leave behind—a fourteen-year-old girl, very bright, who had eating problems which she has now overcome.² I will take a look at her if you will consent in principle to take someone in, and if the parents are able to pay 300 Mark for room and board. She would actually like to bring a second child along as well, but that, I think, would not be suitable for us.

Here on the lake I am swimming Dr. Eitingon out of my system, and I feel very well. But I am sorry that I have to swim him away.[3] The new prosthesis is being tested; it still presses a lot and is very uncomfortable.

You forgot to say on the phone that you would be pleased if we rented the Rebenburg after all.[4] I would be very pleased.

I would like you to feel well again and I would like very much to know what happened.

With a kiss

> Your
> Anna

(Continued, June 12)

Eva dear, this is just a little postscript to my letter of this morning in case the Rebenburg turns from a fata morgana into reality. Through Bernfeld we got in touch with someone who lived in it last year. He says the only disadvantages are the absence of a fence and the public path going through it which, however, can be closed off. Papa thinks I should write to you (because one can't get very far with Mama and Aunt [Minna Bernays] over the phone) in order to find out whether the rental agreement could not include both the closing of the path and the enclosing of at least a part of the garden with a wire fence. (Wire fencing doesn't cost much. I could even pay for it.) Do you think that is possible?

> Your
> Anna

Notes to Letter 26

1. Valti Rosenfeld's plan to get money for the Hietzing house, possibly a mortgage.
2. For a description of the girl (Ann Nederhoud) whose eating problems did follow her to Vienna, see p. 31. The second child may have been Kyra Nijinski (see p. 31), who joined the Hietzing School and Eva's household somewhat later.

3. "Ich schwimme mir den ganzen Doktor Eitingon im See hier weg und es geht mir sehr gut. Es tut mir nur leid, dass ich ihn mir wegschwimmen muss." The humorous effect of Anna Freud's deliberately ungrammatical—transitive and reflexive—use of wegschwimmen (to swim away), i.e., "sich jemanden wegschwimmen," is sharpened and made poignant by being close to the fact and idiom that it was Eitingon who "swam off" ("der ihr abgeschwommen ist") and did not even seem to mind.

4. Rebenburg: residential villa, close to the lakeshore in Grundlsee.

Letter 27

Berlin, June 25, 1930

My dear Eva!

I wanted to welcome you to Grundlsee with a long letter, but now I am too late, and you are there ahead of me. The last days here have been very strenuous because of all sorts of people and excessive heat. All one could do in the evening was to fall into bed dead tired.

So: I welcome you to Grundlsee and will soon follow you there. Until then, I hope it will be lovely and give you what no other place can give you. Let us save all serious matters until we are there together.

But there are still many daily events, external and internal, left to write about. Yesterday Dorothy left in a great hurry. The final decision about the operation [Mabbie Burlingham had appendicitis (M. J. Burlingham, p. 211)] is to be made right now in the afternoon. Dorothy is very calm and sensible, and everything really ought to go well. Bob, Ernst and Erik are here. Bob, radiant and blooming (one could have pictures made up of him as an advertisement: before analysis and after), Ernst quite cheerful, much better than I had expected on the basis of your accounts, Erik in very good shape. In addition, Max [Halberstadt, Ernsti's father] is here from Hamburg with an assignment to take photos for two days. He and Ernst enjoyed each other tremendously, and on Saturday Ernst will go along with him to Hamburg for another three days. All of them are staying with big Ernst [Anna Freud's brother].

Papa and I are very impatient by now. Papa has no patients and is reduced entirely to waiting. The prosthesis still won't quite cooperate. But we make the best of it and just wait, and want so much to get to Grundlsee. I have sessions with Erik and Ernst as often as the distance between us permits; Bob has too little need of treatment.

I am *very* pleased about [Eva's son] Vicki's successful exam [for college preparatory, Humanistic gymnasium] and am waiting for your first letter. This is only an outline, you have to fill it in yourself.

I kiss you,

>Your
>Anna

Letter 28

>(Before June 29, 1930?, Tegel)[1]
>Saturday morning

Eva dear,

I felt so bad when the letter I wrote you three days ago turned up today behind the seat of the car. I gave it to someone to mail and it must have slipped out. But I wanted you to have news from me in Grundlsee right away and at least have company in a letter.

Meanwhile I have your first letter. I think I know what Vicki's fishing means. Ernst's boy, Gabriel [Anna's nephew] has the same thing. It is such a passion with him that the mere anticipation of it gets him excited in all sorts of ways. I'll tell you about it in Grundlsee. I hope that the time you have planned to have alone there, doesn't last too long. I wish I were there to interrupt your solitude.

Now to your questions: Papa would like very much to have a continuous telephone connection,[2] and of course to have the benches removed. But you shouldn't worry too much about us. We will be so glad to be "free" again, and there is no need for everything to be exactly the way one is used to. Meanwhile the pictures and postcards you sent arrived as well, and I think the house looks beautiful. We really enjoyed the pictures.

I am very glad that I already have a boat in my own name: you'll have to be the "light passenger" ever so often and the "Anna" will carry you.[3] I always wanted to have such a boat for myself and will get up very early in the morning and row out on the lake in it. Once again you are doing everything for us all the time. When I get to Grundlsee, I will do everything.

Mabbie is evidently very well again[4]; I spoke to Dorothy this morning, and she sounded quite calm and reassured. I hope there won't be any more obstacles.

These last days of our stay here are hard on us. Papa has no faith in his prosthesis any more and wishes that at least he didn't have to be bothered with it. It would be dreadful, if after all the time he spent here, he could not even count on a good summer. And when he is depressed, I am too. We still can't make any travel plans.

Ernstl is leaving for Hamburg with his father [Max Halberstadt] today and will be back on Tuesday. On Wednesday, he, Bob, Erik and [Ighino] Wimmer[5] will leave from here. He worries me a lot; I was deceived by his joy in seeing me again, and I was also glad to be deceived. But let us leave this for Grundlsee too.

I hope you will know me right away when I come. It's been a long time with so many stages, and in its course I have grown much older. But perhaps it is better this way than it was before.

Perhaps we will soon be sitting in the "Ausleger-Anna" and Berlin will be far away.

I would like to be with you on the anniversary of Mädi's death. But I suppose that for you every day in Grundlsee is an anniversary of her death. Was it wise to move so close to death?

Heartfelt greetings and kisses,

Your

Anna

(still without "outrigger")

Notes to Letter 28

1. Date: prior to June 29, 1930. The "squashed letter" which turned up in the back of the car, is mentioned again, but without requiring explanation, in the following letter (L29).
2. "Daueranschluss": telephones in rural places were frequently connected only intermittently, during certain hours of the day. Despite Anna's and Sigmund Freud's complaints about the obtrusive machine, he required a continuous connection.
3. Apparently, Eva had secured for Anna Freud the rental of a rowing boat named "Anna" and referred to (see below) as an "Ausleger" (outrigger-[boat]), being of a type used for regattas, equipped for one person in the rowing seat and another light in weight ("leichte Person") at the rudder. By virtue of its double meaning, the term *Ausleger* (= 1. outrigger (boat), 2. interpreter, hence also analyst) gives rise to a somewhat elaborate pun in L33.
4. Suggests successful operation on Mabbie's appendix (see L27 n1).
5. Ighino Wimmer, pupil at the Hietzing School, joined others (Bob, Ernstl) in Germany during summer vacations together with their teacher Erik.

Letter 29

Tegel, June 29, 1930

Eva dear,

Even though this is Sunday, I just got your letter of the day before yesterday. That's one of the few advantages of Berlin. Meanwhile you must have received my poor squashed letter and the telegram and my second letter. I would like so much to come myself.

Just a few words in reply. Please don't worry if the Rebenburg cannot do all it is supposed to. Things don't have to be all that perfect. Perhaps it is even better if we don't get to a point where we would feel homesick for it, as in Schneewinkel. After all, one has to leave again.

Ernstl is now in Hamburg, Bob and Erik are in Hiddensee, and it is quieter here again. Schroeder wants to remove the prosthesis tomorrow and give it its definitive shape.

Some changes could still be made even after that. It depresses me that the prosthesis is not what it should be. In addition, various other things oppress me. I also worry about your being so alone in Grundlsee. I talk to Dorothy on the phone regularly and I believe her worries will clear up soon.

As a girl I also knew Käte Eisler, we are exactly the same age. It is a pity about her just as about all the others.

In my thoughts I sit next to you every evening.

    Your
      Anna

Letter 30

Tegel, July 6, 1930

My dear Eva,

I was so sure to be with you on Mädi's day. Not just so that you wouldn't be alone, because I know Omi is with you already and Valti will come too. But I wanted so much to be with you on that day and experience it and Mädi and Grundlsee together with you. It did not come to be, but I am with you all the same. And basically external separation means nothing, for everything real takes place within. And I am always wholly with you, today even infinitely more so than on that day when I came to you from the Semmering [at the news of Mädi's death; see p. 67]. For we keep growing together and becoming more deeply intertwined so that today I can no longer imagine what life would be like without you. This is the truth seen from within.

Seen from the outside, we are sitting like two prisoners on a rock in a sea called Tegel. The ship that is supposed to take us away is a good prosthesis. At times, we think we see it emerging in the distance and then it sails past us, just as it did with Salas y Gomez.[1] Indeed, he got very old waiting; I hope we will be found sooner and that when we sail into the

Rebenburg harbor, you will be standing on the shore. We are having a very strange time here.

I can't write anything about business matters today; I will next time. What comes to you today is nothing but love, shown in an open and simple way that only the "Rosenfelds"[2] can usually achieve.

I kiss you and Omi and Victor (although that won't do if he is still going to go into analysis with me).[3]

I am always

> Your
> Anna

Notes to Letter 30

1. Ballad by Adelbert von Chamisso (1771–1838) about the long solitary life, despair, and final acceptance of his solitude by a man shipwrecked in his youth, spending his years on a bare rock out in the ocean. The scene alluded to is one of disappointed hope: a ship approaches only to turn away again. Regarding the cluster of metaphors "island–ship–castaway" see pp. 95–96.
2. This great compliment to uninhibited spontaneity is not diminished by the fact that "Rosenfelds" is put in quotation marks inserted to mitigate a kind of flippancy otherwise suggested by the use of the impersonal family name.
3. He did not become a patient of Anna Freud. While the rule of separating private lives of analysts from those of their analysands was not observed in the least in the joint set-up of the Freud family, including Ernstl, with the Burlinghams, or with Eva Rosenfeld et al. (see pp. 10–11), the rule against physical tenderness, touching, etc., was observed strictly, by Anna Freud and/or in keeping with her pronounced aversion to close physical contact,—much as it was in her father's rejection of Ferenczi's proposal of an alternative which included kissing (see Freud's letter to Ferenczi of December 13, 1931; Jones III, p. 174–175).

Letter 31

Tegel, July 10, 1930

Eva dear,

For a while our ship was gone, then it reappeared on the horizon and came closer and closer, and now it is turning a little and sailing farther away. We watch it all the time. That is actually our main occupation.

And you? How is it now, with your house full instead of empty as before? Do you have Lizzie there yet, and have things become very turbulent? Have you seen Dorothy yet? You must write me a long letter so that even as castaways we can be with you in all that is going on.

Is the Rebenburg upset that we have not moved in yet?

I thought of many "business" concerns that we share, but would rather leave them for when we can talk.

Write soon!

    Your
    Anna

Letter 32

    July 15, (1930)
    Tegel

Eva dear,

The ship had disappeared entirely below the horizon, but now it has surfaced again and is heading slowly in our direction. If we are lucky, it will reach us in a few days and carry us away toward the end of the week. But we are so terrified by now that we don't dare to mention it out loud for fear of chasing it away.

Eva dear, I really did not expect to get a letter from you during the days Valti was there. I have tried to accompany you in my thoughts, and it makes me unhappy that you are unhappy. If things within you are as you felt them to be in your letter, then I do think you will have to make a great change, which must not be allowed to fail on account of external difficulties.[1] We have to plan this in Grundlsee and it must work out. Omi has already come up with a plan directed toward the same end. She will go to Vienna and take everything that is filling up your house off your hands and into another apartment. Ernsti must not be an obstacle in this. I have the feeling that we can arrange it all if we do it together. But it is silly to write about it because this is the kind of thing one has to talk over. I wish I was there already. In the meantime I am making plans for you in my mind, and later we can compare them with yours.

I suppose I will have four hours every day in Grundlsee. That can't be helped after the long involuntary interruption. But that still leaves 20 free.

All sorts of things are going through my head, but I will have to see what settles down and remains when I am with all of you again.

In the meantime, keep your fingers crossed for our ship!

    Your
    Anna

Notes to Letter 32

1. The great change in Eva's life involved her decision to leave husband and household in Vienna and to start out on a new path, which in fact she did upon her move to Berlin (Tegel). This was followed by a brief journey to Russia, and, finally, in her professional career as an analyst in London, England, and in separation from her husband, Valti, though they remained friends. She took her son Victor with her to Germany (1931–1933) (Marienau), then to Paris (1933–1934), subsequently, from 1934–1936 to live with her in Berlin, and from 1936 onward to London.

Letter 33

Tegel, July 21, 1930

Eva dear,

Our ship must be something quite old-fashioned, a screw steamer, or perhaps a sailship in a calm sea. For a few days it lay out there in plain sight without moving, and only now is it moving again, and quite close. If nothing gets in the way, it will only be a matter of days before we leave.

Thank you for your sweet letter and for your confidence in my thoughts. They have been on vacation for a long time and have created nothing but mischief in my head. What if they have become quite useless by now? But the fact that you have confidence in them may put them back on their feet again. I also like the daily routine that you propose. And I wish we were now in a position to start work in keeping with this new time-table.

I feel sorry for Lizzie that I gave her an opportunity to backslide. She was simply not ready for such a long interruption. If I had suspected that, I would have rather had her come to Berlin. Don't worry about Ernsti. I think Dorothy would be glad to take him on now, despite the fact that, unfortunately, he is so much trouble.

These are all only bits and pieces. Our departure is getting so close that it hardly seems worth writing a proper letter anymore.

In the last two weeks I have been living as I did before I was an analyst and before you and Dorothy knew me: with Rilke poems and daydreams and weaving. This is Anna too, but without "Ausleger".[1] I send you a kiss and nothing but good things,

    Your
    Anna

Notes to Letter 33

1. This is a confession of regression to a state of mind described in "Beating Fantasies and Daydreams," prior to Anna's turn to analysis, thus without "Ausleger," that is, without an interpreter of her condition or analyst, be it her father or herself. Young-Bruehl attributes this regression to the stress of a long wait. I think it still reflects the impact of Anna's break with Eitingon.

Letter 34

    (September 15, 1930)
    Wednesday morning in the grass
    above Sulden (Bolzano)[1]

Eva dear,

We are 1500 meters closer to the sun than usual, and one feels it. It slowly burns away everything that is superfluous in us.

It is very beautiful and at every stage of the way I leave a bit of unrest behind.

I was at the house of a peasant woman who still spins and weaves loden cloth. But not while doing analyses.

I have everything I need in my knapsack. Maybe that is all one ever needs.[2]

Where are you? Is everything all right? You should have only good sessions during this time.

All around cowbells are ringing; perhaps this letter will carry some of it to you.

A kiss

Your
Anna

1. Date: postmarked envelope: Bolzano (Sta. Geltrude in Val Solda). The names in the South Tyrol occur both in Italian and German.
2. On this glorifying of a naive, unconscious, and idyllic condition see p. 98.

IV: 1931

Letter 35

(Spring 1931, Vienna [?])[1]

Eva dear, yesterday I was still so completely in Grundlsee that I didn't write at all, and to everyone's astonishment fell into bed at eight o'clock, and got all caught up on sleep. And today, already, *your letter came*. I am so glad that the "turmoil" didn't come back. I wish I knew exactly how you are feeling every minute. I told Papa everything, and he did not "grunt" but said it is not surprising at all if you find it difficult, for it *is*. I also asked him your question, whether he doesn't think you should leave everything the way it is, and he says no, you would be wasting yourself and that would be a pity. I spoke to Omi right away this morning. She was very happy to hear about you. She doesn't think Vicki will find it so hard to take. Dorothy would be glad if she could be of use to you and get Vicki and Omi on loan at the same time. She will still write to you herself.²

It was so nice in Grundlsee with you, I am glad I came. In my thoughts I am still walking around the lake with you.

Mrs. Sweetser is coming tomorrow on her way through, bringing Adelaide.³ Dorothy is getting a 24-hour-vacation and will spend it with her in the Cottage Sanitarium.⁴ A telegram came today from old Mr. Burlingham. Robert B. had to go back to the sanitarium. Bob will stay two more weeks with them, then he will go to the de Forests.⁵ What do you suppose happened there?

Today was a regular work day with five hours, tomorrow six and the starting of a second vegetable bed (without manure!). Papa saw Pichler⁶ who was very pleased with him. He found the trout especially tasty.

This is a mess, but it is a bit of me for you.

Your
Anna

Notes to Letter 35

1. Date and setting: Although the letter could have been written in fall 1930 after the return of the Freud family from Grundlsee, spring 1931 is more likely. L37 takes up the theme of Anna's "weekend visit in Grundlsee" with Eva, to which the opening of L36 seems to refer, and includes a reference to Marienau, a school which Eva's son first attended in 1931. Moreover, prior to his pneumonia in 1930, Freud did not feel well, and Dr. Pichler should not have been "very satisfied" with his condition. Finally, the opening up of a second vegetable bed suggests either the farm at Hochrotherd acquired late in 1930, or the large garden in Pötzleinsdorf where the Freuds spent spring and summer in 1931 and 1932.
2. All this refers to Eva's decision to leave her husband and Vienna, instead of acquiescing in the status quo, a life which did not satisfy her, and of which Freud said it would be a waste of herself. Her son, Victor, would not, according to Eva's mother, find the breakup of the family too hard to take.

3. The Sweetser children, Adelaide (diagnosed as suffering from an "obsessional neurosis"; to Eitingon, February 5, 1926) and brother Harold were patients of Anna Freud (Young-Bruehl, p. 132) attending the Hietzing School.
4. The "immense Cottage Sanitarium" is located in Vienna (Jones III, p. 109).
5. De Forests (see also pp. 83–84): In view of his father's mental breakdown, Bob Burlingham was to stay with this distantly related American family during his visit in the United States in 1931 (J. M. Burlingham, p. 220).
6. Professor Hans Pichler, a "distinguished oral surgeon," had taken charge of Freud's case since 1923 (Jones III, p. 99).

Letter 36

(Vienna, 1931 [prior to Eva's move to Tegel] ?)[1]
Tuesday evening

My dear Eva!

Thank you very much for your letter. It was a big relief to know that nothing more will happen to you. But you will have to tell me so again and again, or I will feel uncertain. Still, I believe it.

I really don't quite know what to say. I understand perfectly well that you can only do what you want to do from Berlin. But at the same time, I don't want you to go away. I am simply afraid to be without you, and am also afraid that you won't come back, once you are there. But you can't stay here and protect me either. Besides, this isn't about me at all.

After reading your letter it seemed as though things wouldn't have to turn out so badly after all.[2] Perhaps it could all be resolved so that you can stay. That's what I would like.

I don't think I am a very good friend. I want you to belong to me, but I don't make things easier for you. I say good night to you with all my heart,

Your (not-at-all-Valkyrie-like)[3]
Anna

Notes to Letter 36

1. Date and setting: The letter suggests a date at which Eva had decided to move to Berlin, but prior to her actual move to Tegel.
2. Referring to Eva's marital crisis in the hope it might still be resolved without separation.
3. Valkyries: among the maidens of Odin conducting the souls of heroes slain in battle to Valhalla, Wagner's Brunhilde appears as the foremost: Father Wotan (Odin) encloses his favorite daughter in a circle of flame from which Siegfried will liberate her. The identification of Anna Freud with an armored virginal battle maiden might have reflected one of her own ambitions or a familiar criticism of her and her influence on Eva. See also Grosskurth (1986, p. 325): "As John Bowlby sees it, [Melanie] Klein and Anna Freud were mirror images of each other ... Katherine Whitehorn once described them as the valkyries of the psychoanalytical movement." A deeper root for the analogy lies in Sigmund Freud's own conception of his daughter. In his 1913 essay on "The Three Caskets" (1913) he distinguished "three forms taken by the figure of the mother in the course of a man's life—the mother herself, the beloved one who is chosen after her pattern, and lastly Mother Earth who receives him once more" (p. 301). In a letter to Sàndor Ferenczi (June 7, 1913), Freud identified himself with the aged and forsaken father Lear. He pointed out as "subjective condition" for the writing of his essay his own relation to his youngest daughter, Anna. For he identified her—as he had identified his fiancée, Martha, in earlier decades—with Lear's Cordelia, a type "incapable of displaying affection to others" (Young-Bruehl, p. 63), though unfailing in her devotion. "Lear carries Cordelia's dead body on to the stage. Cordelia is Death. If we reverse the situation it becomes intelligible and familiar. She is the Death-goddess like the Valkyrie in German mythology who carries the dead hero from the battlefield" (1913, p. 301); see also Patrick Mahony in Derrida (1985, p. 66).

Letter 37

(Vienna, Pötzleinsdorf, 1931?
6 Khevenhüllerstrasse ?)[1]

Eva dear, your voice on the phone today was not as good as your letter of yesterday. I hope the turmoil hasn't come back. I wish Grundlsee was nearer, then I would have visited you again over the weekend. It seems as though it was terribly long ago that I was last with you. The uncertainty will be over when your telegram to Dr. Simmel has been sent off, but the real uncertainty will only be gone once your letter has arrived in the Wattmanngasse.[2] I wish it were a month later, or rather six months later. Then you'd be back again. So far, I still can't imagine that you won't be here.

Today I was kept busy with many things. Five actual patients, an unhappy family from Romania with a sick child as the sixth, and as the seventh, Mrs. Sweetser and a reunion with Adelaide [see L33n3] who is radiant, tall, and fat. After that I went to a movie with Ernsti because this has been his wish for a long time, and now I feel stupid and sad, as I always do after that sort of thing. But I did plant forty-eight little seedlings and four dahlias in a new garden bed with Ernsti's help. Even so, this is no vacation.

But I feel as though you were immersed in an ocean and I am complaining because a drop has spilled out of a watering can. Papa looks very well and tomorrow is Sunday. Dorothy is still with Mrs. S[weetser] in the Cottage [Sanitarium].

If you decide to leave on Wednesday, I'll still write to you at Grundlsee on Sunday and Monday evening. And then to *Marienau* [Victor's boarding school]? Or right away to Tegel?

I kiss you good night,

    Your
    Anna

Notes to Letter 37

1. Date and setting: Reference to Eva at Grundlsee and to the return of her "turmoil" suggests proximity to the preceding letters. See also L35n1.
2. Refers to Eva's notifying Simmel, as the director of the Tegel Sanitarium, and her husband in Vienna (Wattmanngasse) of her decision to leave and to accept a position at Tegel for a period (see next sentence) limited to six months.

Letter 38

    (Summer 1931; Vienna, Pötzleinsdorf,
      6 Khevenhüllerstrasse ?)[1]
    Sunday evening

Eva dear, we had a hot peaceful Sunday here, and how was yours? This morning it was like a public swimming pool with Mark Brunswick[2] and all the children. There were also a great many visitors in the grown-up department. In the afternoon I wrote twelve letters, and then the Krises [Ernst and Marianne, psychoanalysts] came to play ping pong, which delighted Ernstl, and Kai [Erikson] wet his bed right through the mattress. Dorothy has moved in again, like a prisoner who voluntarily returns from the outside world; the new vegetable seedlings almost died of the heat, and just now I played cards with Papa and won five Schillings. Now you know everything and it is your turn to add your page. I am sure there will be a letter from you tomorrow. Right now I can't imagine what Grundlsee is like when I am not with you. You have only three more days there, but I would rather you were already in Berlin.

This is just a good-night greeting. Today I have been thinking of you with a heavy heart; I feel as if I will know all your thoughts tonight.

A kiss

Your
Anna

Notes to Letter 38

1. Date and setting: The scene described in the first paragraph suggests the suburban setting of Pötzleinsdorf where the Freuds spent the summers of 1931 and 1932.
2. Mark Brunswick, musician, husband of psychoanalyst Ruth Mack Brunswick, both patients of Sigmund Freud (Roazen, 1971, pp. 421–426).

Letter 39

(April/May or summer 1931,
Pötzleinsdorf, Vienna ?)[1]

Eva dear, I didn't want to write until I heard your voice. I had to know first whether you had heard from Valti. Now I know from talking to you on the phone what a difficult day you have had. Simmel sounded so hopeful, as if things would go better for him now. But you? Your letter will surely arrive tomorrow morning, and then I will know more.

I am keeping my fingers crossed for this transition of yours. For Tegel is only a step on your way, and will benefit from your presence, and you will come back to us with a lot of new insight into what can be learned there about this kind of analytical work, and then we can build something good and solid on that here. And you know, perhaps it will turn out the same way with Valti as it did with Victor, that you can speak to each other more forcefully from a distance than close by. Perhaps you can still shake him up and influence him with letters from Berlin. Since yesterday, you have climbed all the way up a mountain and gone down into the nether world, and we haven't moved an inch from our spot. Papa is playing cards, one can look into his window, and outside there is a wind cooling off the dreadful heat. A sculptor was here all day and made a relief of Papa for the house in Freiberg where he was born. It turned out to be a good likeness. Everyone sends you very cordial greetings. Your place here among us remains large and vacant, and in your thoughts you must try it out and occupy it once a day. Tomorrow we will talk again. Perhaps, one day, we will always be able to wish each other a real good night.

Good night Eva, and think of my crossed fingers.

    Your
    Anna

Notes to Letter 39

1. Date and setting: The letter refers to the beginning of Eva's stay at Tegel in 1931: That director Simmel is still hopeful, implies a date prior to the August decision to liquidate. The Czech sculptor Franz Juran (E. Freud, 1978, p. 344) made a bronze tablet, which according to Jones III (p. 242), was affixed on May 6 1931 to the house in Freiberg (Pribor) where he was born. This would suggest a date for L39 at the latest in April or early May, in spite of the reference to the "terrible heat" and the fact that the ceremony and celebration in honor of Freud took place as late as October 25. That

father Freud could be seen from the outside by looking into his window, suggests the villa and garden in Pötzleinsdorf.

Letter 40

(Early July 1931, Vienna ?)[1]
Monday evening

Eva dear, we are sitting here waiting for your call, and because I was so impatient, I called at Omi's, but only Kinderfrau[2] was there and she didn't know anything about you. Then I was annoyed with myself for asking for you. I tried to cover it up again; I hope it doesn't matter. She says Omi was in Tegel all day. So she was with you. But where are you now and why don't you call?

I have a timetable in front of me and am going through it thoroughly. I would so like to be with you on Mädi's day. I can't put in writing what I would like to say to you; that's how it is with me. But I can feel it, and when I am near you, you'll feel it through me like through a glass wall. That is why I would like to come and bring my feelings to you. You will only get this letter if I cannot come earlier than Sunday.

I am worried by your letter to me, and by the one you wrote to Dorothy. All this time I have been afraid that your feelings were still to come, following after the event. Valti's letters are so charming, as if everything were easy and clear with him, and all one had to do was to take him by the hand and make everything right again together with him. But then he behaves so differently again. How can all this be? I haven't shown them to Papa yet, I just mentioned them. I haven't had a chance to speak to him alone. Omi's report on Vicki is the only good thing.

I am still waiting and you still haven't called.

You have so many worries; do you really want to add me to them as well? That isn't right. I am always the same, and so are my affairs and the vegetable garden and the patients. And it's all coming to you not only in my thoughts, I hope, but in reality, on a train.

I kiss you every day of the year with the same love.

>
> Your
> Anna

Notes to Letter 40

1. Date and setting: Eva is in Berlin where her mother Omi is staying. Anna mentioned letters from Valti to Eva to her father for his comments. This suggests a further stage in the separation of the Rosenfelds, as does the mention of Omi's report on Eva's son, Victor, who has by now presumably spent some time in Germany in proximity to Berlin at the boarding school Marienau in the Lüneburger Heide between Lübeck and Hamburg. Mention of the impending return of the day of Mädi's death (July 8) suggests early July 1931.
2. The young woman from the country, always referred to only as "Kinderfrau" (nanny), stayed with three generations of Rosenfelds, as described in a chapter on her in Eva Rosenfeld's memoirs.

Letter 41

> (Summer 1931, Vienna,
> Pötzleinsdorf, 6
> Khevenhüllerstrasse?)[1]
> Thursday evening

Eva dear, today I liked your voice much better. I could only hear Tegel in it, but I am sure that is a good thing, for only through Tegel will everything else come about. I am glad you have so many patients there. When the daily expenses are being covered, everybody is full of hope, and at least one's work isn't going down the drain. I am very curious to get your first letter with your reactions to the patients and your impression of everything.

I told you everything about Valti's letter over the phone. My feeling was the same as Papa's, that it's only words, words you heard before, which carried no weight. But perhaps you will still get him to do something more. On Saturday Minna will be with me. I'll report to you then what she knows.[2] I have already told Ernsti that he is to take a little suitcase along for you. Now you need only write to Minna in a while and tell her what to pack for you. He probably won't leave for another two weeks. Do you have two coats from Grünfeld?

Just think, it looks as if I might be without patients for a while from Saturday on. (I am sending Miss Clark back to her husband in Paris again.)[3] That would be wonderful, but I still can't imagine it. Today was a bad day with the prosthesis, Papa went to see Weinmann twice,[4] I was at Ruth's [Mack Brunswick] who was very surprised about your being in Berlin. I explained it to her very well. I planted a whole bed with beans; I wonder whether they will grow. Dorothy is feeling better and Ernsti is very cheerful.

Many kisses. Are my crossed fingers helping?

    Your
    Anna

Notes to Letter 41

1. Date and setting: Eva is now settled in Tegel. Ernstl, about to return to his boarding school near Berlin, is to visit Eva. Her first report on Simmel's sanitarium is expected.
2. During Eva's absence, Minna Mach, a patient of Anna Freud, is staying at the Rosenfeld house together with Eva's husband Valti, and will report to Anna Freud on conditions there.
3. Miss Clark: a patient of Anna. As she is being sent back to her husband, one would expect Mrs.
4. Starting in 1928 and "for the next two and a half years . . . Freud's surgeon was Dr. Weinmann, a Viennese who had spent some time with Schroeder in Berlin, so as to become familiar with the details of Freud's case" (Jones III, p. 151; see also Dr. Pichler's notes referring to 1931, cited in Jones III, p. 508).

Letter 42

    (Vienna, Pötzleinsdorf, 6 Khevenhüllerstrasse, summer 1931 ?)[1]
    Friday morning

My dear Eva,

I have made up my mind firmly not to make any predictions, because it is too unpleasant when they turn out to be true.[2] But the strange thing is that I did have a premonition that you were going to get sick, almost as though I could see you going straight toward it. But that is not a good way out and no real solution and you must not be sick. So be well again and take care of yourself and don't do more than is humanly possible, because the result would be disastrous. I am already lying in Dorothy's green wheelbarrow in the garden, trying to get well again. I have no temperature now and if it doesn't go up again in the afternoon, I may be all right again. My throat is not quite clear yet, nor is the gallbladder which was slightly irritated, but on the whole I am much better. The whole thing is peculiar.

I am very glad that you like the pictures. I am having some new ones developed but couldn't pick them up yet. As soon as I do, you shall have them.

I promised Ernsti to send you his allowance of $1.00 every week. I am enclosing it here for the first time. I hope the dollar will still be inside by the time this letter arrives. I think he hopes that he will be able to visit with you for a little while every time he picks it up. But you have so little time to spare as it is. I think that he is a little homesick now, but I hope he will soon be acclimated and settle down.

Your letter written in pencil interested me very much. You know, I think that the most difficult thing about dealing with the kind of patients you have in Tegel must be the disillusionment associated with the question of how much pure and how much merely applied psychoanalysis they need and can stand. I have the feeling the therapists there often employ pure analysis where it has long ceased to be appropriate. But this decision and any modification of strict analysis is something which surely requires a widely experienced analyst, thoroughly steeped in analysis (like Ferenczi, or Aichhorn, or possibly Simmel himself). If a young and inexperienced analyst undertakes this, he is in great danger of becoming a "wild" one. But, naturally, the assistants in Tegel have always been young beginners. And one is easily tempted to believe that there is no need to master analysis fully where there is no opportunity to apply it fully. Yet it is just the opposite: one must be an exceptionally good analyst in order to be allowed to modify analysis. Since Tegel cannot have a lot of outstanding doctors, S. would need, above all, to *teach* concurrently with his practice. That is no easy task.[3]

And the patients are of course all beyond the point where they could get well on their own. This establishes an important link to child analysis; however, the element of hope which is present with children because of the incompleteness of their development is lacking. In theory, Simmel is certainly right to keep pushing for a closed institution. Then the two fields could be separated into analytically oriented care and analytical therapy. The first probably has far better prospects as a new factor in the treatment of such patients. The second will perhaps remain disappointing until the right modification of technique has been found. But clearly this could only be done in a place like Tegel.

A shower just chased me into the house. Maybe I'll go back to bed. It's still tempting.

Stay well. I can kiss you because we probably have the same thing.

Your
Anna

It would be best for you to always tear up my letters[4]

Notes to Letter 42

1. Date and setting: The letter, referring to Eva's activity in the sanitarium at Tegel prior to its collapse, responds to a report by Eva on the establishment and its patients (anticipated in L41). Ernstl, preparing for his trip in L41, now left for Berlin, and is to get pocket money via Eva. The setting suggests again a villa with garden.
2. Sigmund Freud, who credited Anna with "telepathic sensibility," conducted experiments in telepathy with her (see Gay, p. 443).
3. Concerning Simmel's psychoanalytical sanitarium, designed for patients with grave mental afflictions (see Bittner, pp. 19–21).
4. The thought occurs in connection with the sensitive subject of criticism of Simmel and his institute; but see Ross, p. 38.

Letter 43

(Vienna, August 1931, (?)[1]
Saturday, very early

Eva dear, yesterday your voice sounded bad to me again and that was because of Valti's two letters. How will you manage to combine working over there with keeping track of what is going on inside him over here? And then I was alarmed that you want to do night duty. Surely, you won't take the next day off in return, and it is impossible to do both. I have done a lot of night duty lately and I know that one is only a quarter there the next day, and that one gets quite dizzy. I suspect you want to do it because you can't sleep anyway. But that makes it much worse.

I will call the bookstore right after eight A.M. and have them send you Frau Mathias's cookbook. It has wonderful specialties, with little hints and shortcuts. If it should be too fancy for Tegel, I will send you still another one. We use it in Neuhaus and I learned how to make real Italian risotto and Palatschinken[2] that don't stiffen up, and other such things from it.

Ernstl is very well. He has gained 2 kilos. When he is wearing his gym shirt, I tell him he looks like Schmeling. On the 25th he wants to go back to Scharfenberg[3] for a week of farm work before school starts.

Yesterday Aichhorn was here and was especially nice. He follows your plans with great interest. He is really making tremendous efforts on behalf of the school. The prosthesis was somewhat better today. We may still leave for Neuhaus today, so naturally it's raining.[4] I still have four hours today, but I might not have any on Monday. Minna is coming today.

Are you doing the shopping for the sanitarium already? Write everything about the housekeeping to me as well. Who are the most seriously ill patients? The morphine addicts or the melancholics? And what are the doctors like?

Stay well and take care of yourself.

Your
Anna

Notes to Letter 43

1. Date and setting: Eva has begun to take up regular work at the sanitarium. Ernstl's wish to return to his boarding school "on the 25th" suggests late summer or early autumn, prior to the beginning of the school year.
2. Palatschinken: Austrian dish; thin pancakes (crepes) filled with jam. Eva took charge of the housekeeping, shopping for food and meals at the sanitarium.
3. Ernstl stayed with his aunt Anna during summer vacations. He was a small and fragile boy, though an admirer of the boxing champion Max Schmeling. Ernstl wished to return to the Scharfenberg boarding school prior to the beginning of the school year for a week of farm work instituted at this progressive institution to supplement learning with "practical," manual labor.
4. For a weekend resort, Dorothy and Anna rented a place at Neuhaus, and furnished it. Though they purchased a farm at Hochrotherd in fall 1930, it took apparently many months before it was restored and the furniture from Neuhaus could be moved to the new place. In the meantime, they still went to Neuhaus for short vacations.

Letter 44

(Neuhaus near Vienna, summer 1931 [?])[1]
Monday morning

Eva dear, I haven't spoken to you for two evenings now. We didn't leave for Neuhaus until Sunday. On Saturday evening I joined the tarok game because Alfred Rie's wife is gravely ill,[2] and yesterday morning we finally drove out here. Neuhaus is as beautiful and peaceful as ever. I plunged right into the housework, and then we lay in deck-chairs on our woodland meadow for a while and toward evening it began to pour and it is still pouring. By noon we will be home again. I dreamt all night that I will have to take final exams[3] and I introduced myself to the various examiners. It was very unpleasant.

On Saturday Minna came to see me. All things considered, she seems to be doing fairly well. From her account one would not get the impression that anything unusual is happening with Valti. He is apparently depressed—until Fritzi calls.[4] I would think it is the same as always, with the same changes of mood as when you were with him. Of course, I don't want to draw Minna out, and actually she doesn't know all that much anyway. But if there were any serious change in him, she would notice.

I had a letter from Lizzie, asking for advice. She is apparently afraid of the Pappenheim idea and would like to take a room at Gusti's [Koerner]. If it is not for long, it hardly makes any difference. I will write to her.

Papa is well. Weinmanns says his mouth is fine, in spite of his smoking. That is the most important thing. I have had a funny idea here in Neuhaus where I can always think differently from the way I think in Vienna: It occurred to me that I hadn't been completely alive since the night he came down with pneumonia, and that I just didn't notice it.[5]

What have you experienced in these last two days? They seem to have been so terribly long to me. I am glad that I can speak to you again tonight. Berlin is far away, after all.

I kiss you with all my heart

    Your
    Anna

Notes to Letter 44

1. Date and setting: L44 is in sequence with L43 in which the visit to Neuhaus, described here, is announced.
2. Father Freud's weekly card game (tarok) with partners of his own generation, including Dr. Rie (the father of analyst Marianne Kris), is in jeopardy. Daughter Anna has to substitute and postpone her projected weekend visit to Neuhaus.
3. The Austrian (and German) "Gymnasium" (college preparatory school) concluded its exacting curriculum with comprehensive written and oral examinations ("Matura," "Abitur") administered to candidates, who were usually eighteen years of age, over a period of several days.
4. Fritzi Löwi: Valti Rosenfeld's sturdy secretary and girl friend held a record in free style swimming at the Jewish sport's club (Hakoah) of which Valti was a leading member. Victor recalls that she was allowed to drive his father's car and that, after the termination of her relationship with Valti, she complained about Valti to Eva.
5. Sigmund Freud's pneumonia: October 17 to November 1, 1930.

Letter 45

(Vienna, 1931 [?])[1]

Eva dear, I gathered on the phone that you weren't working as furiously any more, and felt a little less worried about you. Even one week of it would have been too much for you, and it wouldn't have been right anyway. An enterprise that can only be kept going when people are fed into it to be devoured and annihilated by it, is not viable in this day and age. This is how dragons were served in the olden days. But that cannot possibly be the purpose of a sanitarium. By the way, I know about this in Tegel; it always goes this way with the most seriously sick patients. They cannot be kept in open wards for long; their treatment is possible only in locked wards, which would afford quite different alternatives and facilities for long-term patients.

Now that I know your daily schedule, I follow you through the building in my thoughts and have a guilty conscience when I consider how lazy I am right now. How is the vegetable garden doing? Has it been properly cared for? Don't you get any breaks?

Everything is very quiet here. The sun has disappeared and the garden feels unpleasantly autumnal. I'd like to get the sun back. The stay in Neuhaus didn't agree with Dorothy very well, although she enjoyed being there very much. She looks miserable today and is tired. I have only one patient and am not used to that yet.

I returned Valti's letters to Omi.[2] I don't understand them, but then I don't know him well enough. I am glad for Omi that he does not want her and Vicki to come. That wouldn't have worked out. I made up my mind not to think of any plans for you that go beyond the next two months. The future is too obscure. Perhaps there will be a change in Valti after all.

Dr. Eitingon wants to postpone the Congress. I hope he succeeds!

Heartfelt greetings to you

Your
Anna

Notes to Letter 45

1. Date and setting: The letter (see 3rd paragraph) follows upon the visit to Neuhaus described in L44.
2. Letters of Valti to Eva which she had sent to Anna Freud (see L41).

Letter 46

(Vienna, Pötzleinsdorf, 6
Khevenhüllerstrasse, August,
1931?)[1]

My dear Eva, it seems to me that I haven't heard from you in a long time. But it is only a day and half, and this evening I am going to call you up again. Everything is peaceful with us. I am sitting in the garden in Papa's lawn chair and all three dogs are pestering me. Actually, it is not all that peaceful. Miezi was called home by a telegram yesterday because her mother is gravely ill, our temporary cook injured her hand and it had to be operated on, and last night a small pipe burst and we had no water. Tomorrow morning the American dental wizard is coming for one day to give his opinion on the prosthesis, and a sculptor—yet another one—is making a bust of Papa for a change and we will have to keep Wolf from devouring him (the sculptor).[2] But I feel much more peaceful inside, which is good. Can you hold out and can Tegel hold out? When you have a chance, write what you think of the analyses they do there and about what the chances are for such serious cases. Papa was often very skeptical. Does Dr. Eitingon know that you are in Berlin? Last night I was at Mariandl's who is not doing very well. I hope she can carry the baby to term.

To my great surprise, I took some very pretty little pictures of the place here. I will send them to you tomorrow, as soon as I get the prints. But you won't forget us in any case.

Greetings and kisses

Your
Anna

Notes to Letter 46

1. Date and setting: The dental "wizard" (first paragraph) was Professor Kazanijan of Boston and Harvard who treated Freud, seeking to improve his prosthesis, during August 1931 for a fee of $6,000 (Jones III, pp. 171–172, 510).
2. "Yet another sculptor" (cf. L39): "In 1931, on the insistence of his pupil and collaborator, Paul Federn, Freud had declared himself willing to sit for a bust to be made by the Yugoslavian sculptor Oscar Némon (born 1906). Later a statue was made." This entry in E. Freud: *Sigmund Freud. His Life in Pictures* (1978, p. 324), refers to a photo (p. 254) of the sculptor and Freud in the garden at 6 Khevenhüllerstrasse.

Letter 47

(27.8.1931)[1]

My dear Eva, I just spoke to you on the telephone, and right afterwards I got all your letters and enclosures, and am still quite confused by it all. I guess it must be my mistake. Ever since I have known Tegel, the specter of dissolution has hovered over it, yet somehow I never really thought this could happen. It was so beautiful and perfect in its principles and objectives, like a sort of dream; its insufficiencies and defects and the tight money situation didn't seem to fit in but to be added on as if by accident. I always had the feeling that they might disappear and then Tegel would be what it can be. I regret terribly the loss of Tegel as a possibility.

But you are so right in everything you say. As I read what you wrote on Eitingon, I had the feeling for the first time that someone understood what I went through with him during the last years. It was that feeling that devastated me. I felt as though I was in a desert where nothing could grow. Wandering around in it, one dries up.[2] And I also know that everything you say about Simmel is right. Dorothy felt the spirit of the sanitarium in exactly the same way when she was there as a guest. At the time I kept hoping it wasn't that bad, but it really is.

Wednesday

I was interrupted yesterday. Nowadays, I always go along for the treatments in the morning and the afternoon. I feel less nervous when I can see it all. In the evening I had such a fierce headache that I couldn't function. I have these headaches often now, almost every day. Somehow I can't shake off my fear that something might go wrong. I am afraid that some growth might develop again, at one of the many pressure spots which always result from the work that is being done. And things like that. I can't even imagine what it is like not to have such worries. But that wasn't what I wanted to write about.

This afternoon Dorothy will go to Schnitzler with Tinky, so he can set a date for the operation. She will move into the Berggasse on the first of September[3] and would like it to be done right after that. It will be good for her to get this over with.

Vicki came to lunch with us after spending an hour with me. I find him flourishing physically, strong, healthy, and manly as never before. I don't believe that the school influenced him much up to now. Apparently, he enjoys being there very much and participates in the entire life there with great zeal and interest. But it is a different kind of relationship from Ernstl's at Scharfenberg. There is no underlying ideal of what kind of person one should become. I could not speak to him about more intimate matters. He has his two old defenses, evading by joking or going into the technical and matter-of-fact. I didn't want to press him but I regretted it a little. In answer to your question yesterday on the phone, I think one should still give him a while at the Bondy school. He enjoys it so much. If you can't do it, I always can.[4]

I enclose a letter from Lizzie's mother that arrived yesterday for you. I opened it and read it anyway. I haven't heard from Lizzie for a while.

Your long letter with all the doubts about which direction you should take, has been overtaken by events. Once Tegel has been liquidated, you must come here and make this a resting station from which you can make further plans. Your place here is always ready for you, in every sense. I would have come to Tegel if I could have helped in any way, but I have been to so many consultations there, and if one wants to help, one has to come with money, and that I don't have. But I would still have come to you, if it weren't for the hope that you would come to us very soon. As long as the American is here, I won't budge.[5]

Last night I dreamt that I murdered our cook, Anna. I chopped off her head and cut her into pieces and had no guilt feelings at all, which was very funny. Now I know why; her name is Anna and that's me [see p. 7].

Think of what you wrote about the relationship of the staff to Dr. S., and think of Aichhorn. Then you will realize why Aichhorn's institute was so wonderful. He accomplished exactly what has been missing in Tegel, and held everyone in the palm of his hand. But why are we all children who need to be held?

That is all for today and I kiss you. You are going to have a terrible week. Ernst should pay the bill for Ernstl.

I advised Omi not to write another letter to Valti. It seemed too dangerous to me. Wholly

    Your
    Anna

Notes to Letter 47

1. Date and setting: The express mail envelope of this letter on the demise of the Tegel enterprise in August 1931 is postmarked August 27, 1931 (a Thursday). The first part was written on August 25, the continuation on Wednesday August 26, and the letter mailed the following day.
2. The final judgment on Eitingon and their relation (see pp. 8, 91–94).
3. The move in question here is a return of the family to their residence in Vienna at Berggasse 19 where they first moved in 1929.
4. Concerning this paragraph, Anna Freud's educational ideal, the characterization of Eva's son, and her offer of financial support for his education (see Bittner, pp. 15, 22; Ross, p. 31).

5. A reference to Professor Kazanijan (see L46) who worked on Freud's prosthesis "for twenty days" (Jones III, p. 172).

V: 1932

Letter 48

(26.[25.?] 3. 1932)
(Vienna, Berggasse 19 ?)[1]

My dear Eva!

How do you feel in Grundlsee? Is it stronger than what one brings to it? Is it still Mädi's Grundlsee? In my thoughts I walk around the lake with you until our feet are tired. In the houses on the far side one is even farther away from everything than in Hochrotherd. But I can't imagine it all in the snow, and I am glad that Hochrotherd is nearer to the Berggasse. As we decided last time, the Berggasse is the center of everything, and we revolve around it sometimes in smaller, sometimes in larger circles.

Valti called me and gave me your news. Minna was with me and all is quiet in the house. We are well. Papa has a week's vacation from Pichler now and is glad that he can at least rest after lunch. On the whole, he feels much better, the stomach too, and he needs orthoform[2] only once a day at the most. The wound is healing very well.

This morning was a high point in Hochrotherd (H[och]R[roth]E[rd]). Frau Josefa moved in with child, dog and rabbit. A lot of furniture, our belongings from Neuhaus, are lying about and need to be unpacked, and the whole place needs to be occupied. We almost did not get back by eleven. This double life is not so simple when things get serious out there. But tomorrow I only work until three, and then we'll drive out there again and unpack. It is so beautiful there, and I am glad that you could really see it the other day.

Ernstl is very good; Bob is still not well at all. I would so much like build up my strength but find only occasions to spend it. Let me know how you are. I would like to be with you. You too must take root in HRE, so that we can grow in the same soil.

A kiss

>   Your
>   Anna

Notes to Letter 48

1. Date and setting: The envelope is postmarked Saturday March 26; the letter was probably written on March 25. The furniture from Neuhaus has been moved to Hochrotherd; the wife of a local farmer, Frau Josefa, will keep house and do some farming on the property. This marks the stage of full use of HRE as a weekend and midweek resort for Anna and Dorothy. Meanwhile Eva Rosenfeld, on a visit from Germany, is staying in her beloved Grundlsee, still wintery in March. The hope that she too would take roots in Hochrotherd was not to be fulfilled.

2. "It was Dr. Weinmann who suggested the use of orthoform, a member of the novocain group and therefore a benefit derived from Freud's early work on cocaine. This proved a great boon for some years, unfortunately it later caused irritations leading to a local hyperkeratosis, a precancerous condition. After that its use had to be considerably restricted" (Jones III, p. 151 in an account of the year 1928). According to Schur (1972, p. 414), it was in 1931 that Weinmann suggested to Freud "that he try insufflations of Orthoform—a novocain derivative in powdered form used for local application to painful sores."

Letter 49

>   (Vienna, March [25]26, 1932?)[1]
>   Friday evening

My dear Eva!

I am sending just another quick greeting for Easter Sunday. Your letter came right after mine had gone out. I am so glad that you found Grundlsee lovely, and that it was in Grundlsee that you found yourself again. Perhaps that always remains the most important encounter one can have with anyone.

Only two important bits of news from here; Papa is very well and a host of primroses appeared under the cover of the snow in HRE. Today we were able to dig out the first ones. It is so beautiful out there, and I am getting to know a lot of feelings that I only knew about from books!

Last night I dreamt there was a fire and I couldn't untie the cow to get her out of the stable. Today we went to get the first six chicks for Tinky's birthday.

In the mornings I have patients, and afternoons are free. Only Sunday and Monday am I free all day.

Come back soon filled with Grundlsee air.

    Your
    Anna

Notes to Letter 49

1. Date and setting: The letter, written on Friday evening, March 25, 1932, was postmarked, like L48, on March 26, a day before Tinky Burlingham's birthday on Easter Sunday March 27.

Letter 50

(Vienna, 1932?)[1]

My dear Eva!

I am so disappointed; I was so absolutely sure that I would be sitting with you at Kretzer's tonight that I stored up everything for our talk together. Your first letter startled me because I did not realize that the decision would already be made now, prior to the sale. But you are probably right.[2] I wanted to tell you all that and a good deal more as well. Tuesday is all right with Papa.[3] Write to me quickly saying when you will arrive and when you will leave again. Then I will postpone the Tuesday–Wednesday Hochrotherd "week-middle"[4] by a day. I have only three patients now. I can easily shift them and I want to have a cozy evening with you. Imagine, Martin [Anna's brother] had a bad attack of kidney colic and had to go to Childs Hospital, but he is over it by now. As of yesterday we have a two-month-old chow, a daughter of Ono. Dorothy is leaving next Saturday evening. Jeanne [Lampl-de Groot] is coming Monday to visit for four days; Aunt Miezi, who has had the guest room, left today. I was not feeling too well myself, but I am better now. My lecture for the Congress[5] is coming along slowly.

I am worried about you and your future, but I almost believe that without a house you will find it easier than with one.

Come soon, I kiss you lovingly,

    Your
    Anna

Notes to Letter 50

1. Date and setting: Presumably, Eva Rosenfeld, who has been staying in Grundlsee during a visit from Germany (see preceding letters), is about to visit Vienna. The possibility of selling the Rosenfelds' house in Hietzing is being discussed. An hour of analysis with Sigmund Freud is set for Tuesday. All this, and the fact that midweek visits to Hochrotherd are by this time a standard feature, points to spring 1932, as does Anna Freud's preparation of a lecture for a congress of which there was one in 1932, in Wiesbaden, from September 3 to 7, where she lectured on "neurotic mechanisms under the influence of education" (Peters, p. 194; probably, "Psychoanalysis and the Upbringing of the Young Child" (*Writings I*, 1932).
2. Presumably, concerning the sale of the Rosenfeld house which did not materialize.
3. Probably for an analytical session on the occasion of Eva's visit.
4. "week-middle": in English in the original.
5. See above, n1.

Letter 51

(Vienna, Pötzleinsdorf, 6
Khevenhüllerstrasse?)
August 21, 1932[1]

My dear Eva!

I would have liked so much to have heard from you since you have been gone. How is Gar? How are your innards? How was your arrival in Grundlsee? Have you been able to rest a little, body and soul? When will you come again?

Dorothy left last night. She must have had a terribly hot day for traveling today. Bob [Burlingham] will leave tomorrow for the seaside in Normandy to await the return of the others. That is a very good thing, I pushed hard for it.

We are floating in the heat wave, but stay on top. Papa is writing, and my lecture for the Congress is wandering from one corner of my head to the other. Tuesday I want to whitewash the chicken coop in HRE, perhaps that will help. After all, I am now learning that one must spread manure on everything that is supposed to grow.

Jeanne is still visiting. Today I was in HRE with her and Mathilde and Robert [Hollitscher]. It was quite different than usual, but it is always beautiful. Wednesday Ernst is supposed to come.[2] Write soon!

Your
Anna

Notes to Letter 51

1. Setting and date: Probably the summer villa in Pötzleinsdorf, after Eva's visit to Vienna, with Eva staying once again in Grundlsee. It is vacation time. Dorothy has left Vienna, her son Bob is about to leave. Sigmund Freud is working, probably on his *New Introductory Lectures* (1932) (see L52). Anna Freud, in keeping with her father's method, is preparing her lecture for the impending congress (see L50n1) by conceiving it and committing it to memory, rather than by writing it down. Jeanne Lampl-de Groot, whose visit was announced in L50, is still staying with the Freuds (M. J. Burlingham [p. 240], mistakenly dates the letter August 21, 1933; the date is in Anna Freud's handwriting).
2. Ernst—here probably referring to Anna's nephew—on vacation from the boarding school at Scharfenberg.

Letter 52

Vienna, August 25, 1932

My dear Eva!

I am quite alarmed by your letter and if my trip to the Congress were not so imminent, I would get up and visit you right away. But it can't be done and I feel very uneasy about you. If only you hadn't gone to Grundlsee, it didn't do you any good this year, it only brought you worries and unrest! Do you have a doctor? It doesn't sound that way. I was counting on having Friday with you again.

You were so miserable last time; it was only a question of how it would manifest itself.

We are well, Papa's Lectures[1] are almost finished. Lün[2] keeps cheering us up as a relief from work. It isn't quiet here: Brill is already in Vienna, Saturday Ernst is coming, Sunday Radó, Tuesday Levys, Jeanne just left, and Ruth[3] is having fits and there is lots of Congress business to attend to. When I don't escape to HRE, as I do now and then, I go crazy. I must leave here on Wednesday at the latest; my lecture isn't finished yet either.

But you be well again or come to Vienna as you are. You could find what you need more easily here. Write to me right away!

    Your
    Anna

Notes to Letter 52

1. The *New Introductory Lectures*.
2. Lün was originally the name of the chow lost by Eva in the summer of 1929 (see L14), but the same name came to be used for another chow.
3. Psychoanalysts Abraham A. Brill, Katá and Lajos Levy, Sándor Radó, Jeanne Lampl-de Groot, Ruth Mack Brunswick.

Letter 53

    (Vienna, Pötzleinsdorf, 6
      Khevenhüllerstrasse, or
      Hochrotherd, late August 1932?)[1]
    Friday

Eva dear, I wonder whether I will still reach you in Grundlsee. It seems to me as though you are facing a whole battlefield. What can I contribute by telling you about myself? Yesterday I finally planted my vegetable garden with a border of twenty little blue lobelias around it and fifteen heads of lettuce, fifteen kohlrabi and a few cucumber seeds that I don't have much faith in. Now sensational developments have occurred all by themselves. It was indescribably hot today and at noon I thought everything had wilted. But in the evening they all perked up again. Is this enough to write a letter about?

It is a pleasure to look at Ernstl these days. I haven't had a session with him yet so I don't know what is going on inside him, but his external appearance couldn't be better. He is enthusiastic about Scharfenberg and has a real friend. He looks a bit younger, sunburnt and lean, and he is not at all lazy any more. He will stay here for at least a week.

Otherwise everyone, from Papa to Taltoun,[3] just feels hot. We lie peacefully in the garden. Papa, unfortunately, had to go into the city yesterday and today, to see Weinmann. At the moment, the prosthesis is not right at all. Dorothy is still no tower of strength but thinks she has done more than her share of resting. There is a bit of me in all of them, not only in the vegetable garden. You must dig me out of there, as well as out of you; there is no real "I" as yet.[3]

But what there is of it kisses you. What will Simmel have to say? Probably nothing good.[4] I am so sorry that you must leave your one place of rest. Traveling will be very strenuous. Call me from Berlin.
   Always

      Your
      Anna

Notes to Letter 53

1. Date and setting: The continuation of summer heat suggests the nexus with L52, as does the arrival of Ernst from his boarding school, announced in the preceding letters. The vegetable garden precludes Berggasse 19, but

could have been planted either at Pötzleinsdorf or, more likely, in Hochrotherd. The doubt whether the letter will still reach Eva in Grundlsee, and the wish to get a phone call of hers from Berlin (last paragraph) suggest that L53 is the last in the series addressed to Eva at Grundlsee.
2. Taltoun: Tinky Burlingham's black chow?
3. Concerning this metaphoric confession and its connection with Anna Freud's sense of a lack of identity, see pp. 97–98.
4. Eva continued to work for Simmel during and after the liquidation of the sanitarium at Tegel (see p. 39).

Letter 54

Vienna IX, Berggasse 19
December 11, 1932[1]

My dear Omi!

You are always so good to me and I am behaving so badly toward you. Many thanks for your birthday wishes and for the charming things you sent me. The rolls of paper are charming (Dorothy calls them doll's toilet-paper) and have solved finally the problem of our not-so-rust-free knives. Our teapot is wearing its drip catcher around the neck, and the napkin rings are waiting for the next guests to come for tea. Mama wanted to take one of the extra rolls for the Berggasse, but I rose to its defense and would not surrender it. I did get your first long letter, Omi, it did not go astray. But it was so difficult to answer that I kept putting off the reply. I don't know what to say. But I know one thing: Papa was very much in favor of Eva's leaving now and starting to see the whole situation in perspective from a distance. And since, as we say, he is always right, he is surely right this time too, and one should take care not to interfere with her or disturb her. He thinks she still has an entire, vigorous life of her own ahead of her and shouldn't let it be taken away from her and let herself be destroyed. I can well imagine that it will be very hard for you if she goes to Moscow.[2] But surely it isn't dangerous, for so many people go there and most of them come back filled with enthusiasm. I have the feeling it will mean a lot to Eva to see the potential for the future and the constructive things going on there, and perhaps this will give her ideas which she could then use and develop when she is back here again. Being confined and constricted would be the worst thing for her, I think, and that is precisely what her life was like in Vienna in the recent past. I miss her very much. Even though I didn't see her every day, she was part of everything. But I do hope she will be back again soon. Things were just too hard for her lately.

We also had long talks about this with Uncle Max and Yvette [Guilbert]. They are very worried and cannot quite grasp the whole situation as yet. Actually nobody really knows how it will turn out. I saw Valti repeatedly at concerts. He was especially nice and surely hasn't the faintest notion of what is going on with Eva.

Did you get much enjoyment from Eva's stay with you? How is your health? I will call you tomorrow evening.

With a heartfelt kiss

    Your
    Anna

Notes to Letter 54

1. This typed letter to Eva's mother, observing a convention of almost child-like deference to an elderly lady, is, in substance, a defense of Eva's decision to lead an independent life of her own.
2. In her memoirs (ER, pp. 256–269) Eva was to describe her "study trip" of six weeks to Soviet Russia, arranged by relatives of the "eminent Hungarian communist [Béla Kun] and his family" whose lives lawyer Valti Rosenfeld had "saved" "with great skill." The trip proved both an adventure and a disappointment.

Letter 55

Vienna IX, Berggasse 19
December 15, 1932[1]

My dear Eva,

I think this will be the next to the last letter that will reach you in Berlin. I am glad that you are really looking forward to your trip now. Be sure to wear many layers of underwear and take a hot water bottle along for the trip. At a pinch you can always get hot water from the engine. I am terribly curious about how it will all turn out for you and what you will see. I hope you feel free for the moment, and curious. Lou[2] always said Moscow was marvelous in the winter, and that in spite of the fact that it is many degrees below zero, it is not colder in winter than Vienna, because it is not windy. To be sure, they hardly went anywhere on foot in those days but always drove in one-horse sleighs, and had many facilities and conveniences besides, which probably don't exist any more at all. Do you happen to have an Orenburg shawl? Lou says that one wears them over one's face in Moscow to prevent one's nose from getting frostbitten. In any case, you should take something like that along.

Your request for the Lectures is two days late. Papa already asked Martin to send a copy for you to Omi.[3] There is nothing inscribed in it, I am afraid, but it was sent by him after all. You will have to keep this one, I guess, and then give it to him to inscribe for you. Don't you think so? I am rereading the Lectures, actually reading them carefully for the first time, which one can't really do very well with a manuscript, and I find them wonderful.

Papa is still suffering from many minor after-effects of the last operation.[4] He can't open his mouth very well, and chewing is also still difficult. Jofi [another chow] still gets most of his food. But looking at him, you wouldn't notice anything wrong with him.

I am looking forward to the week between Christmas and New Year which I am keeping completely free this time. I am rather tired already, and right now there is so much to do and I am more impatient than usual. The weather is horrible too; we need to have lights on almost all day. Also, I did not get to HRE during the week, and I always miss that.

It is a good thing that you are still seeing Victor. Does Valti know he [Victor] won't be coming here for Christmas? At the concert he still seemed to be counting on him.

I send you very many greetings. Your voice over the phone sounded so near.

    Your
      Anna

Notes to Letter 55

1. The opening and the conclusion of this letter to Eva seem to anticipate the end of Anna's close and intimate relationship to her.
2. Lou Andreas-Salomé was a native of Russia.
3. "The publication of Sigmund Freud's *New Introductory Lectures* was dated 1933, but they actually appeared on December 6, 1932" (Jones III, p. 180). Freud's son, Martin, had become manager of the Psychoanalytische Verlag (Jones III, p. 178).
4. Jones III (p. 186), about 1932: "It had been altogether a bad year, with five operations, one of which, in October, was pretty extensive."

VI: FROM A LATER PERIOD

Decades lie between the preceding and the following letters and excerpts. The Rosenfelds and the Freuds became refugees from Hitler's Reich in England. The Second World War was underway when the most shattering event in Anna Freud's life, the death of her father, took place in 1939. In "the terrible summer" of that year she still had some hope that his condition might be due to the radium therapy. No one, she wrote soon afterwards, should have to suffer this treatment; it was "too cruel a way to perish" (to Simmel, November 25, 1939). That Freud had himself ended his life with the help of his doctor was left unmentioned. Though "everything personal" was over, she wrote to Eitingon there was so much left of the world her father had built, that it should suffice if one were not "too immodest." For she had not "destroyed herself" (to Eitingon, October 19 and November 15, 1939). The new phase in her life included as her private sphere the relationship with Dorothy Burlingham. It was centered on her work, the Hampstead Nursery in wartime, later the Hampstead Clinic. Successful as she was abroad, she was in a constant struggle for recognition in Britain, where psychoanalysis was claimed by the opponents of Anna Freud and "the Anna Freudians," the followers of Melanie Klein, who was, to begin with, also Eva Rosenfeld's second analyst (see pp. 44–45). Perhaps this had something to do with the fact that we could not find further correspondence between Anna and Eva until 1946, and from that year onward virtually all personal and certainly all extant intimate communications are those of Eva to Anna, "the silent one," as Eva called her in her last letter to her, dated February 22, 1977.

Undoubtedly, Eva was now and for the rest of her years, the one who wooed Anna. Yet Anna must have permitted her to do so, and to have responded to Eva's solicitous, maternal affection to some extent; possibly even, now and then, by way of a "long, sympathetic" letter, "like in olden days," if Eva's references (see below) to such—missing—responses are to be trusted. The altered relationship, in which Eva's voice predominates, is illustrated by the following quotes from more than 120 letters which she wrote to Anna between 1946 and 1977.

Thus, in 1946, after asking for permission to attend Anna Freud's psychoanalytical sessions, unless her presence would be disturbing to her friend (May 7, 1946), Eva confessed: "I am thinking constantly of you." She wrote to Anna:

> Just about as long as I have known you, between age 30 and 50, you have maintained a superhuman effort and achievement for the sake of a unique task—the care of your father. Now that this task has come to its natural end, you need to develop another side of you. I can feel how your body and soul cry out in protest against the compulsion and hardness which were necessary for your former way of life. "Is that so, or am I right?" as Victor would say. And so your motto should be: Walberswick [Anna Freud's and Dorothy Burlingham's country place], joy, pleasure, physical exercise and the right to some mindless relaxation.

In 1947, in answer to Anna's "long, sympathetic letter," mentioned above, Eva attempts to review and to reestablish their relationship, as she prepares to leave on a professional journey to Brazil. To Anna she writes:

You know how communicative I am by nature. If it were up to me, there would be no end of things to tell one another. But I am now a mature woman, and still alive and sound, inspite of many fateful events. And so I cannot come to you any longer like a young girl to woo you. Our friendship has been and remains the most important and valuable thing in my life. The year of 1924, when I had the privilege of meeting you and your family, remains anno Domini 1 of my existence. And you, my Anna, your life as analyst notwithstanding, are still a very shy and exceedingly delicate being; and you know it. But to overcome your shyness is getting harder and harder for me. I do hope very much that one day you will be simply there for me as I am for you, and then our common goal and work will also become evident. I am so grateful to you that you have said it for once, how much I hurt you in 1938 [i.e., through Eva's association with Melanie Klein]. But since then I have done penance. It is nine years now that I have given up completely all ambition to accomplish anything in the context of the [psychoanalytical] movement, so that you would never be offended by me and I could never even seem to be in your way. And so it was also from 1927 onward to 1938 that I removed myself and took myself out of your way in order that your relationship to Dorothy could develop fully, which at that time became the most important for you. In 1938 my life hung by a mere thread. The raft to rescue the shipwrecked could not be you, my dear one. For this was all about you. The renunciation which drove me away from Vienna, was for your sake. Valti was just a minor figure. Also, I know from my second analysis that this need to remove myself—which I had failed to do in my youth—with the consequence of the collapse of our family, the death of my father, the downfall of my brothers, and even the death of my mother—now finally had caught up with me and come to a head, to prevail against my inner innocence. I almost abandoned myself. And that too was for your sake. Without finishing my analysis I could not find my place in your vicinity. You had to forge a life together with Dorothy for yourself, and I was so horribly in the way, and therefore in the way—an obstacle—to myself. For then as now your happiness came first for me, it was the prime requirement. But you, my Anna, had no use for me, just as you did not have any use for me in London. And yet I ask myself in vain how that could be possible. Surely you realize to what extent you are repeating together with Dorothy the "impregnable fortress" which your mother and aunt once represented for you. And I believe I am always to be poor little Anna who can stand being excluded. I don't believe that we have different aims in our work, but I had no other choice than to grow silent. I do understand how very much I had hurt you. That is: it would not have needed to be a hurt or offence. For there is a lot in my work that I want to share with you, learn from you, and also show you. Just give me an opportunity, when the time is right. Whether I get a visa to Sao Paulo is uncertain ... but I do believe that the people over there would learn true and useful things from me in however modest a measure. I'll take along no confusion from Kleinian work, but rather matured and tested thoughts. For I will not go there in anyone's name or on anyone's orders. If we don't have "one" single analytic conception, we have none; and in that case one would have to seek out error rather than truth. But that seems to be even more difficult for human beings than the search for truth. So, please, show me my errors, clearly and plainly. Meanwhile I am showing you my friendship, loud and clear. Ever your Eva. [to Anna Freud, March 3, 1947]

Did the relationship ever approximate its former condition? In 1950 Eva wrote: "Every summer I am sad not to be with you and this time especially, because I feel that you need the right kind of care for once, the thousand details which would occur only to someone who has the right notion of what you need. . . . For me, summer vacations have been a terror now for years, because my loneliness then weighs me down as a heavy burden" (to Anna Freud, August 22, 1950). The next year she regrets that she will not to be with Anna and Dorothy—"probably for the first time"—on the 23rd of September, Sigmund Freud's birthday (September 22, 1951). There is no lack of written or oral communications—on practical matters or professional topics, including appreciative comments by Eva on Anna Freud's "An Experiment in Group Upbringing" (to Anna Freud, March 2, 1952). In 1953 Eva thanks Anna "a thousand times" for a letter "quite like in olden days." Yet she adds: "I always have a problem knowing whether I treat you better when I leave you alone or when I make myself known to you" (August 18, 1953). In 1954, ruminating and writing on a maternal love "fixated on her 'dead' child, because it is the only one secure from death," Eva acknowledges and enjoys Anna's comments on her work as tokens of genuine intimacy ("lauter echte 'Du's' ") and "fruit" of their friendship (September 16, 1954). However, three years later she asks, as a "belated present" for her sixty-fifth birthday, whether Anna could once call her up in London "all on her own initiative" ("ganz 'von selber' "). Would that be possible?" (to Anna Freud on Easter Friday 1957).

The final expression of Eva's nostalgia is a letter she wrote when she went back to Grundlsee for a visit there in the summer of 1957. She wrote:

My thoughts are with all the people I love, and they are not memories but relived presence ("Wieder-Lebendigkeiten"), which deeply touches my heart. I guess I knew I would have to come back here, but I didn't know that this would so awaken me from the dead. Thank God that you have in your "Far End" [Anna's and Dorothy's house in Walberswick] something really alive and nearby, and don't have to seek far and wide until you find yourself again. Perhaps you succeed in that even every week. I have had to search and to wait for a long time; but now I am satisfied. The beauty of the place is indescribable, and the timeless washed-away sin is indescribable as well! All is real again which made life so precious once upon a time, and perhaps I myself am still the least real. To my right I look at the Rebenburg, in front of me at the lake. During daytime the sun glitters upon it, at night the moon. All is silent, only the faint sound of the saw-mill from far away, just as it always has been. And the gentian! The high-stemmed bell-flower is blossoming right now. Two old childhood friends of mine live five minutes away from here and are within reach in every sad moment. Alone I should not have stood it. But after all that I "am" now, isn't it touching that I am here, from one house to the next, still the mother of Mädi? With the most fervent love, Your Eva, and a kiss to Dorothy and the children.

"As far as Vienna goes," she adds in a second letter, "I feel as you do, but Grundlsee is different, every reed of grass and every fragrance of the meadow amount to so much more than the good or evil men can do. And now I'll go on travelling across Europe with mixed feelings—and will be home on the 4th of September. And at long last London will be home after all" (to Anna Freud, August 12 and 21, 1957).

Eva's relationship to the past and to Anna is in a sense no longer subject to change at this point. But as her memories take on definitive shape in her memoirs, and specifically in the chapter which, for discretion's sake, will not be called "The Professor and Anna" but merely "1924–1939," nostalgia and longing seem to give way increasingly to reflection and insight. She quotes Leonard Woolf to the effect that "the attachment of daughter to father... was not properly understood until after the second eating of the apple of knowledge by Sigmund Freud," and finds this "unforgettably witty and clever bon-mot" evidently most appropriate for the "clever daughter Anna" (to Anna Freud, January 14, 1970). She distinguishes now between Anna and herself: "For really clever matters I am not clever enough, but the human element—that has always been my thing" (September 10, 1972). "Naturally," she writes to Anna on April 24, 1974, "you could not write the story of your life. You have had a mission in life which extinguished everything else; but such a one as I am plucks at her life with constant curiosity. For my own story has been fed at the same time by a new kind of knowledge which lends importance to all the unimportant things; and in the end all important things will be unimportant, and then I will step down from the stage of life" (April 24, 1974). And finally: "We can say that we have lived through an eventful half-century: I in a personal and you in an impersonal life," and she adds once more: "my life owes its value to you"—"Euch": meaning not merely Anna and Dorothy, but Anna and Sigmund Freud and their circle.

Such is the character of Eva's side of the later correspondence. But there are also two late letters by Anna personal enough to bring the present collection to its conclusion in that they suggest the way in which Anna did communicate on her part with her old friend.

The first is a letter written while Eva was recuperating from some ailment in London and Anna Freud was resting at the house she and Dorothy owned in Suffolk by the sea, after the 25th International Psychoanalytical Congress at Amsterdam. The house of Anna's brother Ernst and his wife, the latter suffering from a heart condition was close by; and so were the houses Dorothy had bought there for her children, as well as analyst Willi Hoffer's house (later passed on to W. Ernest Freud). In the fifties and sixties Walberswick became a summer gathering place for analysts, including many temporary visitors who had long lived in the United States, such as Ernst and Marianne Kris.

Anna Freud wrote from Walberswick on August 11, 1967:

Letter 56

Dear Eva,

I have no news of you and don't know whether you are making any progress. Too bad you missed Walberswick. The heat, which is oppressive in London, is just the right thing here. I am lying in my hut on the beach, hear nothing but the sea, and am trying to forget the Congress and the whole year's work. Not so easy!

At Ernst's it is always the same: not too bad, but far from good.

Let me know how you are.

    Your
    Anna

Anna Freud's last letter in our collection is a response to Eva who wrote to her on September 9, 1975: "My Anna, am I really to believe that you will be eighty this year? I don't like that at all. But Mathilde assures me it is so. I thought it was rather the unassuming 79th. What shall we do about it? So far, I only know of a wish of Mathilde's—a low bathtub so that she can step into it easily. Shall we—Dorothy, you, Gusti, and I—make it a collective present? She herself has to take care of the formalities by obtaining the required medical certificate from her health-service physician. Do you have any special wish? Meanwhile, I can only wish you two that the weather will keep on being beautiful. With much love to both of you, Eva."

To this Anna Freud replied from a country place she and Dorothy had in Ireland:

Letter 57

    Rathmore nr Baltimore, County Cork,
    Eire[1]
    September 12, 1975

Dear Eva,

I am very enthusiastic about your plan for Mathilde's bathtub. She really needs this. I could finance it alone, but perhaps a joint gift might give her greater pleasure. Could you set this in motion, please? It will surely take some time.

I have no wishes at all. Perhaps I would like to be a little younger.

My strength is sufficient for the life here.

All the best,

>   Your
>   Anna

Eva answered on September 15, 1975:

> My Anna,
>
> This letter has several points of departure: 1) Thanks for your letter; 2) I duly noted and understood the innuendo about your strength being sufficient for the life in Eire. But what are we to do about your other half-sentence—which I understand equally well? 3) The physician does not want the shallow bathtub. He doesn't want to tempt Mathilde to take a bath on her own. As he would have had to provide the certificate to get this project on the way, it won't work. Who knows, perhaps his prohibition is a wise judgment. 4) And now I am moving ahead a week in the calendar to tell you that the 23rd will be dedicated by me to one single thought, the last one in the life of your father before he entered into immortality, which he knew he would even in the letter he wrote when he graduated from high school.* Yesterday we had stormy weather, today is the Day of Atonement—hence: the most beautiful sunshine. Love to you both, Eva.

---

*In a letter of June 16, 1873, Sigmund Freud told his friend, Emil Fluss, jokingly, to guard and keep his letters—"you can never know"—and expressed his concern to rise above mediocrity (1873, pp. 6–7).

References

Aichhorn, A. (1935), *Wayward Youth*. New York: Meridian Press, 1955.
Andreas-Salomé, L. (1923), *Ródinka*. Jena: Eugen Diederichs.
——— Freud, S. (1966), *Briefwechsel*, [Correspondence] ed. E. Pfeiffer. Frankfurt: S. Fischer, 1980.
Atwood, G. E., & Stolorow, R. (1979), *Faces in a Cloud. Subjectivity in Personality Theory.* New York: Jason Aronson.
Bannach, H.-J. (1971), Die wissenschaftliche Bedeutung des alten Berliner Psychoanalytischen Instituts [The scientific significance of the Old Berlin Psychoanalytic Institute]. *Psyche*, 25: 242–254.
Bernfeld, S. (1925), *Sisyphos oder die Grenzen der Erziehung* [Sisyphus or the limits of education]. Vienna: Psychoanalytischer Verlag.
——— (1969), *Ausgwählte Schriften* [Selected Writings]. 3 vols. Frankfurt: Ullstein.
Bittner, G. (1974), *Das andere Ich. Rekonstruktionen zu Freud* [The Other Self. Reconstructions to Freud]. München: Piper, 1974.
——— (1977), *Tarnungen des Ich. Studien zu einer subjektorientierten Abwehrlehre* [Disguises of the Ego. Contributions to a subject-oriented theory of defenses]. Stuttgart: Bonz.

———— Heller, P., eds. (1983), *Eine Kinderanalyse bei Anna Freud* (1929–1932). Würzburg: Königshausen & Neumann.

———— (1988), *Das Unbewusste—ein Mensch im Menschen?* [The Unconscious—A Human Being within the Human Being?]. Würzburg: Königshausen & Neumann.

———— (1989a), *Vater Freuds unordentliche Kinder. Die Chancen post-orthodoxer Psychoanalyse* [Father Freud's unruly children. The chances of a post-orthodox psychoanalysis]. Würzburg: Königshausen & Neumann.

———— (1989b), Maria Montessori und das Unbewusste [Maria Montessori and the Unconscious]. In: *Montessori-Pädagogik und die Erziehungsprobleme der Gegenwart* [The pedagogy of Montessori and the educational problems of the present], ed. B. Fuchs & W. Harth-Perter. Würzburg: Königshausen & Neumann.

Burlingham, M. J. (1989), *The Last Tiffany. A Biography of Dorothy Tiffany Burlingham*. New York: Atheneum.

Chamisso, A. von (1829), Salas y Gomez. In: *Chamissos Werke*. Leipzig: Bibliographisches Institut, n. d., Band 1, pp. 259–267.

Chapple, G., & Schulte, H., eds. (1981), *The Turn of the Century*. Bonn: Bouvier.

Coles, R. (1970), *Erik H. Erikson. The Growth of His Work*. Boston: Little, Brown.

Derrida, J. (1985), *The Ear of the Other. Texts and Discussions with Jacques Derrida (Otobiography, Transference, Translation)*. Lincoln: University of Nebraska Press.

Deutsch, H. (1975), *Confrontations with Myself*. (New York: Norton, 1973).

Erikson, E. H. (1930), Psychoanalysis and the future of education. In: *A Way of Looking at Things. Selected Papers (1930–1980)*. New York: Norton, 1983, pp. 14–30.

———— (1931a), Children's picture books. In: *A Way of Looking at Things. Selected Papers (1930–1980)*. New York: Norton, 1983, pp. 31–38.

———— (1931b), The fate of the drives in school compositions. In: *A Way of Looking at Things. Selected Papers (1930–1980)*. New York: Norton, 1983, pp. 39–69.

——— (1970), Identity crisis. In: *Life History and the Historical Moment.* New York: Norton, 1975, pp. 17–47.

——— (1974), Peter Blos: Reminiscences. In: *A Way of Looking at Things. Selected Papers (1930–1980).* New York: Norton, 1983, pp. 709–712.

——— (with Joan M. Erikson) (1980), Dorothy Burlingham's school in Vienna. In: *A Way of Looking at Things. Selected Papers (1930–1980).* New York: Norton, 1983, pp. 3–13.

——— (1983), *A Way of Looking at Things. Selected Papers* (1930–1980), ed. S. Schlein. New York: Norton.

Ferenczi, S., & Groddeck, G. (1986), *Briefwechsel* [Correspondence] (1921–1933). Frankfurt/M: S. Fischer.

Freud, A. (1922), Beating phantasies and daydreams. *The Writings of Anna Freud*, Vol. I. New York: International Universities Press, 1974, pp. 137–157.

——— (1926), Four Lectures on Child Analysis. *The Writings of Anna Freud*, Vol. I. New York: International Universities Press, 1974, pp. 3–69.

——— (1927), *Introduction to the Technique of Child Analysis* (German version revised. See 1926: *Four Lectures*).

——— (1927), The theory of child analysis. *The Writings of Anna Freud*, Vol. I. New York: International Universities Press, 1974, pp. 162–175.

——— (1930), Four Lectures on Psychoanalysis for Teachers and Parents. *The Writings of Anna Freud*, Vol. I. New York: International Universities Press, pp. 73–133.

——— (1932), Psychoanalysis and the upbringing of the young child. *The Writings of Anna Freud*, Vol. I. New York: International Universities Press, pp. 176–188.

——— (1936), The Ego and the Mechanisms of Defense. *The Writings of Anna Freud*, Vol. II. New York: International Universities Press, 1966.

——— (1965), Normality and Pathology in Childhood. Assessments of Development. *The Writings of Anna Freud*, Vol. VI. New York: International Universities Press, 1965.

——— (1968), Wege und Irrwege in der Kinderentwicklung. [Revised German version of *Normality and Pathology.*

Schriften der Anna Freud, Vol. VIII. Munich: Kindler, 1980.

Freud, E., ed. (1978), *Sigmund Freud. His Life in Pictures and Words*, compiled by E. Freud, L. Freud, I. Grubrich-Simitis, with a biographical sketch by K. R. Eissler. London: André Deutsch.

Freud, S. (1873), *Briefe*, ed. E. Freud. Frankfurt: S. Fischer.

―――― (1900), *The Interpretation of Dreams. Standard Edition*, Vol. 4 & 5. London: Hogarth Press, 1953.

―――― (1909a), Analysis of a Phobia in a Five-Year-Old Boy. *Standard Edition*, 10: 3–149. London: Hogarth Press, 1955.

―――― (1913), The Theme of the Three Caskets. *Standard Edition*, 12: 289–301. London: Hogarth Press, 1959.

―――― (1914a), Remembering, repeating and working through. *Standard Edition*, 12: 147–156. London: Hogarth Press, 1959.

―――― (1914b), The Moses of Michelangelo. *Standard Edition*, 13: 211–236. London: Hogarth Press, 1955.

―――― (1915–1916), Introductory Lectures on Psycho-Analysis. *Standard Edition*, 15 & 16. London: Hogarth Press, 1963.

―――― (1921), Group psychology and the analysis of the ego. *Standard Edition*, 18: 67–143. London: Hogarth Press, 1955.

―――― (1924–1932), *Gesammelte Schriften* (Collected Writings), ed. A. Storfer. Vienna: Psychoanalytischer Verlag.

―――― (1926), The question of lay analysis. *Standard Edition*, 20: 179–258. London: Hogarth Press, 1959.

―――― (1927), The future of an illusion. *Standard Edition*, 21: 3–56. London: Hogarth Press, 1961.

―――― (1929), Civilization and Its Discontents. *Standard Edition*, 21: 59–145. London: Hogarth Press, 1961.

―――― (1932), New Introductory Lectures on Psychoanalysis. *Standard Edition*, 22: 239–248. London: Hogarth Press, 1964.

―――― (1938), Ergebnisse, Ideen, Probleme. (London, Juni 1938) *Schriften aus dem Nachlass—Gesammelte Werke*

[Posthumous Writings], Vol. 17: 151–152. London: Imago Publishing, 1941.
────── (1960) *Briefe,* [Letters], ed. Ernst Freud. Frankfurt: S. Fischer, 1960.
────── Andreas-Salomé, L. (1966), *Briefwechsel* [Correspondence] (ed. E. Pfeiffer), Frankfurt/M: S. Fischer, 1980.
Freud, W. E. (1985), W. Ernest Freud and J. Martin—A Conversation. *Psychoanal. Ed.,* 4: 36–37.
────── (1987), Die Freuds und die Burlinghams. In: *Sigmund Freud House Bull.* (Vienna), 11/1: 3–18.
Gay, P. (1988), *Freud. A Life for Our Time.* New York: Norton.
Göppel, R. (1991), Die Burlingham–Rosenfeld Schule in Wien (1927–1933). Schule und Unterricht für die Kinder des psychoanalytischen Clans. [The Burlingham–Rosenfeld School in Vienna (1927–1933). School and instruction for children of the psychoanalytic clan]. *Zeitschr. für Pädagogik,* 37/3: 413–430.
Gordon, D. E. (1981), Oskar Kokoschka and the visionary tradition. In: *The Turn of the Century.* German Literature and Art, 1890–1915, ed. G. Chapple & H. H. Schulte. Bonn: Bouvier, pp. 23–52.
Grosskurth, P. (1986), *Melanie Klein. Her World and Her Work.* New York: Alfred A. Knopf.
Hauptmann, G. (1893), Hanneles Himmelfahrt. Traumdichtung in zwei Akten. [Hannele's Ascension. A Dreampoem in two acts]. *Ausgewählte Werke,* Band 2, Berlin: S. Fischer, 1925.
Heller, P. (1990), *A Child Analysis with Anna Freud.* New York: International Universities Press, 1990.
Humboldt, W. von. (1910), *Briefe an eine Freundin* [Letters to a female friend], ed. A. Leitzmann. Leipzig: Insel.
Jones, E. (1957), *Sigmund Freud. Life and Work,* Vol. 3. London: Hogarth Press, 1957.
Kardiner, A. (1979), *Meine Analyse bei Freud* [My analysis with Freud. Reminiscences (1977)]. Munich: Kindler.
Laplanche, J., & Pontalis, J.-B. (1967), *The Language of Psychoanalysis.* Norton: New York, 1973.
Leupold-Löwenthal, H. (1984), Zur Geschichte der "Frage der Laienanalyse" [Concerning the history of "The Question of Lay Analysis"] *Psyche,* 38: 97–120.

Peters, U. H. (1979), *Anna Freud. Ein Leben für das Kind* [Anna Freud. A Life for the Child], rev. ed. Frankfurt/M: Fischer Taschenbuch Verlag, 1984.
Pfeiffer, E. (ed.) (1980), Commentary and notes. In: *S. Freud and L. Andreas-Salomé: Briefwechsel*. Frankfurt: S. Fischer, 1980.
Roazen, P. (1971), *Freud and His Followers*. New York: New American Library, 1976.
Rosenfeld, E. M. (1950), The Pan-headed Moses: A parallel. Paper presented to the British Psycho-Analytical Society.
────── (unpublished), *Recollected in Tranquillity*. Memoirs.
Salber, W. (in collaboration with W. E. Freud) (1985), *Anna Freud*. Reinbek bei Hamburg: Rororo.
Schottländer, F. (1959), *Das Ich und seine Welt* [The Ego and Its World]. Stuttgart: Klett.
Schultz, U., & Hermanns, L. M. (1987), Das Sanatorium Schloss Tegel Ernst Simmels—Zur Geschichte und Konzeption der ersten Psychoanalytischen Klinik [E. Simmel's Sanitarium in Castle Tegel. Concerning the history and conception of the first psychoanalytic clinic]. *Psychotherapie. Psychosomatik. Medizinische Psychologie.* (Stuttgart). 37/2: 37–67.
Schur, M. (1972), *Freud: Living and Dying*. New York: International Universities Press.
Young-Bruehl, E. (1988), *Anna Freud. A Biography*. New York: Summit Books.

Index

Asterisks following L (letter) or n (notes) point to information contained in a letter or the respective notes: L1*n* points to significant information on a given topic in both Letter 1 and its notes; L1n* points to the notes only.

Abraham, Hilde: L24
Adelaide Sweetser: *see* Sweetser, Adelaide
Aichhorn, August (1878–1949; psychoanalyst, city-councillor in Vienna): 13–14, 18–19, 80, 81, L1n, L6n, L8 (he and his institute a model for Hietzing School), L47 (and for Tegel Sanatorium), L42, L43
Aichhorn, Walter: 13
Altruism, "altruistic surrender": *see also* Freud, Anna
  self-sacrifice: 5–8, L1*
Amsden, Dr. (psychoanalyst): L12n
Andreas, Lou Salomé: *see* Salomé
Atwood, G. E. & Stolorow, R.: 9

Berchtesgaden (Schneewinkel): 4, L9n, L11, L12 , L13n, L9–L14 (Letters from), L15n, L29
Berggasse: 6, 29, L8, L16, (L25)n, L47n, L48 (the center of everything), L54
Berlin (see also Tegel): 3, 19–20 (Berlin versus Vienna): 27, 32; 39, 41, L6, L8, L20n (Berlin and Vienna), L24, L27, L28, L29, L36n, L53n, L55
Bernays, Minna (b. 1865, Wandsbek; d. 1941, London; Martha Freud's sister): 75, L26
Bernfeld, Siegfried (b. 1892, Galicia; d. 1953, San Francisco; psychoanalyst): 8, 28, 79–80, 94, L3, L25 (his seminar), L26
Binswanger (psychoanalyst): 13
Bisexuality: 41 (Eva on subject)
Bittner, Günther: ix; on Anna Freud's Letters to Eva Rosenfeld: 3–22
Blos, Peter (teacher, psychoanalyst): 14, 16–17, 32, 82–83, L17n
Bonaparte, Marie (psychoanalyst): 8
Bondy School (= Marienau): L47
Bourgeois acquisitiveness (Anna Freud on subject): 27
Bowlby, John (psychoanalyst): (L36)n
Briehl, Mary (teacher, psychoanalyst): 13
Brill, Abraham A. (psychoanalyst): 8
Brontës (Eva on subject): 42
Brooch, story of lost: 30–31
Brunswick, Mark: L38n

195

Brunswick, Ruth Mack (1897–1946; psychoanalyst): L38n, L41, L52n

Burlingham family: 74–78. *Dorothy and family:* 12–14 (as Anna Freud's "enlarged," artificial family in symbiosis with the Freud family); 29–30 (B. family part of Freud's solar system; the Burlingham children), 15–16, 74–78, 83–86, L2, L4n, L10, (L9)n, L12n (relation to Eva Rosenfeld), L13n, L14n, L16n, L17n, L18, L23n, L24, L25n, L27, L28, L29, (L30)n, L31, L33, L35, L37, L38, L40, L42, (L43)n, L45, L47, (L48)n, L49n, L51n, (L53)n, L54, 180–186 passim. *Bob Burlingham:* 12 (girlfriends), 16, 29 (patient of Anna Freud), 74–75, 83, L11*n, L12n, L27, L28, L29, L48, L51. *Charles Cult Burlingham* (father-in-law of Dorothy): L35. *Dorothy Burlingham* (née Tiffany; b. 1891, New York; d. 1979, London): 11, 13 (S. Freud's patient), 74–75 (relation to Anna Freud), 75 (S. Freud on Dorothy), 43 (negative "Burlingham" effect" on Eva's relation to Anna Freud), 77–78 (personality of Dorothy), L21. *Mabbie (1917–1974):* 15, 74–75, L5, L10, (L23)n, L24, L27, L28n. *Mikey (Michael):* 74, 76, L25. *Dr. Robert* (Dorothy's husband): 29, 76–77, (L12)n, L25, L35n. *Tinky* (b. 1919): 74, 76, L4n, L49n, (L53)n *Dorothy B. as initiator and founder of the Hietzing School:* 13, 16–17, 29–30, 78, 87 (later calls Hietzing School a mistake).

Burlingham, Michael John (biographer of Dorothy Burlingham): 12, 16, 87

Chamisso, Adelbert von (1771–1838; poet, author of "Salas y Gomez"): 7, 146

Child analysis: 4, 12 (comparison to patients at psychoanalytical sanitarium)

Clark, Miss: L41n

Congresses (psychoanalytical): L2n, L3 (in Bad Homburg, 1925), L4n (Innsbruck, 1927), L20n (11th, in Oxford, 1929), L45, L50n (in Wiesbaden, 1932), L51n, L52, 185, L56 (in Amsterdam)

De Forest, Izette (Judy's mother): 14, L10, L35n

De Forest, Judy: 14, 83–84, L10, L19n, L23n, L35n

Delinquents (treatment of by Aichhorn): 81

Demeter and Kore: 69

Dewey, John: 17

Dogs: Jofi (chow): L55. S. Freud's chows named Lün: L14n, L52n. Eva's dachshund Racker: 65. (Tinky's?) Taltoun: L53n. Anna Freud's German shepherd Wolf: 65, L10, L46. Love of dogs: L14n

Education: 17–18, 32, 80–82, L8*. *Anti-authoritarian:* 17–18, 80–82. *See also entries under* Aichhorn, Bernfeld, Blos, Burlingham (Dorothy), de Forest (Judy), Erikson, Freud (Anna, Sigmund, W. Ernest),

Hietzing School, Rosenfeld (Eva), Marienau, Scharfenberg, Settlement)

Eissler, Kurt (psychoanalyst): 70

Eitingon, Dr. Max (b. 1881, Galicia; d. 1943, Jerusalem; psychoanalyst): 7–9, 91–94, (L2)n, L4, L20n, L24, L25n, L26n, L45, L46, L47*n

Elsa Houtermans: see Houtermans, Elsa

Emigration: 28, 43–44, 46

Erikson, Erik (Homburger) (b. 1902, near Frankfurt; psychoanalyst): 10–11, 13–14, 16–17 (on Hietzing School with Joan Serson Erikson); 22 (on psychoanalysis and human enlightenment), 32, 37, 82, 86, L4n, L17n, L19n, L24, L27, L28, L29

Erikson, Joan Serson: 16–17

Erikson, Kai: L38

Ernstl (Ernsti): see Freud, W. Ernest (Anna Freud's nephew)

Erzsi Toszeghi: see Toszeghi, Erzsi

Ferenczi (psychoanalyst): 11, 77, 84, (L9)n, L12n, (L30)n, L42

Fichtl, Paula: 75

Fluss, Emil: 187

Freiberg (Pribor): 156

Freud family: see also Bernays, Minna; 29–31 (Freud solar system), 63–69 (circle of the Freuds and Lou Salomé), 75 (the Freud household), (L9)n, L30n

Freud, Anna (b. 12/3/1895, Vienna; d. 10/10/1982, London): see also Aichhorn, Burlingham(s), Eitingon, Freud (Sigmund), Hietzing School, Psychoanalysis, Rosenfeld (Eva), Salomé, Tegel

Personality: ix–x, 5–9, 95–98; attitude toward work and leisure: 5–6; empathy, shyness, depth of feeling, tension: 5–6; dreams: 7, 12; as a child: 8; knitting: 10; sense of humor: 9–10; *virginity–sexuality–relation to men:* see "relation to Eitingon," "relation to father," "relation to Lou," and Freud (Sigmund); *also* Burlingham (Dorothy); 6 (role as confidante), 8 (Vestal virgin); 10, 93 (masturbation), 80 (sexual enlightenment), 8 (S. Freud on Anna's sexuality), 93 (relation to men), L33*n (regression to daydream-phase), L36n (not "Valkyrie-like"). *Later years:* 180–187. *Characteristic traits:* L4 (generosity); L6 (on vanity: ball dress), L8 (happiness not as important as other things), L13 (on life), L30 (everything real takes place within), L42n (photos; predictions telepathy). Concern over indiscretion: L42; see 38 (Eva should tear up her letters) *and* L46 (photos). L49 (self-encounter most important of all)

Health, well-being, work, leisure: see also Neuhaus, Hochrotherd; L1 (convalescence, narcissism), L4 (exhaustion; wish for weekend retreat), L9, L10n, L15 (wish to be safe and protected); *see also* Tegel *and* Freud, Anna, style (Tegel as island of safety); L16,

197

L17, L19n, L22 (near [psycho-somatic?] breakdown, wish for peace and quiet), L23n (recovery from near-breakdown), L24 (partial recovery, well-being), L25 (recovery; hay-fever; work; wish for farmhouse), L33, L35, L37, L42 (sickness and convalescence), L47 (headaches), L48, L55, L57 (old age)

Self and self-analysis: L4*n* (Freud's "Group Psychology" and her own analysis; generosity; daydreams), L8 (on her own analysis), L17*n* (her analysis with her father), L18 (compelled to give lectures), L22* (trying a long retreat into herself; dream of finals), L25*n (on her being rejected, and her choice of rejecting love-objects as a child), L34n (weaving and analysis)

Idealism and "altruistic surrender": see also views on psychoanalysis; ix, 21–22; "altruistic surrender": 5–9, 12, 96; self-overcoming and sublimation: 5, 21–22; "narcissism": 5, 9, L1; self-surrender: loss of self, abandonment, withdrawal, renunciation: 7–9; aversion against public exposure: 38, 46; escape from everyday life, wish to retreat and be protected: 7; *self-dedication, service, self-sacrifice, self-realization, self-fufilment:* ix, 7–8; self-devaluation: 94; sense of lack of self and self-effacement: 95–98 passim; conflict between inwardness and realism, self-involvement and self-abnegation: 97–98; her style: 95–97 (metaphors: traffic-island: 95; metaphors of withdrawal: 96; and of lack of self or self-effacement: 97). L11, L25 (ideal of selflessness), L47 (dream of murdering Anna), L49 (dream of cow in burning stable), L53 (no real "I" as yet). Asceticism: 5; strong will: ix; wish to be good: 5; ethos of Anna Freud and her early circle: 22, 37

Ideal of natural (unreflective) state of being: see also above; 98 (her love of the unconscious, naive, simple, and of nature), L24*, L34*n* (mountains; see also wish for farm [weekend house], Hiddensee), L56 (the sea); gardening: L35, L37, L38, L49, L51, L53*. Schoolfarm: L5

Psychoanalysis: see also above "idealism" *and below* "relation to father": ix (psychoanalysis all-encompassing to Anna Freud); professional life: 4; an analyst even in private: 5; her own analysis and case: 4, 10–11, 92–93; views on psychoanalysis: 10–11; analysis equals love and goodness: 10, 72, L8*; defense mechanisms (*see also* "altruistic surrender"): 4, 6–7, 22; children in analysis with her: 13–14

Publications, professional activ-

ity: 4 ("Beating Fantasies and Daydreams," "Four Lectures on Child Analysis," "Four Lectures on Psychoanalysis for Teachers and Parents," "The Ego and the Mechanisms of Defense" [*see also above:* "altruistic surrender"], 64 ("Introduction to the Technique of Child Analysis"), 6 (the case of the "young governess" in: "The Ego and the Mechanisms of Defense"). "Writings," Vol.1: 4, 106, 124; Vol. 2: 6; Vol 6: 18. "Beating Fantasies and Day Dreams": 93. L4n (how to study S. Freud's writings; lecture and positions in International Psychoanalytical Association), L8* (analysis = love = goodness), L16n ("Introduction to Psychoanalysis for Teachers"; her seminars on child analysis in Berlin and Vienna), L17 (Psychoanalytical Association; her seminar), L20*n* (her seminars in Vienna and Berlin), L24 (her seminar; Psychoanalytical Association), L25 (Berlin seminar), L30n (no kissing in analysis, and "neutrality rule"), L33n ("Beating Fantasies and Daydreams"), L42 (on analysis pure and modified), L51n (work on lectures)

On *education, psychoanalytical pedagogy, and Hietzing School: see also* Aichhorn, Bernfeld (Siegfried), Blos, Burlingham, de Forest (Judy), Education, Erikson, Freud (W. Ernest), Hietzing School, Marienau, Rosenfeld (Eva), Ross, Scharfenberg); 14–19; Anna Freud as pedagogue: 14, 18; retrospective doubts about, and evaluation of, "psychoanalytical pedagogy": 13–14, 18, 32 (incl. project method). Attitude toward "progressive education": 80–81, L8*n; her child patients at Hietzing School: 83–90; (L50)n

On Simmel's "Psychoanalytical Sanatorium": 19–21 (incl. remarks on psychoanalytical therapy and psychoanalytic nursing care: 21), 38, L42

Her attempt at a "psychoanalytical reform of life": 12–22 passim

Relation to Dorothy Burlingham and Burlingham family: see also Burlinghams *and* Burlingham, Dorothy; 29–31; 30 (Anna, Dorothy, Eva as "firm friends"), 45, 74–78, 182

Relation to Eitingon (see also *Etington, Max*): 7–9, 91–94, L4, L20n, L25*, L26*n, L47* (judgment of Eitingon)

Relation to father: see also Freud Sigmund (especially sickness, cancer), Tegel, *and* Freud, Anna, style (prosthesis–metaphor): x, 3–6, 9, 11–12 (on reading her father's works and the study of psychoanalysis), 12 (dependency on father giv-

199

ing meaning to her life; refusal of a "substitute" for the relation to her father), 93–94. In the Letters: L4*n (how to read his writings), L7 (talk with Papa), L8 (sense of freedom and insight when away from Berggasse, but cf. also L48), L11*n (giving meaning to her life), L14n (loss of Lün, Heinerle, Sophie), L17*n* (her analysis with her father), L19 (his sickness), L36n (Valkyrie and Cordelia), L38 (playing cards with Papa), L42n (used by father for experiments in telepathy), L44n (must substitute as partner in father's card game; his pneumonia), L47 (worry about his health), L54 (Papa "always right"), L55 (on S. Freud's "New Introductory Lectures")

Relation to Eva Rosenfeld: see also Burlingham, Dorothy *and* Rosenfeld, Eva: ix; affection, empathy, and almost daily contact during early period of friendship: 3, 41; Eva as her alter ego: 7, 12, 48; dreams about Eva: 7, 12; shared humanistic ideal: 22–23, 37; Anna at Mädi's death: 24, 67; first connection with Eva and her establishment: 28; relation to Eva and Eva's household: 65–66; presents to Eva: 28–29 ("Handarbeiten," poem); praise of Eva's "establishment": 31; waning of friendship: 40–44; physical distance: 40–41; preoccupation with father's condition: 41; rebuffs of Eva by S. and Anna Freud: 41–42; negative "Burlingham effect" on relation to Eva: 43. Anna's loyalty despite Eva's relation to Melanie Klein?: 45–46; Anna on Eva's death: 48. Relationship in later years: 180–187. In the Letters: L5 (sense of intimacy), L8 (closeness; on Eva's analysis), L9 (identification with, and sense as if Eva experienced things for her, thus sparing herself; wish to help her), L11 ("you are I and I am you"; dream about Eva; interprets Eva's relation to Obermann). Intimacy: L18, L20 (undo Eva's depression). L22 (dream about Eva), L28n (concern about Eva's solitude; misplaces letter; Eva as Anna's factotum), L30 (closeness: physical separation means nothing), L36 (concern for Eva), L38 (as if I knew all your thoughts), L39 (wish for closeness), L40 (intimacy: impossible to express it in writing), L42 (concern with Eva's health), L43 and L45 (concern: Eva overworked), L47 (Eva's place in Freud family; offers to pay Victor's tuition at Marienau), L50n and L52 (concern with Eva's condition), L54n (on Eva's marital and career crisis; her trip to Mos-

cow, sense of closeness to her; relation to Eva's mother, Omi), L55
Relation to Lou Salomé: 63–65 passim
Letters to Eva Rosenfeld, Anna Freud as writer: ix, 95–98; when written and from where: 3, 37. *Character of letters:* ix (graceful sobriety), 3–5, 9; 7, 12 (L11 as illustration of a "psychoanalytical letter"), 38, 38–39 (letters: possible cause for cooling of relationship), 40–41, 46 (letters kept secret by Eva). *Style* (especially: use of metaphors): L15n, L16, L18*n, L19, L20n, L22n, L23n. Tegel as metaphoric "island of safety": L14, L15, L16, L18, cf. L24n (real island; also L25); Tegel as desolate rock in the sea: L30; and the nexus to the metaphoric use of the prosthesis as ship: L30; ship and island: L31, L32 (ship), L33 (ship and "Ausleger" boat). "Ausleger–Anna" (boat): L28n, L33n

About individual letters: L1: 5–6, 9; *L3:* 64; *L4:* 5, 11, 22, 33; *L5:* 15; *L6:* 20, 31, 38; *L8:* 6, 10, 17–18, 35, 37; *L11:* 7, 12 (analysis of L11), 32, 48; *L12:* 15; *L13:* 22; *L15:* 7, 20; *L17:* 9, 14; *L19:* 9; *L20:* 20, 27; *L22:* 7, 22; *L24:* 7, 10, 14–15; *L26:* 11; *L30:* 7; *L32:* 38; *L33:* 15; *L34:* 10; *L35:* 39; *L36:* 39; *L41:* 39; *L42:* 20, 29; *L47:* 8–9, 15, 21–22; *L55:* 40; *L57:* 47

Freud, Ernst (brother of Anna Freud; architect; and his son Gabriel): 19, 40 (Eva's analytical couch), L26, L27, L28 (Gabriel), L47, L56

Freud, Martha (née Bernays; b. 1861, Wandsbek; d. 1951, London; Anna Freud's mother): 75, L13n*, L23, L26, L54

Freud, Jean Martin (b. 1889, Vienna; d. 1967, England; Anna Freud's brother): L14n, L50n

Freud, Sigmund (b. 1856, Freiberg [Pribor]; d. 9/23/1939, London; *see also* under Freud, Anna): x, 5 (autobiography; Interpretation of Dreams), 8–9 and 94 (on Anna Freud's sex life), 13 (patients: Anna Freud, Eva Rosenfeld, Dorothy Burlingham), 46 (emigration; in London, 1938), 86–87 (on the educational system), L11n, L14*n* (loss of Lün, Heinerle, Sophie), (L16)n, L23n (transference), (L30)n (versus Ferenczi's physical expression of intimacy with patients), L38 (playing cards), L39 (playing cards; bronze relief made of Freud), (L42)n (ascribes "telepathic sensitivity" to Anna), L44 (tarok card game), L46n (sculpture made of Freud; skeptical about psychoanalytic treatment for severely ill patients of Tegel), 187 (desire to rise above mediocrity)

Sickness: cancer, prosthesis: 3, 6, 38, L6*n, L17 (prosthesis in resistance), L19n (prosthesis in resistance: metaphoric treatment), L22, L23. Further mention of the prosthesis: L24, L25, L26, L27, L28, L29, L30, L41, L43, L46 (American dental wizard), L53. Other health concerns: L35n (Pichler), L37, L44n (pneumonia), L47, L48n (orthoform), L49, L55 (after an operation), 180–181 (last year and death), 187

Writings: 24 ("Future of an Illusion"), 26 (lectures at University of Vienna), 86–87 ("Civilization and its Discontents"), L4*n (Anna Freud on how to read Freud's writings [cf. also 11–12] with reference to "Introductory Lectures"; "Totem and Taboo"; "Case Histories"; "Mourning and Melancholia"; "Group Psychology"; "The Moses of Michelangelo"), (L19)n ("Interpretation of Dreams"; cf. 2), L23n (articles on psychoanalytic technique; "The Question of Lay Analysis"; "Remembering, Repeating and Working Through"), (L36)n ("The Three Caskets"); "New Introductory Lectures": 98–99, (L51)n, L52, L55n; aphorism on the psyche: 98

Relation to Dorothy Burlingham and her family: 13 (symbiosis with the Burlingham family), 75 (on Dorothy)

Relation to Eva Rosenfeld: 23, 26 (on marriage between first cousins), 29–30; Eva's analysis with Freud (*see also under* Rosenfeld, Eva): 33–37, 70–72. Freud's attitude toward Eva's marital crisis: 39, L35n, L40, L41, L54. Reaction to Eva's writings: 41–42 (rejects Eva's interpretation of the riddle of the Sphinx), 45 (on Melanie Klein and Eva; does not accuse Eva of betrayal), L8n, L50n

Relation to and correspondence with Lou (Andreas Salomé): 4, 7–8, 63–65 passim

Freud, Sophie (b. 1893, Vienna; d. 1920, Hamburg; mother of W. Ernest; Anna's sister): 66, L14n

Freud, W. Ernest (Ernsti) (= Ernstl [Ernsti] Halberstadt): x, 13–16, 44, 66; on Hietzing school and education: 80, 84–88. In the Letters: (L3)n, L6n, L7n, L8, L9n, L11, (L14)n, L16n, (L17)n, L18, L24, L25, L27, L28, L29, L32, L33, L37, L41n, L42, L43, L47, L48, L51n, L52, L53

Freund, Anton von: (L4)n
Freund, Vera von: 66
Fritzi Löwi: *see* Löwy, Fritzi

Gay, Peter: 8, 91, 94
Glockner: L14n
Gmunden (summer resort): L23
Goethe, Johann Wolfgang von: 40
Gordon, D. E.: 69
Grosskurth, Phyllis: (L36)n
Grundlsee (summer resort): 4, 31, 67, L13n, L24, L26n, L27, L28, L32, L35, L37, L38, L48n, L49, L51, L52, L53n, 183–184
Guilbert, Yvette (b. 1886, Paris; d. 1934, Aix-en-Provence; Eva's

aunt; French chansonnière) and husband Max: L16n, L54
Gurewitch, Marinka: L4n, L5, L8, L19, L20
Gusti Körner: *see* Körner, Gusti

Halberstadt, Heinerle: L14n
Halberstadt, Max (b. 1882, Hamburg; d. 1940, Johannesburg; phtographer; father of W. Ernest (Ernstl) Halberstadt Freud): L7n, L27
Halberstadt, Sophie (née Freud): *see* Freud, Sophie
Hampstead Nursery/Clinic: 180
Hauptmann, Gerhart: 64 (his play "Hannele")
Haydn: Toy Symphony: 32
Heinerle: *see* Halberstadt, Heinerle
Heller, Grete: 14
Heller, Peter (and father [Hans]): ix (bias of), 4, 10, 13–14 (Hans), 16, 22, 69, 86–87 (views on Hietzing School), (L9)n, L16n, L18, L19, L24
Hermanns, L. M.: 19
Herta Huber: *see* Huber, Herta
Hietzing (suburb of Vienna): 65
Hiddensee (island in the Baltic sea): L23n, L24, L25n, L29
Hietzing School (Burlingham–Rosenfeld School): *see also entries under* Freud (Anna), Rosenfeld (Eva); 11 (Bittner), 13–19 (Bittner), 31–33 (Ross), 68 and 75 (school founded by Eva Rosenfeld and Dorothy Burlingham), 78–90 (Heller). *Pupils, teachers, parents:* 13 (pupils; many in analysis with Anna Freud, one with Dorothy Burlingham; some not in analysis; staff in analysis with S. and A. Freud, and training to be analysts), 14 (parents connected with analysis), 16 (teachers), 32–33 (pupils and teachers), 82f (teachers), 83–90 (pupils) Literature on the school: 16. Relation public school system: 18–19; L6n. The school (tangible result of Freud-Burlingham–Rosenfeld relationship; a monument to Mädi, meant to "replace Mädi"): 32, (L5)n. Building, location: 32. Teaching by the project method: 17, 19, 32. The issue of compulsion and freedom at the Hietzing School; its inadequacy: 32, L8, 86–87. Educational climate and perspective: 78–83. L5n (Hietzing school and school farm), L6n (certification of curriculum), L8 (problem of discipline), L16, L17, L18, L43
Hochrotherd (location of Anna's and Dorothy's farm, near Vienna): 75, (L25)n, (L35)n, (L43)n, L48*n, L49, L50, L51, L(53)n, L55
Hollitscher, Mathilde (née Freud; b. 1887, Vienna; d. 1978, London; Freud's eldest daughter): 48, L15, L16n, L24, L51, L57, 186–187
Hollitscher, Robert: L51
Houtermans, Elsa: L21
Huber, Herta: 12, 66, (L9)n, L11n, L17, L23
Human and humanistic ideal: 21–22, L13n (human ideal: Mädi)
Humboldt, Wilhelm von (and family): 19, 21–22 (letters to Caroline cherished by Eva Rosenfeld), 37, 40

Iona, Mario and Elisabeth: 13
Island: *see* Freud (Anna, style [metaphor]), Hiddensee, Tegel (safety island; desolate rock in the sea)

Jeanne Lampl de Groot, *see* Lampl de Groot, Jeanne
Jekels, Ludwig: 14
Jews: 24 (emancipation–assimilation, Rosenfelds), 77 (Burlinghams)
Jones, Ernest (psychoanalyst): 8, (L9)n, L10
Josefa, Frau: L48
Juran, Franz (sculptor): (L39)n

Kardiner, Abraham: 8
Kazanijan, Professor (dental wizard): L46n, L47n
Klein, Melanie (b. 1882, Vienna; d. 1960, England; psychoanalyst): 4, 44–45 (as analyst of Eva; repudiates Eva for lack of allegiance; accusing her of having sacrificed her analysis to the friendship with Anna), (L36)n, 181–183
Königsee: L13n
Körner, Gusti: 66, L5, L16, L44
Kokoschka, Oskar (painter): 26 (Eva asked to be his model), 69
Kraus, Trude (Pfandl): 14, 66, L11n, L24
Kris, Ernst and Marianne (psychoanalysts): L38, 185

Lampl, Hans and Jeanne de Groot: 8, 93–94, L21n, L50n, L51n, L52n
Landauer, Karl (1887–1945; psychoanalyst): L2n
Letters to E. Rosenfeld: *see* Freud (Anna), Letters to Eva
Levy, Katà and Lajos: L4n, L52n

Lilli Sachs: *see* Sachs, Lilli
Lizie Wellenstein: *see* Wellenstein, Lizzie
Loos, Adolf (architect; furnished Rosenfeld house): 26
Löwy, Fritizi: 73, L44n
Lün: *see* Dogs

Mach, Minna (patient of Anna Freud): 28, 66, L13n, L19n, L21, L24, L41n, L43, L44, L48
Mädi (Rosenfeld): *see* Rosenfeld, Mädi
Mahony, Patrick: (L36)n
Marienau: 15, (L35)n, L37n, L47 (Bondy School)
Marinka Gurewitsch: *see* Gurewitsch, Marinka
Mathias, Frau (Cookbook): L43
Menaker, Esther: 13
Miezi, Aunt: L46, L50
Minna Mach: *see* Mach, Minna
Money (in Rosenfeld family): 24, in Tegel breakdown: 38
Montessori, Maria: Montessori system: 17
Moscow: L55

Narcissism: L1*
Nederhoud, Ann: 11, 31, 66, (L11)n, (L26)n
Némon, Oscar: L46n
Neuhaus (near Vienna): 75, L43n, L44, L45, L48n
Nietzsche, Friedrich: 24, 36
Nijinsky, Kira: 31, 66, (L11)n

Obermann, Julian N. (b. 1888, Warsaw; d. 1956, New Haven; Professor of Semitic Languages): 12 (lover seeking mother), 22, 72–74, L9*n, L11*n (seeking mother; his letters), L13n

Oedipus and the riddle of the Sphinx (Eva on subject) 41
Omi Rosenfeld: *see* Rosenfeld, Rose Schiller
Ophuijsen (psychoanalyst): L23n
Orthoform: L48n

Patients (referred to in the Letters): L1, L4, L11n, L14n*, L16n, L17n, L18, L19n, L23n, L24, L26, L27, L30n (patients: interweaving with private lives; no physical intimacy), L33, L35n, L37, L40, L42, L43, L45 (at Tegel), L47, L49, L50
Period prior to World War II: ix, 22
Peters, Uwe Henrik: 6, 8, 13, 64, 91
Pfeiffer, Ernst (editor: correspondence Lou Salomé–S. Freud): 64
Pichler, Dr.: L35n, L48
Psychoanalysis: *see also* Child analysis: x; Bittner on necessary subjectivity and emotional relationships in psychoanalysis: 9–10; "interweaving" of psychoanalytic and "real" relationships, and "rule of neutrality": 10–11; psychoanalysis as theme of the letters: 9–12 (Bittner); A. F. on going into analysis: 10 (analysis = love = goodness); Eva Rosenfeld's later judgment on analysis and character: 10; how to approach psychoanalysis (Anna Freud–Bittner): 11–12; intuitive knowledge of psychoanalysis: 11–12; futility of priority disputes in psychoanalysis: 11–12; "pure" and "applied": 20, 32. Psychoanalytic nursing care as distinct from therapy: 13, 32 ("active therapy" and "pure analysis"). On patients at Tegel: 12–13. *"Psychoanalytical community"*: 21. British Psychoanalytic Society: 42, 44. Congresses: 4. Psychoanalysis and character: 36. Psychoanalysis and medicine: 43. Psychoanalysis and Socratic ethic: 22. *Psychoanalytic paedagogy, education* (*see also* Hietzing School; A. Freud on education; S. Freud on the educational system): ix, 14–19, 18 (Anna Freud on changing emphases, successes, and contradictions in psychoanalytic paedagogy), 32 and L8 (issue of discipline), 22 (Erikson on psychoanalysis and education of mankind); L8 ("psa paedagogy"). *Psychoanalytical "reform of life"*: 22 (Hietzing School and psychoanalytic Sanitarium Tegel); *Tegel*: 19–21, 37–40, 90–91

Radó, Sandor (psychoanalyst; 1890–1972): L23n, L52n
Rank, Otto (psychoanalyst): 8
Rcbcnburg, Villa (in Grundlsee): L26, L28n, L29, L31 (personified)
Regine: *see* Toszeghi, Regine
Reinhard Simmel: *see* Simmel, Reinhard
Reik, Theodor (psychoanalyst): 74
Rie, Alfred: L44n
Rilke, Rainer Maria: 98, L33
Roazen, Paul: x, 71, (L38)n
Rosenfeld (Family history): 24–25 (relation to arts, theatre; move from Eastern ghettos to

the West; cultural–intellectual interests and debates); Eva's brothers: 24–25 (delinquency), 24 (cultural superiority of women in family), 25 ("nouveau riche Jewish middle class"), 33 (the hypnotist's party). L38n (Rosenfeld directness in expression of love)

Rosenfeld, Eva Marie (b. 1892, New York City; d. 1977, London): *see also under* Freud, Anna and Sigmund; Hietzing School, Obermann, Rosenfeld (Mädi, Omi, Theodor, Valti), Settlement, Tegel, Zellerhaus; 23–48 (Ross on Eva); 63–74, 180–187

Character: ix–x, 23–24, 29–30; loss of children, her tragedy, backdrop of despair: 23–24, 26–27; bravery, zest, sense of drama: 24–25; attitude toward coincidence and omens: 30–31; individualism, strong will: x; wit: x, 29; attitudes toward Vienna and Berlin: 27; 34 ("a Prussian Jew," a "free-thinker," curious, not strenuously "intellectual"); her education, position in parental family, relation to father: 24–25, 42; to brothers: 24; her social conscience (devotion to care for underprivileged, indifference to status, attitude toward authority): 25–28, 32–33; conception of the New Woman: 27; admirers: 29. *Idealism, humanism:* human *ideal* shared with Anna Freud: ix, 21–22; "uncompromising scale of values": 29; "what we did was less important than who we were": 22, 37; *dedication, service* (self-sacrifice: self-realization): ix, 21–22; joy in selfless service: 24–25, 29; tendency to excessive "service" role as factotum: 34; *"teaching, helping, healing":* 25, 28 (healing presence), 32–33. Rosenfeld directness in expression of love: L30n

Her household and "establishment(s)" ("model of household management," "foster-children and helpers," role vis à vis "Hietzing School"): 10–11, 14, 27–28 ("a model of household and gardening"), 33 (breadwinner). The new establishment: foster children and helpers: 13–14, 16, 31–32, 63–68 passim, L3*, L6, L7, L11, L16n, L17n, L19, L24, L26, L32. *Eva and Hietzing School:* 14–17, 31–33, 82 (attitude toward education), (L5)n, L8*n (for "compulsion")

Loss of Mädi (see also *Rosenfeld, Mädi), mourning, depression:* x; mourning for Mädi: 23–24, 33, 66–69, L4, L5, L18, L20*, L35 (turmoil, "der Wirr"), L37 (turmoil), L52 (depression-sickness?), 184 ("the timeless washed away sin")

Relation to Anna Freud, the Freuds and their circle, and the analysis with Sigmund Freud: see also Freud (Anna), Freud (Sigmund); *Initial phase:* 28 (first contact, friendship with Anna, central to Eva from 1924–1932); presents to Anna: 28–29; Anna introduces Eva to her father: 29; relationship to Freud family: 29–31, 34; meets Lou Salomé: 63–64; approach to psychoanalysis: 33 (hypnotist in Eva's family); how to read Freud: 11, 33, L4*n* (intuitive knowledge of psychoanalysis; later paper on "Pan-Headed Moses"); Anna decides Eva needs analysis: 33. *Analysis with S. Freud, and related topics:* 10–11, 33–37, 39. 34 (another father, honor, privilege, concerns over analytic relationship, how to repay), 34–35 (analysis does not disturb intimacy with Anna Freud family, but may have been factor promoting drift away from Anna), 34–35 (role of analysis in resolution of Eva's marital–professional crisis), 36 (transference, repression), 36–37 and 71 (Eva on how the analysis affected her and her life; wish to be analyzed by Anna Freud; characterization of Sigmund Freud as a "glutton for truth"), 70–72 (analysis with S. Freud shaped her thinking; clarified all except central trauma: loss of Mädi; relation to father), L8*n (analysis with Freud), L55 (relation to S. Freud). Abortive attempt to resume analysis with S. Freud: 45. *Eva as factotum of the Freuds:* 34, 41, 43–44, L14 (loses Lün), L57n. *Eva's retrospective view of her relationship to Anna Freud, Sigmund Freud, their circle, and to psychoanalysis:* 182–185. *Relationship to Dorothy Burlingham:* (L12)n, L16n, L17*n* (acting as foil to Dorothy), 182 (in retrospective)

Eva's marital crisis and turn to analysis as her profession: marriage: 26 (married at 19); *marital crisis:* 3, 33, 38–39 (decision to leave husbband and Vienna); relation to Obermann: 72–74. *Tegel:* function of her stay there for her, her job at the Sanatorium prior to and after its collapse: 3, 22, 37–40. Trip to Russia: 40; L54n. This development as reflected in the Letters: L18, L26 (financial worries), L32n, L35n, L36n, L37, L38, L40, L41n, L43, L44n, L47, L50n, L54; work at Tegel: L42*, L43, L45; trip to Moscow: L54n, L55. *Training to be, and being, an analyst:* early untutored knowledge of psychoanalysis: 11; psychoanalysis and love: 37, and the analysis with S. Freud (*see above*). Relationship and analysis with Melanie Klein: 44–45 (case assigned to her by M. Klein revives her own afflictions: 44); success as therapist and trainer of therapists: 35, 43; status in her profession: 45, 182. Eva Rosenfeld as writer and thinker: 41–43; writings: on Oedipus and Sphinx: 41–42; on the Brontës: 42; "The Pan-Headed Moses": (L4)n. Negative assessment by A. and S. Freud, and her self-assessment: 42–43. Role of psychoanalysis in Eva's life and impact on her view of the world: ix–x, 43

Later years: 180–187; on Anna's relation to her father: 184–185; Eva's relation to Freud family after 1932: 43–44 (helping Ernstl to leave Nazi Germany). On her work as analyst in later years: 181–183; relationship and correspondence with Anna Freud in later years and old age: 45–47, 46 (Anna's anger at Eva's BBC broadcast), 47 (inequality in final relationship); *see also* 182–185. *Eva's unpublished memoirs:* ("Recollected in Tranquillity," abbreviation: ER): 22, 47 (source for the essay by Victor Ross), 63–73 *passim*, 178, (L5)n

Rosenfeld, Mädi (Rosemarie) (b. 8/2/1912, Vienna; d. 7/8/1927, Grundlsee): 5, 16, 23, 66–69; L14n; death and image of M.: L5n, L17, L30, L13*n (M.'s character: maturity, true humanity, belief in God; her grave, her writing; her ideal), L25 (ideal of selflessness [needing nothing for oneself]), Mädi's day: L30, L40; Mädi's Grundlsee: L48

Rosenfeld, "Omi" (Rose Schiller; b. 2/20/1863, Jasi (Iasi), Romania; d. 8/10/1942, Oxford; Eva's mother): 25 (perennial mourning), 41 (central role in Eva's childhood resumed in endphase of Eva's marital crisis; the "indispensable Omi"), L5n, L6, L7, L8, L15, L16, L19, L20, L21, L22, L30, L32, L35, L40n (O. and Kinderfrau), L45, L47, L54 (letter to Omi; Omi's presents to Anna and Dorothy)

Rosenfeld, Theodor (Eva's father): 24–25, 71

Rosenfeld, Valti (Valentin; b. 1886, Vienna; d. 1970, London; attorney; Eva's husband): 14, 16, 26 (early interest in Freud), 27 (disorientated, dissatisfied), 31 (avoiding Eva's "establishment," and alienation), 33 (defends socialists; diminished legal practice), L1n, L6, L18, L26n, L32, L37n, L40, L41, L44n, L45, L47, L48, L54n, 182

Ross, Victor (= Rosenfeld, Vicki) (b. 1919, Vienna): x, 13–16 passim, 22. On Eva Rosenfeld: 23–48. 27 (birth of Victor), 28–29 (role in, and attitude toward, mother's friendship with Anna Freud), 39, L4, L5, L16n, L17n, L18, L22, L27, L28 (fishing), (L32)n, L35, L37 (Marienau), L40n, (L44)n, L45, L47* (characterization), 181

Russia: 40, L54, L55

Ruth: *see* Brunswick, Ruth Mack

Ruths: L15n

Sachs, Hanns (psychoanalyst): 14

"Salas y Gomez" (ballad by Cham-

isso): 3–4, L30n, L31n
Salber, Wilhelm: 4, 6, 8, 12, 14
Salomé, Lou Andreas (b. 1861, St. Petersburg; d. 1937, Göttingen): 4; correspondence with S. Freud: 4, 7–8. 28 (Ródinka, a book by her: Eva's present to Anna), 34, 63–65, L3, L6n, L7, L8, L55n. *See also under* Freud, A. and S.
Scharfenberg (school): 15, L43n, L47, (L51)n, L53n
Schmeling, Max (boxer): L43n
Schmutzer (artist): 97
Schneewinkel (Berchtesgaden): 4, 77
Schnitzler, Julius: 68; L47
School, The: *see* Hietzing School
Schopenhauer, Arthur: 24
Schroeder, Dr.: 3, 31, L6n, L18, L23, L29
Schultz, U.: 19
Schur, Dr. Max (internist): L19, (L48)n
Seidmann, Tom (Martha), Jankew, and child: L21n
Semmering (resort): 4, 64–65 (Villa Schüler), L1n, L3, L5, L30
Settlement, The: 32–33 (The Settlement and Hietzing School); L1n
Simmel, Dr. Ernst (b. 1882, Breslau; d. 1947, Los Angeles; father of Reinhard): 3, 14, 19–21, 37–40, 66, 77, 87, 88–90, 91, L7, (L8)n, L24, L37n, L42n, L47, L53n, 180 (Anna Freud's letter to E. S.)
Simmel, Mrs.: L8
Simmel, Reinhard (b. 1920; son of Ernst S.): 13–14, 31, 88–90, (L7)n, L8n, L15n, (L16)n, (L17)n, L25
Sphinx, riddle of: 41
Suse (Susy) (lover of Ruths; and baby): 14, L16n, L17, L24

Sweetser family (Adelaide, Bob, their mother, and Harold): 13, 15, 67 (Harold), L35n, L37

Tegel (psychoanalytic sanatorium, castle, park): *see also* Freud (Anna), Freud (Sigmund), Rosenfeld (Eva), Simmel (Dr. Ernst); 7 (island of safety and confinement), 14, 19–22, 37–40, 66, 90–91, 95, L6n (beauty of T.), L14n, L15*n (island of safety), L16, L17 (lake; Tegel Inc.), L18*, L28, L30 (rock in the sea), (L36)n, L37n, L41 (sanitarium), L42* (patients; parallel to child-analysis; only experienced analyst may modify analysis; analytical care and analytical treatment; pro closed institution), L43, L45 (excessive workload), L47*n (wishful idea of Tegel sanitarium, and liquidation), L53n (liquidation). Letters from Tegel: L6 to L8, L15 to L17, L18 to L33
Tiffany: *see* Burlingham family
Toszeghi, Erzsi: 14, L4n, L24
Toszeghi, Regine: L6n
Toszeghi, Vera (von Freund): 14, 27, 66, L4n, L6, L8, L25
Tropp, Mr. & Mrs.: 14
Trude Kraus: *see* Kraus, Trude

Ustobal, Gretl: L17

Vicki (Victor) Rosenfeld: *see* Ross, Victor
Vienna: *see also* Berggasse; 3, interweaving of "real" and analytical relationships in early Viennese circles of analysts: 10–11; public schools: 13, 17, 18; Vienna versus Berlin:

209

26–27, 32, L20n; Eva deciding to leave Vienna: 33, 39–40, L19, L20, L37n, L44, L50, L51; Vienna Woods: 30; (L25)n; Pötzleinsdorf: L38n, L39n, 184

Wagner, Richard: 24, (L36)n
Walberswick (summer resort in England): L56, 181, 184–185
Weigand, Mary: x
Weinmann, Dr.: L41n, L44, (L48)n, L53

Wellenstein, Lizzie: 14, 66, L1n, L16, L17n, L24, L25, L31, L33, L44, L47
Wimmer, Ighino: L28n
Wolf: *see* Dogs
Woolf, Leonard: 184

Young-Bruehl, Elisabeth: 4, 6, 8–9, 12, 74–75, 77, 93

Zellerhaus: 25–28 passim, 32, 38

NO LONGER THE PROPERTY
OF THE
UNIVERSITY OF R.I. LIBRARY